The Story of Steve
An Immigrant's Tale

by

Dan Remenyi

Printed by Lightning Source POD

Academic Publishing International Ltd, Reading, RG4 9SJ, UK
info@academic-publishing.org
www.academic-bookshop.com

Contents

Preface

This book has been written in part from memory of actual events and incidents and from stories I heard as a child in Dublin from my parents, grandparents and others. Other parts of the book are based on research conducted on the web and in books and also stories told by Hungarians I have met over the years. The book also draws in information which I was given by my Polish guide during my visit to Auschwitz. It is not intended to be a fully accurate and complete account of the life or times of my father, Steve Remenyi. A large tome would be needed for that. The objective is rather to present some of the major features in his life and times and to give as a by-product of that story, some little impression of what it was like to live in the family that he and Patsy created for themselves. The last few chapters offer some background information about Hungary and Auschwitz and some reflections on the whole story as well as a tribute from an Irish poet.

Dedication

I have written this book for a number of reasons, the most important of which is that I believe that Steve would himself have liked to tell his story if he was not so deeply steeped in a culture of secrecy. I believe that in time he could have been brought out of this secrecy culture. He didn't live long enough.

The second important reason is that I know we have been especially lucky to have been able to get a glimpse of Mariska Reményi and I believe that what happened to her in the last days of her life should be made known to a wide audience. At present that chapter is elsewhere only available in Hungarian.

Finally I have written this book for Louise and Kate who one day may want to know something about my side of our family.

Acknowledgements

I have been helped with this book by loads of people, especially with regards to the typesetting and the proof reading. There are too many names to list them all but I would like to tell everyone I am very grateful for the help I have received. I had not realised just how much work there is in producing a relatively short story like this.

However I would like to acknowledge the encouragement which I received from Seamus Fox to complete this book. Without his encouragement the book would have stayed as a draft for another seven years at least.

Finally I would like to thank Margit Izsaki. I have never met her and I have no idea what she was like. But to write a book which clearly showed sympathy for those who were victims of Hungarian Nazism was a brave deed in post World War 2 Hungary. Most Hungarians simply airbrushed the events of this period out of their personal and collective consciousness.

Sheehan Family Tree

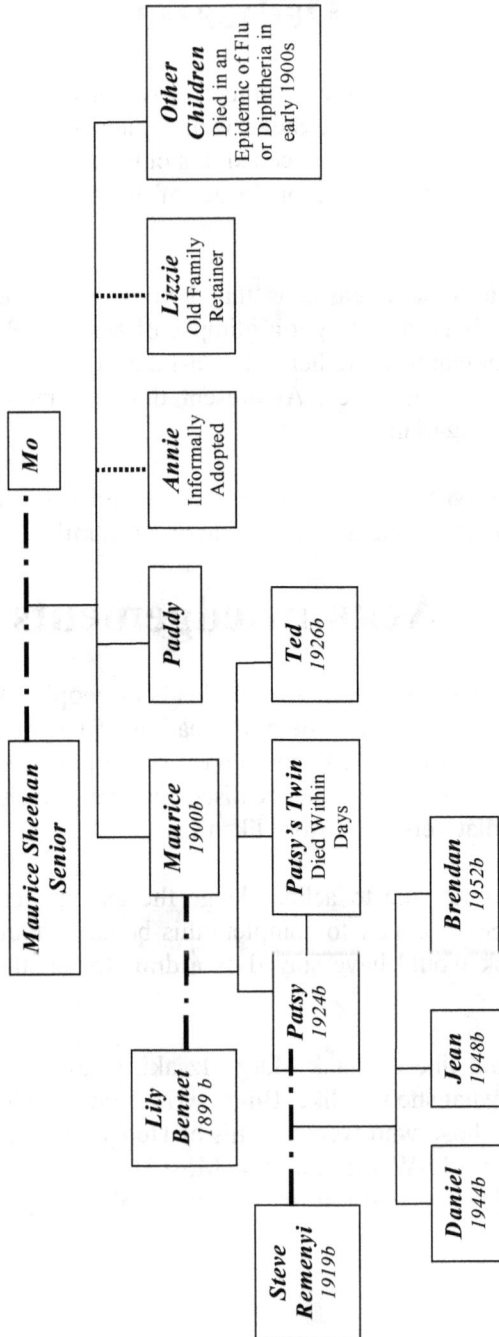

Maurice Sheehan Senior

Mo

Other Children — Died in an Epidemic of Flu or Diphtheria in early 1900s

Lizzie — Old Family Retainer

Annie — Informally Adopted

Paddy

Maurice *1900b*

Ted *1926b*

Lily Bennet *1899 b*

Patsy *1924b*

Patsy's Twin — Died Within Days

Steve Remenyi *1919b*

Jean *1948b*

Daniel *1944b*

Brendan *1952b*

Remenyi Family Tree

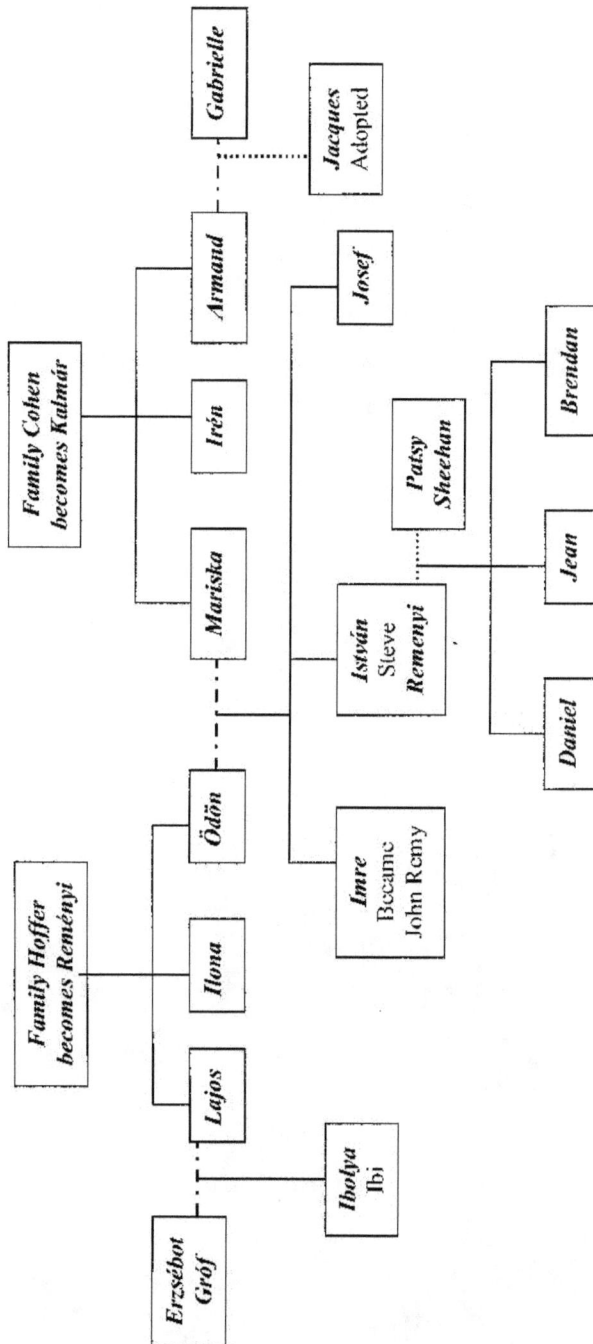

The Story of Steve

Chapter One

Out of Hungary and into Ireland

I have wanted to tell this story for a long time, but I kept procrastinating. I'll do it next year was my attitude. And so the years have passed. As the eldest child in Steve and Patsy's family I have come to feel that it is *now or never*.

The Second World War destroyed the lives of many tens of millions of people and completely changed the course of the lives of many hundreds of millions more. The story of Steve is just one example of a life sent, by the chaos of the times, in a completely different direction to what he and his family expected.

Steve Remenyi turned up in Dublin, out of the blue in 1941. It wasn't so much that he wafted in on a breeze but rather he drifted in from the Irish Sea on the high tide. Steve sailed into Dublin Bay on the VICIA[1], an elderly cargo ship registered in Finland, towards the end of November. As far as the crew were concerned this was a routine stop in a port in a relatively welcoming country, as Ireland was neutral in the war, and they looked forward to a few days in a safe haven. The VICIA was an old cargo boat, constructed in 1896 that had sailed across the Atlantic Ocean in the early years of the war. It was a very run down looking ship which was clearly the worse for wear and which badly needed a coat or two of paint. It was the sort of ship that was sufficiently small and old, not to have been a prime target for a German U-boat torpedo. One could well image the U-boat commander seeing the VICIA in his periscope and thinking that he would do well to save his torpedo for a bigger and better target.

Steve, working as the ship's Radio Officer was one of the younger members of the crew, the rest of them being old sea-dogs from just about every part of the world. The photograph of the members of the crew shows that they were certainly a bunch of weather beaten old salts who took all the dangers of the north Atlantic in 1941 in their stride. But the end of November that year was not an auspicious time to be working on a Finnish ship in allied waters. On December 8, 1941 the United Kingdom declared war on Finland.

---

[1] There is a photograph of the Vicia on the cover of this book taken after 1943 and before the end of the war when it was renamed the Irish Spruce. The painted Irish tricolour and the word EIRE were attempts to discourage attacks by either the German's or the Royal Air Force or the Royal Navy.

Such was the turmoil of World War Two that one day the Finns were allies and the next day they were enemies. This is, to say the least, all quite confusing, as Ireland was not at war anyway. The official line was that Ireland was neutral. Ireland or to be absolutely correct *Saorstat Eireann - the Irish Free State* or Southern Ireland was in a transition period from being an integral part of the United Kingdom to being an independent sovereign state i.e. a republic. But in 1941 the Irish Free State was still working towards breaking all ties with the United Kingdom. Due to the physical proximity of the Irish Free State to the United Kingdom it could not stay out of the war altogether and thus it declared a State of Emergency which could be argued showed some sort of solidarity with the allies. The term State of Emergency was an official euphemism which allowed the Government to intern foreigners, censor the press and control the economy, of course many Irishmen both from the South and the North signed up to fight. Such was the political diversity in Ireland that some fought against the Germans, some fought for King George (i.e. their King and Country) and some fought because there wasn't another job available. There were even some Irishmen who wanted to see the Germans defeat Ireland's old enemy or at least give Britannia a good bloody nose.

It seems that it may have been the intention of the owners of the VICIA to sell her to the newly formed company Irish Shipping Limited. However this information was not conveyed to the crew who had signed on for a return trip to North America. When it became known that the ship would be sold to the Irish, four officers including Steve sued the owners for breach of contract and for repatriation expenses to the USA. However having won his case it then occurred to Steve that Ireland was probably not such a bad place to see out the war. He had spent some time in the USA and had not found it congenial. Thus Steve Remenyi chose to stay on, eventually becoming an Irish citizen, and he made his life in Dublin for the next 17 years. The other members of the crew, in dribs and drabs moved on to other parts of the world. Concerning the ship itself, the VICIA was eventually taken over by the state owned marine transport corporation Irish Shipping where it became part of the fleet for a number of years. The ship was renamed the Irish Spruce and remained in the Irish Shipping fleet until 1949 when it was sold to Turkish interests.

So Steve's arrival in Ireland was really unplanned. He found himself "accidentally" and, some might say fortuitously, in a neutral country at the height of the Second World War. He spoke very little English but had some money from suing his ship's owners, and so he began to make a life for himself in Ireland.

Steve Remenyi had been born in Hungary on August 19, 1919, the year the Austro-Hungarian Empire imploded as a result of losing the First World War. The name on his birth certificate was István Reményi[2], Istávan being the Hungarian equivalent of Stephen. He was known to his childhood friends as Pista which is the Hungarian equivalent of Steve. Post World War One was a time of considerable upheaval in Hungary but the Remenyi family managed well even in those times of unprecedented turmoil. The Remenyis were not rich but they were more than financially comfortable being able to afford a generous life style and also being able to help less financially fortunate parts of their family.

Steve was the third son of Ödön and Mariska Reményi who was born to them a full sixteen years after their first son. His eldest brother, Imre, had been born in 1903 and their middle son Joseph was born in 1911. Thus the three boys were each eight years apart in age.

Steve was the baby of the family and by all accounts a spoilt child with an especially close relationship with his mother. He was a confident young boy with what was clearly a well-balanced personality. He was outgoing by nature and easily made friends and these friends were important to him. When he left Hungary he carried with him a pile of photographs showing his group of friends. These photographs showed mostly young people swimming in the Danube or relaxing on the shore of the river. There were other photos taken in the busy streets of Budapest. He was a good-looking young boy who had been taught from an early age to be careful of his appearance. There is no doubt that he was a likeable child and subsequently a popular young man. His mother was especially attentive to him and this attention increased considerably from the age of about seven when Steve's brother Joseph died. At that time Joseph was in his early teens. It is not clear precisely of what condition Joseph died. It seems that he had a protracted illness that did not respond to treatment.

Ödön and Mariska Reményi went to considerable lengths to find a cure for Joseph, eventually taking him to Switzerland, which would have been, in the 1920s, one of the main centres of modern world medicine. This was typical of the Remenyis that they would try to leave no stone unturned in finding a solution to their problem. However all this effort was to no avail and Joseph died in a sanatorium in Davos in Switzerland. It was thought at the time that it had to be some sort of cancer. Joseph's body was brought all the way back to Hungary where it lies at rest in the same graveyard next to his father, Ödön.

---

[2] Steve did not use the original spelling of Reményi with the accent on the second e.

With regards to the older brother Imre, as he was all of 16 years older than Steve, these two brothers really never knew each other at all well. As Joseph died so young Steve was really brought up as if he had been an only child. To add to Mariska's problems Steve's father also died relatively young, of a heart attack, when Steve was about fourteen, which of course drew him even closer to his mother.

Steve had been brought through a relatively typical middle class academic education. However, for his final years of schooling he had been sent to a college which specialised in commercial subjects including bookkeeping, economics and some business law, as it was intended that he would go into business as his parents had done. The Remenyis, especially Mariska, had done some planning and had worked out the type of career they wanted for Steve and he was happy enough to go along with that. But the 1930s was not a good time for long term planning.

Quite some years before Ödön and Mariska had already chosen a similar type of career path for Imre, although Imre's attempts to run his own business had failed. This failure was not due to Imre's inability as a businessman or to political upheavals but rather to his interest in pursuing the life of a playboy. Of course this activity was pursued at considerable expense to his parents. In later life Imre was to admit that he had made a big hole in the family fortune during that period. But in the 1920s and early 1930s Ödön and Mariska had enough money to allow Imre to be a regular visitor at the nightclubs and casinos, not only in Budapest but also further afield especially the French Riviera. He was known as a man with deep pockets, which were regularly refilled, by his father and mother. Imre had certainly from a young age acquired a taste for *la dolce vitae*. But Ödön and Mariska's funds were, at the end of the day, limited. Furthermore world events were going to change the world of the Remenyis in a profound and irreversible way and Imre's ability to live this sort of life was soon to cease.

Steve's schooling in Budapest finished in 1937 and he was now ready to help in the family business. However by that time it was clear to a lot of people including Mariska that war would soon come and change everything. With the Nazis having taken over Austria, Hungary was right on their doorstep. Hungary was poised precariously right next to the forthcoming conflict with borders with both Austria and the Soviet Union and other vulnerable Central European countries and it didn't take much foresight to appreciate that there was a considerable likelihood that much of Central Europe would soon be consumed in this awful conflict.

4

Thus Mariska considered that it would be a good idea for Steve to get out of Hungary and even out of Central Europe. As a result in 1938 a decision was made which changed the thinking about Steve's future career. He would not go into business in Hungary but would acquire a qualification, which would take him abroad to the new world. Mariska knew that this was a matter of some urgency. She knew that he would have to do something quickly and that he could not take several years to obtain a qualification. At this stage time really was of the essence.

After reviewing the options Steve was sent to a technical institute in Budapest to study marine radio systems and operation. This would give Steve a qualification, with which he could get away from Hungary and which he could use elsewhere in the world – or at least that was the plan.

Steve had quite a technical flair and he was really good with his hands, a gift which he retained all his life. Within the year Steve was highly competent in Morse Code as well as the basic electronics required to operate the large and complex radios in use on pre-war ships. He obtained his diploma demonstrating that he was a qualified radio operator and with this he set off for an exciting job on a merchant marine ship on the high seas.

The decision to send Steve abroad was made by Mariska alone, because as mentioned above, Ödön had died a few years earlier. Mariska was no doubt a very astute and strong willed woman as she took over as head of the family and ran the business on her own after Ödön's death. Her eldest son Imre was not around to help her. Some years before Ödön and Mariska had set up a business for Imre but it did not work out well. Imre, having failed in the business, had also taken up employment in the merchant navy. For Imre it was just a question of getting away to do his own thing in a world which was much wider than the Hungarian world he had left behind. By 1938 Imre had already been working at sea for a number of years and had made many trips to America where he was ultimately to settle. Like many others from Central and Southern Europe to be in America was the prize for Imre.

So the somewhat unusual idea of going abroad was already well established in the Remenyi family. Joseph had died in his early teenage years after an extended illness and thus Mariska's decision to send Steve overseas was indeed, an amazingly brave one as it left her alone in Hungary with no husband and no children and only a few relatively distant members of her family.

Although Steve was a very gregarious young man with many friends in his own age group, going abroad actually suited him quite well. He had a certain sense of curiosity and adventure and a great desire to see the world. So except for leaving his mother, it was no real hardship for him to say goodbye to his friends and other members of his family and to set sail on the high seas. In any case from Steve's point of view he was not necessarily planning to be away from Hungary for a long time. He had thought that the forth-coming troubles in Europe would certainly blow over in a few years. The First World War had after all only taken four years and this new war, in his view could not take any longer. He would come back to Hungary, being well travelled and settle down into the family business or some other business that he would start.

At almost the same time as Steve was getting ready to leave, Imre who had not only been through a failed business, but had also been through a failed marriage and been divorced, returned home for a short stay. During this visit it was decided that Imre would re-marry and that he would emigrate with his new wife and that they would live in Australia. This was chosen as it was as far away from the on-coming war as it was possible to get. His new wife was to be Magda, who was the young cousin of Mariska's great friends and neighbours. The story of Imre and Magda is an interesting but complicated one in its own right, but suffice to say that this second marriage of Imre's didn't last long either. Despite the fact that Magda was a pleasant and attractive person Imre was a very complex man and he was not able to settle down with Magda. She set up home in Sydney and Imre moved on to New York. Imre was a restless, adventure seeking man and couldn't stand being so far away from the action of the war, and he left Australia in order to go to America and continue to be actively involved in the war. He joined the supply transport section of the United States Navy which followed and supplied the American invasion tactics in the Far East. He worked on these ships for many years even after the war ended.

Adventure was in the air for the Remenyi brothers in 1938.

Mariska equipped both her sons with some money to help get settled in their new lives and bade them farewell in the hope of seeing them again in Hungary in more settled times in the not too distant future. At that stage Steve was not yet 20 years old and it is clear that neither Steve nor Mariska thought that he was leaving his mother and his home for good when he departed on his long journey in 1938.

By the outbreak of the war in September 1939 Steve was already established in the merchant navy as a radio officer. He had made many trips across the world visiting the USA as well as South America, the Far East and Australia. The radio operator's job was not a difficult one, in fact it was considered by many to be a very comfortable number. On board ship radio officers worked a normal eight hour shift listening to radio broadcasts. They confirmed international time signals for the ships' clocks and listened out for weather forecasts. There was not much else for them to do. Of course they were always on standby in case an emergency message needed to be sent. This job gave Steve a satisfactory income as well as the status on board ship of being an officer. In his photograph collection there were several snap shots of Steve in his officer's uniform on the bridge with the captain. During 1939, 1940 and 1941 he had held jobs on a number of different ships. Correspondence home showed that he had spent some time in and enjoyed being in Sweden and Argentina. In the United States of America, out of which he worked for a while, he had a post-restante address in Texas.

In those early years during 1939 to 1941 he enjoyed the life away from home and on the high seas and he did not seem to be personally much affected by the on-going war. The war was a great adventure to him which he found fascinating and he followed all the details of the military and political developments of that time. In later life he was always glad to recall the detail of these times which he remembered well.

At this stage he spoke Hungarian and German fluently and had some knowledge of French and a very small smattering of English. In later years Steve would occasionally mention difficulties he had had in Miami in the USA when on one occasion it was known that he spoke German and was therefore regarded by the authorities as a potential German spy. What happened was that he was using the ship's radio to talk across the airwaves to a friend in German and this was picked up by the American Coast Guard who initially thought that German speakers must be up to no good.

During 1941, as hostilities grew on the Atlantic, Steve came close to the realities of the war a few times. He had always been interested in photography and had taken with him a small box camera. With what is now a very primitive photographic device he had taken shots of burning and sinking ships in the North Atlantic and pictures of desperate looking men in lifeboats being rescued after their ships had been sent to the bottom of the ocean. These were quite eerie photographs of wartime tragedies which he kept as souvenirs of this period.

On one occasion Steve had been caught in a bombing raid. The German bomber had not got a direct hit but in diving for cover Steve hurt his back which resulted in his having a slipped disk, a problem which haunted him again and again for the rest of his life.

The politics behind the Finnish ship being stranded and the crew's detention in Ireland are interesting. Shortly before the United Kingdom declared war on Germany on September 3, 1939, Nazi Germany had, to the shock and amazement of the world, made a non-aggression pact with the Soviet Union. The surprise was because Hitler and the Nazis were so obviously anti-communist it was thought that it was impossible they would collaborate on anything. The Nazi-Soviet pact meant that at the outbreak of war the Soviet Union was not an allied power, in fact it was generally regarded as potentially hostile, being at least in one sense an ally of Nazi Germany.

The 1930s were troubled times in other parts of the world besides Western and Central Europe. At this time the Soviet Union was engaged in its own war with Finland, which had been an ongoing affair for a number of years. As Russia had occupied Finland for many years from 1809 until the end of the First World War, the Soviet Union regarded Finland as some sort of break away province and they wanted it back. On the other hand the Finns, a very independent minded people, had no desire whatsoever to return to 'Mother Russia'. It was always thought surprising that the huge Soviet Union had not been able to just walk all over the Finns who were after all a small nation with not all that much in the way of resources. In general the British public sympathised with the Finns as they saw them as a little country standing up to the gigantic Russian bear and to boot the Russian bear was in cahoots with the Nazis. In this conflict the Finns had received moral support from the United Kingdom. However when Hitler invaded the Soviet Union on June 22, 1941 the position of Finland drastically changed. Pretty well from the instant of the German invasion of the Soviet Union, the latter became an ally – albeit one that was not all that well trusted especially by the British. This meant that Finland was at war with a British ally, and an important one, whether trusted or not. The Finns clearly saw what was coming and they tried to argue that they had no cause to be regarded as an enemy of the United Kingdom. They employed the word co-belligerent but this was not taken as seriously as it should have been. It is clear that the powers who were running the United Kingdom did not really want to go to war with the Finns but in reality the politics of the situation was that the pressure from the Soviet Union was ultimately just too strong. Thus on December 8, 1941 the United Kingdom declared war on Finland. That was the fateful day when the course of the war directly affected Steve and on which the VICIA sailed into Dublin Bay. Before that date the VICIA was part of allied shipping and therefore under the protection of the Royal Navy and the Royal Air Force. After that day the VICIA was a target for the Royal Navy and the Royal Air Force and to have steamed out of Dublin Bay would have been highly problematic if not suicide.

The ship hadn't struck a rock like the Irish Rover but by visiting Dublin her sailing days under her old flag were over.

The island of Ireland had been effectively partitioned by the British in 1920 when they passed the Government of Ireland Act which created two parliaments in Ireland. Thus was created two political entities, one called the Irish Free State and the other called Northern Ireland. The Irish Free State consisted of 26 of the original 32 counties of Ireland. Northern Ireland contained the remaining 6 counties in which most of the population were not Roman Catholic. In the Anglo-Irish Treaty which was signed in London on December 6, 1921 these six counties remained an integral part of the United Kingdom, a decision which has plagued the island of Ireland to this day. The status of this transitional Irish Free State was that it looked after its own domestic policies and affairs, but that it was subsidiary to the United Kingdom on certain other matters relating to affairs such as foreign policy. It was only on January 1, 1949 that the Irish Free State became a fully independent republic with total control of all aspects of its affairs and its destiny.

So Steve found himself with a completely new set of challenges and opportunities which he could not possibly have envisaged when he sailed into Dublin just a few weeks earlier. But Steve was essentially a resourceful man and he saw these new arrangements as an opportunity. Whether Ireland in 1942 was a good place to be marooned really does depend on your point of view. It was generally a cold, damp country with shortages of food, fuel and just about everything else. Although it is true to say that rationing was only introduced into Ireland in May 1942 it was, even before that time a country with shortages of just about everything.

To many Ireland is famous for its welcoming attitude. The Gaelic expression *cead mile failte*, which translates as *a hundred thousand welcomes,* is a well known Irish greeting. As is expressed in the tourist guide books, the Irish are usually very affable to tourists when they encounter them casually. But like anywhere else in the world the casual 'friendship' and hospitality only goes so far. It could be arguable that the Irish are not especially high on the xenophobic scale, but at the same time the Irish are not exactly magnificently welcoming to foreigners. There probably is a certain amount of basic xenophobia inherent in the Irish psyche due to nearly 700 years of struggle, often very bloody with the English. But on the other hand in the United Kingdom at this time foreigners, and perhaps especially seamen, were not treated all that well. It was after all a time of a life and death struggle with Germany and foreigners were generally suspect. In addition to this general attitude it was known that Hungary was in a number of respects pro-Germany and was likely to join the war on the German side.

Irrespective of the hospitality of the Irish or the lack thereof, Ireland had one overwhelming positive characteristic in 1942, which commended it to Steve. Ireland was not at war. Unlike Imre, Steve had a much more balanced attitude to adventure and by now he had more than three years sailing the high seas in wartime. So enough was enough and staying in Ireland meant that Steve could achieve his own and his mother's ambition of getting out of the Second World War.

As it turned out the war was not that far away. Flights over Ireland by both German and American air force planes caused some degree of anxiety. The Irish population knew that the Free State could have been drawn into the war by either a British or German invasion, against which the country would have no defence. Dublin was bombed a couple of times in January and May 1941 by the Luftwaffe. There are several quite different stories told about these bombings. The first story goes that on January 2, 1941 a German plane lost its way and needed to dispose of its bombs to reduce its weight to be able to have the flying range to get back home to Germany. The pilot is alleged to have lightened his aircraft by disposing of his bombs over Dublin. However other sources say that this bombing raid was a deliberate warning by the Germans that if the Irish Free State allowed Royal Navy bases to be established in the South they would be targeted by the Luftwaffe. To think that an Irish Government would willingly allow British troops back on its soil having only just got rid of them after a 700 year struggle suggests that the Germans were not fully informed about attitudes in Ireland. The third story is that the British, probably the Royal Air Force, were able to divert wireless beams so that the Germans thought that they were over Britain and that while they were actually bombing Dublin, they believed they were hitting a United Kingdom city. It is hard to know which of these stories would be true. Our image of Germans does not go along with the suggestion that they would be lost and not know they were over Ireland. Maybe they were misinformed about the possibilities of Cobh being used as a Royal Navy base but the fact that the last story was believed in Dublin sheds a lot of light on the cynical attitude of the Irish towards the British – an attitude which was probably justified. In any event the German Government in the 1950s paid an amount of £327,000 to the Irish Government in compensation for the damage done by the bombing.

Of course whichever story about the bombing incidents is true, by and large, the Irish Free State was a safe place to be, and for a young man who had left his home to escape the war, it was sort of logical for him to stay on there and build a new life in that country.

However, living in Ireland was not all plain sailing for Steve as it offered him a whole new set of language and social challenges. As mentioned before Steve's spoken English was not good – in fact it was quite poor. With a vocabulary of perhaps only a hundred words and a very heavy accent he had trouble making himself understood. There were stories which were told about how he used to get the language wrong and the funny situations in which this landed him. The structure of Hungarian is very different to English and most other European languages and it is no mean task for a Hungarian to become perfect in English as Steve eventually did. In the early months of being in Ireland he would frequently reverse subjects and objects in a sentence and place the verb in the wrong place and choose quite inappropriate words. The sort of situation he faced was well portrayed in the Monty Python film sketch where the bogus Hungarian-English dictionary gets its user into trouble. Of course the Irish are always good for a laugh and in these early days it was just as well that Steve had a sense of humour and that he proved to be strong enough for a good laugh at his own expense. Steve's robust sense of humour was one of his most important and lasting assets. In the end he spoke flawless English. Of course he spoke English with a distinctively Irish accent.

The second problem was a bit more serious. It was the question of how Steve would earn his living in this strange country. Everything Steve had learnt had been in Hungarian and or German. He had prepared himself for a technical career with radio technology. He had no other qualifications. All commercial ships were required to have a radio officer since the early part of the 20th century. This regulation came into effect shortly after the sinking of the Titanic. The training for radio operation was delivered largely by the Marconi Company which was the major supplier of ships' radios. Although the radio operator's certificate was supposed to be international it was not usable in Ireland. The reason for this was that on British (and Irish) ships there was a regime of 'job reservation'. The three jobs of captain, chief engineer and radio officer required the incumbents to be British. At a time of war this was hardly surprising. In Steve's case being Hungarian would have been especially unsatisfactory to Allied Governments as after all the Hungarians were in league with the Germans. Steve had taken some high school courses in business but these were in no way a qualification and were thus of little value except that they were probably somewhat instrumental in helping set up his own business in Ireland.

Establishing a business was not a great problem for Steve. He had money from the law suit against the company and he had savings from his radio operator's salary. The Remenyi family had in addition to their main business interest, some property on the banks of the Danube. On their property they grew grapes, as did most people in that area, as vines grow like weeds on the banks of the Danube. But the Remenyis also pressed some of these grapes and made their own wine. In addition they also made charcoal. Steve as a youngster had taken a special interest in the charcoal making. Perhaps this had been the natural interest of a young boy in building fires and keeping them going during the charcoal manufacturing process. Whatever the reason, Steve found his knowledge of how to make charcoal invaluable in Ireland in 1942 and this allowed him to go into business for himself[3].

One of the main shortages in Ireland during the war was fuel in general. Coal had been rationed, initially to two bags a household but this was quickly reduced to a ration of zero as all coal was needed for industry. That was when Irish peat or turf came into its own. Generally regarded as an inferior sort of fuel, turf as it was colloquially called, burned well and was used extensively after the end of the War. Gas was also rationed with its availability being limited to a few hours a day during meal times, so meals had to be eaten to a specific schedule. However it is not possible to cut household gas off entirely without having considerable problems in re-instating the service so a small trickle of gas remained in the pipes which allowed Dubliners to have, what they called, a "glimmer" of gas to boil a pot or kettle of water. This was illegal and the government set up "glimmer men" to go about catching those indulging in this practice. Times were certainly hard. Petrol was also in short supply but of course there were not all that many motor vehicles around in those days.

---

[3] During World War II about a million vehicles were converted to run on gas which was the product of charcoal. This technology had been around for many years but it was not as convenient as simply filling up the tank with petrol. Charcoal was an inexpensive fuel and when there was no petrol around it kept people moving.

The war in the Sahara Desert had severely disrupted the flow of oil to the British Isles and there was little petrol available for Ireland or to the Irish motorist. As late as May 1942 Rommel and his Afrika Corp were dominant in the desert war and this remained the case until the German defeat at El Alamein in November 1942. Thus there was little or no oil coming through.

Fortunately, the few motorists in Ireland in 1942 had mostly converted their cars to gas burning vehicles, fuelled with charcoal. Steve found it easy to get into this market and quickly he set up business in the countryside, in the Irish midlands, manufacturing and marketing charcoal. Steve's technical and organisational skill came to the fore and he enjoyed developing this venture. His business prospered and within the year it appeared that Steve, although only in his early twenties, was well on his way to financial prosperity. At this time he thought that turning up in Ireland had been a most fortuitous event and that he had really landed on his feet. However as the German success in the desert war was the main driver of Steve's business it was to be short lived.

During this 'charcoal' period Steve worked and lived during the week in the Irish countryside, but on the weekends Steve came to Dublin for his social life. He was an outgoing, gregarious and sociable person, who really enjoyed the company of others but who, oddly enough, was at the same time also quite contented to be on his own. Steve had developed from a good looking boy to a very handsome young man. He was tall, six foot; he was slim; and he had a big mop of black hair[4]. He always took time and paid a lot of attention to his appearance. Furthermore in those early days spoken English with a very pronounced accent was said to be attractive. He also stood out from the crowd in that he had a business going and he had some money to spend.

To many, Dublin was and still is the main centre of entertainment in Ireland, having if nothing else a very fine collection of public houses. There were also a wider range of cafes and restaurants. And there were dance halls. On one of his frequent trips to Dublin Steve met the woman who was to become his life long companion, Patsy Sheehan. At this time Patsy was barely 18 years old and was a very good looking young woman. She was tall and slim with a head of flaming red hair.

She had already been out of school for a few years, in fact since she was 14 years old. Patsy like many other Dubliners of her generation had fin-

---

[4] This can be seen in the photos at the end of the book.

ished school at this age because of financial problems which were simply that her family needed the money she could earn, albeit the fact that the wages for a 14 year old girl were very little indeed. Still it was better than nothing. Also Patsy had not coped well at school. There is little doubt that she was at least slightly dyslexic and the schooling system in the 1930s did not recognise this as anything other than backwardness. The dyslexia showed itself in her inability to spell, and this made writing very difficult for her and this problem haunted her all her life. She had been to a convent school and her only memories of these years were the unpleasantness of the nuns. According to Patsy the nuns' only interest in her was to ensure that the catechism had been properly drummed into her.

By the time she had met Steve she was working as a shop assistant which she disliked intensely. She, like Steve, was also very concerned about her appearance and boasted for many years that she had a 22-inch waistline when she met Steve. She dressed fairly well, at least as well as her limited income would allow, and at that stage of her life she used cosmetics skilfully. She was a very flighty woman who always had a lot of attention from the young men of her acquaintance. Both curvaceous and equipped with a red headed temper she stood out in a crowd. She was highly spirited and she certainly knew how to get to the head of a queue. She naturally or instinctively knew how to catch people's eyes and she loved being the centre of attraction. She retained this skill well into her later years. Whereas Steve was from a prosperous middle class family, Patsy was from the distinctly poor working classes of Dublin. Ireland was a very class conscious society which was probably a left over from the centuries long English occupation. There were clear distinctions between the working classes and the middle classes in several respects. At least they were both Catholic and thus did not have the complication of the differences in the Irish society due to the Catholic-Protestant divide. However Steve's and Patsy's attraction for each other made these class differences irrelevant to them.

Patsy Sheehan had found her home life with her parents very hard. Not only was it dull and tedious but it was a clearly deprived way of life. To escape this she was always drawn to things that were unusual and Steve would have been a very unusual character on the scene in Dublin in 1943. It was thus inevitable that Patsy would have found Steve very attractive and in turn Steve had an eye for good-looking women. Thus it did not take Steve and Patsy long to become involved with each other. Once this relationship started it did not take long before the inevitable happened and Patsy fell pregnant.

Being pregnant and unmarried in Ireland in 1943 was undoubtedly a highly undesirable condition for any young woman in which to find herself. In fact it is really quite hard to imagine just how much of an encumbrance this must have been. Many women found that their lives were largely wrecked by such a happening. Unmarried pregnant women were certainly disgraced as were their families. Such women were seen, not as unfortunates who needed help but rather as living witnesses to the existence of the devil. In fact what they were in reality were living witnesses of the superficiality of Catholic piety. They were often sent to convents or sent abroad to have the baby. In fact Patsy was well aware of The Magdalene Sisters and the spectre of being sent to one of their institutions hung over her. It would not have been beyond her father's austere sense of justice to have sent her to such a place. The Magdalene Sisters took unmarried pregnant women into their convents where they put them to work under hard conditions including working 12 or more hours per day in their laundries. These women who were treated astonishingly badly were often made to spend the rest of their lives in these institutions. They were not automatically released when the baby was born. These babies were generally given away to childless couples. The Mother Superior of the order had it in her gift to release or detain for as long as she thought necessary the hapless women who entered their institution. In general the Mother Superior could deem these women to be sinners and capable of returning to the sinful life style which originally got them into trouble. As such it was argued that they were kept in the institution for their own protection. The system supported by the Catholic Church and the Irish State was little less than institutionalised slavery. Recent exposés of this system have shocked Irish society.

Fortunately Patsy didn't have to endure the Magdalenes. There was some discussion between Patsy and Steve about terminating the pregnancy but this would have been a very risky and illegal business in 1943. Even today abortion is not legal in Ireland and it is said that thousands of Irish women cross the Irish Sea each year to have this procedure performed. So it was out of the question for Patsy. Thus although Patsy really did not want the baby and always resented how this pregnancy had encumbered her life, she really had no choice but to go through with it. She was simply not ready emotionally for the role of motherhood. Thus with no real options available she consented to marry Steve and become a wife and a mother.

Of course it was no easy matter to find a priest to marry them. It was not considered a wise thing to marry a foreigner in Dublin at that time. There was the worry that the foreign man would not settle down in Ireland. He might stay a year or two and then just pack up and move on to another part of the world with or without his Irish wife. There were stories about how foreign men had passed themselves off as bachelors while they already had a wife and a family back home. Marrying a foreigner was indeed risky. The Catholic Church was aware of this and did not rush to agree to marry them. Patsy recalled how the priest she approached tried hard to talk her out of marrying Steve. Irish Catholic priests told her about the tricks a foreigner could get up to. She was advised that she was too young to marry. She was told that a good looking girl like her should not get involved with a stranger from a distant part of the world.

"To be sure there are plenty of handsome and eligible young Irishmen who would be delighted to make you a wonderful husband", the old priest said. "Why go and marry a foreigner?" "Well I love him," said Patsy. "Well if I were you my child I would think this over very carefully and come back in a few months and see me again if you still want to go through with this". The priest went on to dish out the old cliché; "Always remember the wisdom in the old saying – *marry in haste and repent at leisure*". Patsy knew she could win an agreement based on love against such enormous common sense. She realised that she had to announce that the matter was perhaps a little more complicated and pressing than the priest had been led to believe. She was after all pregnant. So she decided to confess. "But I am pregnant," Patsy finally blurted out. "Holy Mary Mother of God, what a terrible thing for a lovely Irish Catholic girl to have done" said the priest. "That is a mortal sin", he said. "I had better marry you next week! Get that man over here at once". There was no further delay or indeed discussion about the suitability of the groom. Ireland in the 1940s had clearly not awoken to the issue of women's choices.

In January 1944, while three months pregnant and still only 19 years old, Patsy married Steve in the little Catholic University College Church on St Stephen's Green in Dublin. To this day it is a very picturesque church tucked away rather obscurely on the West side of Dublin's most fashionable Georgian square.

This whole business was a great shock and a great shame to the Sheehan family from which it took them a number of years to recover. Patsy's parents Maurice and Lily Sheehan were faced with both a 19 year old pregnant unmarried daughter as well as the prospect of a foreign son-in-law with an unpronounceable and definitely unspellable surname. For a conservative Catholic working class family this was no small burden.

As Patsy's whole family refused to go to the wedding it was attended by only a few friends and without any of the normal family celebrations which accompany such events. Steve certainly had the money at that stage to hold a wedding reception but with no family members present on either side it appeared to them that a normal wedding reception would only aggravate the bad or perhaps the hurt feelings within the Sheehan family. Thus a few close friends attended the wedding and after the ceremony they all went to lunch at one of Dublin's well known restaurants. Despite Steve's interest in photography there are no surviving photographs of the wedding. Neither Patsy nor Steve ever spoke of this occasion. It was done as simply as possible and as quickly as possible. They had been cheated out of, or maybe they cheated themselves out of a celebration. There is little doubt that this was not the most satisfactory way to start a married life.

As mentioned before the newly weds seem to have had no concern about the different backgrounds from which Steve and Patsy had come and the different values which emanated from these very different upbringings. Essentially they were a handsome couple who under difficult circumstances were going to try to make the best of the situation in which they had found themselves. As they lived together for 40 years until Steve died the difficult circumstances with which they started their married life did not seen to have unduly impaired their relationship or their future life together.

There is no doubt that Patsy had multiple expectations from marrying Steve. She often said that when she got married, Steve and she had intended to return to the Remenyi family home in Hungary as soon as Mr Hitler was taken care of by the allies. After all, the Remenyis had a large family house, an established business and a country estate. But it is not clear that Patsy would have even known where to find Hungary on a world map. She would have had no idea of the difficulties presented by the Hungarian language or of the challenges in living in such a foreign society. In such respects she had no ability to be able to think practically.

As to Steve's expectations, that question is more difficult. Clearly Patsy would not have expected anything that Steve had not specifically suggested to her. On the other hand Steve was fairly politically astute and he would have known that post war Central and Eastern Europe would have to be very different to what he had been used to as a child. He must have known that his middle class family could not survive the Second World War as well as they had survived the First World War. Perhaps the alternative life in front of him in Dublin relative to what he had left behind was so abysmal that he just wanted to focus on the best possible scenario of one day getting home. He probably could not have guessed at that time the dreadful outcome the war would have for the peoples of Central and Eastern Europe.

But whatever Steve's expectations were for himself and Pasty concerning going back to his family home after the war, Joseph Stalin and others had different plans for Hungary and the Hungarians which resulted in keeping Steve in Ireland for quite some time.

The Sheehans of Cuffe Street

Steve was now 24 years of age, married, living in Dublin with a business that was in terminal decline. His wife Patsy Sheehan was an attractive but pregnant young woman of 20 years old. Patsy was a complicated person with deep insecurity problems which were clearly the result of the unfortunate circumstances of her upbringing and background.

To understand Patsy Sheehan it is necessary to know a little about Patsy's family. Most of Patsy's upbringing was in what is best described as an extended family in which there were nine people. Huddled together nine people are a lot, spread over three generations, but this was not all that unusual for Ireland in the first half of the twentieth century. All of these people had some direct influence on Patsy, not the least of which was her paternal grandfather whose dreadful misfortunes effectively made Patsy's early life a proper misery.

Patsy was born in Dublin on February 29, 1924 as one of twin girls to Maurice and Lily Sheehan. Maurice and Lily had not been married long. It had been a difficult pregnancy and birth for Lily and Patsy's twin sister did not survive more than a few days. It transpired that Lily Sheehan had some congenital difficulty with child carrying and childbirth. As that sort of thing was never spoken about in those days no one ever quite knew what the problem actually was. But she fell pregnant again reasonably soon and after the even more troublesome arrival of the next baby, Ted, only a year or so later, she was advised by the doctor that any more children would put her life in jeopardy. She took this advice seriously. As she was a devout Catholic this brought to an end the physical side of her relationship with her husband.

Lily Sheehan was a tall elegant looking woman in her youth. She was born Lily Bennett and she came to Dublin from County Meath at the age of sixteen to go into service with a parish priest on the north side of the city. Not much was ever said about her family except that it was large and that her father seems to have been somewhat of a rover and had gone to America on a couple of different occasions on his own to make his fortune and had returned to the family home in county Meath without any great sum of money to his credit. After trying life in America a second time, old man Bennett returned to stay in Meath thereafter. Lily had quite a few brothers and sisters, a number of who emigrated to England but who stayed in touch with her on a Christmas card type basis for much of her life. After a few years in service with the priest she met Maurice and they decided to marry and start a family. Lily was by most standards an intensely devout Catholic. In the last days of her life the neighbours used to refer to her as the 'saint' in the street. What this meant was that she would attend mass daily, if she could, and she would go on her knees on a stone floor to say a rosary[5] or two whenever she could.

Maurice Sheehan was employed by a large international company and when Patsy was born he had a reasonable job and every prospect of a good career with the organisation. He was a hard working and loyal employee. He was proud of his education which consisted of staying in school until 16 years of age. He had the Irish Catholic equivalent of the protestant ethic and he took great pride in the fact that he had never been unemployed for a single day, even during the worst days of the Great Depression. Whenever it was appropriate he would say, "I never had a single day out of work". He really did define himself in terms of his job and his responsibilities to his family, at least to his original family. He was a large big boned man with a bald head. He was conscious of the baldness to the extent that he grew the hair on the left side of his head to about six inches and then he used some sort of greasy hair dressing to plaster the long hair over the bald middle patch. He was a complete tea-totaller who had a strong aversion to the 'drink'. He had very strong opinions and he did not readily listen, at least too readily, to anyone else's opinions. Unlike his wife Lily he was not much of a Catholic. He would go to mass on Sundays but he liked arriving late and being at the back of the church so he could get out quickly when it was over. He was a heavy smoker of Woodbines so as he exited the church he would light up a new fag.

So the immediate family into which Steve married was Patsy, the surviving twin, and the younger brother Ted, also known as Terry and the parents Maurice and Lily. But these four people had not really had a chance of ever living together as a family. Circumstances had prevented that from a very early stage long before the time Steve met them. For all of Patsy's conscious life the four younger Sheehans had lived within the extended family.

As mentioned Maurice had been caught up in the grave misfortunes of his father. Maurice's father who also went by the name of Maurice and who will be referred to as Maurice Senior came to Dublin as a young man

---

[5] For those who are not familiar with the Catholic praying regime a rosary consists of five sets of prayers. Each set contains one Our Father, 5 Hail Marys and one Glory Be. It is normally said on one's knees and if the discomfort of kneeling can be increased through a rough surface all the better. From a child's point of view a rosary is pretty close to torture.

from somewhere near the village of Castletown in County Wexford towards the end of the 19th century as he had a job on the railways. He was one of many who were attracted to the big city at that time and he saw it as an opportunity to make his fortune. He was an energetic and talented man and initially he had been very successful and he quite quickly rose to a senior rank at one of Dublin's larger railway stations. At that stage he had a fairly prestigious and well-paid job and the family enjoyed the relatively high income that he earned. Like most Catholic families of that period they had a large number of children, somewhere in the order of twelve. The exact number of children was never mentioned by any member of the family. It was probably too painful to be specific about how many of the children had died. At that time the Sheehan family lived in a large house at a good address on the North side of Dublin.

This rather large family did not last long as a considerable number of the children passed away in one of the great diphtheria or flu epidemics which struck Ireland, and for that matter the rest of the world, in the early years of the 20th century. It is hard to imagine eight or nine of your children dying in the space of a few months and the repercussions of such an event can only be devastating. As can have been expected, this tragedy had a catastrophic effect on Maurice Senior and he began to drink more than he should. Drinking has been and some would say still is, a major problem in Ireland. Some people refer to excessive drink as the 'Curse of the Irish'. Anyway Maurice Senior took to the drink. Soon his income could only just cover his drinking and the family moved into much more difficult financial circumstance. However more tragedy was yet to come. Due to some accident while at work at the railway station Maurice injured his eyes. Again the nature of the accident was not discussed. He did not go blind immediately but over a period of a few years he eventually totally lost his sight.

As the blindness was slow but steady the railway company knew his sight was deteriorating. Eventually they let him go and he thus lost a well paid job as well as having a drinking problem. In those days there was no compensation paid and little or no state benefits for the blind. So the family was now in serious financial trouble. Maurice Senior was able to find some fairly routine and very low paid work in a hardware shop. The hardware shop, unlike the railway, stood by him and kept him on the payroll even after he was totally blind. He was able to do some unpacking type jobs. However in reality he went there more to pass the time than anything else as his pay at the hardware shop was a tiny fraction of what it had been before.

This old man Maurice Senior died in about 1950 and although I cannot say that I knew him well as I was only six years old at that time, I do not recall any hint of the bitterness which the loss of so many members of his family and his blindness could so easily have engendered. Misfortune was what happened to some people. Catholicism taught the faithful to live with their lot and maybe even see hardship in some sense as a blessing.

But Maurice Senior's personal misfortune brought misfortune on the whole of his family including Patsy and Ted. At that time, in the second half of the 1920s, Maurice Senior's household consisted of himself, his wife who was known as Mo, two children, Paddy and Annie and an old lady who went by the name of Lizzie. She was not a member of the family. It would be unusual today but no one seemed to know what Lizzie's surname was. It was never mentioned in the family. It was almost as though she didn't have one. Thus there were five people who had relied directly on Maurice Senior for support.

Mo died in the late 1930s before the Second World War and nothing much is known about her except that she was very fondly spoken of by the other members of the family. The large photo of her which hung on the wall made her look like a very old woman but she was probably only in her sixties. As will be seen shortly she must have been a very generous lady.

Probably the most colourful member of the Sheehan family was Maurice's younger brother Paddy. He had a direct influence on Patsy who regarded him as a man who had known how to live his life with some success. Paddy Sheehan was quite a few years younger than Maurice and was the only other member of the original Sheehan family who survived. He was still at primary school when his father went blind. He stayed on until he was legally old enough to leave. Paddy left home as soon as he could and like so many other Irishmen before him, he joined the British Army. He was a big strapping man and no doubt he made a fine looking soldier. Being picked up as a recruit or taking the "king's shilling" as they used to say was probably the easiest way for a young Irish lad with no money and little education to get away from home quickly. This adventure of Paddy's took place in the early 1930's.

But like so many Irish men before and after him, he did not enjoy the military life and returned home as soon as he could. It is probable that he left the British Army without a proper discharge. Like so many other things, the Sheehans did not speak directly about Paddy's time in the army. He had a couple of souvenirs from his military days, a big bear skin and a bugle.

In the years Paddy had spent in the British Army he had been based near London. In this time he grew to know the city and the environs very well indeed. One of Paddy's party tricks was to recite all the street names you would encounter if you went from various points in London to different destinations. It was almost as though he had once been a London taxi driver and had acquired the "knowledge". But I am quite certain that he had not ever trained for this job. Paddy would say, "Now if you want to go from Victoria Station to King's Cross Station you would go along such and such a street and then along such and such a road, etc." He never appeared to be aware of how boring this little display of knowledge could become.

Having had his one adventure abroad he spent the rest of his life living with the other members of the Sheehan family, never marrying or moving out of the Sheehan home to live on his own. He was entirely dependent on that family for his emotional well being. On returning to Ireland Paddy decided to join the Irish Health Service. He did not have the right qualifications so he obtained the necessary books and worked hard to acquire the qualifications, which he needed. He was successful at this. This left Paddy with an unusual respect for books and he kept piles of them in his room. The Irish Health Service suited him and he settled down to spending the rest of his working life working in a hospital.

Paddy Sheehan became an orderly in an institution for the seriously mentally ill. He would have been quite a formidable figure working with disturbed people. Everyone in the family believed that he had many stories to tell about his job. However he was very professional and also he was a very private man who did not relate much of his experiences.

He was an unusual man who spent much of his later years, after retirement, behaving much like a hermit. In effect the day he retired from his job in the mental institution he went to his little room and spent 30 years there hardly ever coming out. Most of his meals were brought to his room as was the daily newspaper. He had a collection of short wave radios and through the press and the radio kept himself fully informed of world affairs. In the early years of his retirement he would go out to pick up his pension and buy books but in the later years of his life, he had his pension picked up for him and he hardly ever left his room at all. This eccentric if not bizarre behaviour was always a mystery to the other members of the family. Maurice and Lily would say, "Well working for 35 years in that mad house has rubbed off on to Paddy". However it is certainly possible that he may have suffered from some form of agoraphobia during the last couple of decades of his life. But a doctor was never consulted and no diagnosis was ever suggested, never mind made. Paddy was simply perceived to be eccentric, although he may well have actually been ill.

The other member of the Sheehan family who had a direct influence on Patsy was Annie. She was a few years younger than Paddy and thus considerably younger than Maurice. Annie Sheehan who was always presented as Maurice's sister was not born into the Sheehan family at all. Annie's natural mother had been a great friend of Mo's, Maurice's mother. This great friend had become pregnant out of wedlock in the earlier years of the century and this caused the father to disappear. Mo's friend had done one of the few things which a woman on her own could do in those days which was to go to England and have the baby, and then give the child away. The baby would normally have been given away in England but this woman insisted that she wanted to bring the baby back to Ireland. Mo took the baby girl into her family and Annie lived her life as Mo's child and as Maurice and Paddy's sister. This was one of the ways the Irish managed to cope with unwanted children – give them away privately to friends or relations. No doubt this was not entirely legal.

When Annie became 60 or perhaps it was 65, and was eligible for a State Pension she needed her birth certificate in order to claim her money. A search was made for the document but it could not be found. This clearly caused Annie some distress. It does not appear that the others were able to create a plausible reason why all the other members of the Sheehan family had their own birth certificates and Annie did not have one. Annie said a few times that she had begun to think that she was not really a Sheehan. It is not clear why a missing birth certificate should produce such a thought. I have always believed that deducing this lack of lineage from a missing birth certificate is quite a feat and perhaps demonstrates that Annie was really quite sharp. But as far as can be made out Annie's parentage was never admitted to her. The Sheehans made no distinction between Annie and themselves in any way. She was never made to feel in any way that she was an outsider. She was the last of the older Sheehans to die and after Paddy's death she inherited all that was in the Sheehan estate – not that there was much to speak of.

Annie Sheehan left school as early as she could and spent most of her working life employed as a cleaner. Although she was said to have been quite an attractive child, Annie grew up to be a plain looking woman. She was short and plump for most of her life, with a rather round moon type face. She always dressed in dowdy clothes. No doubt as a child she was dressed from charity shops and she continued this as a life time habit. The Sheehans often went to jumble sales especially those that were associated with St Vincent de Paul. Annie was very shy. Annie was both slow at movement and rather slow in speech. Thus she could give the impression of being slow-witted. Of course she had very little schooling which would have been typical of a poor working class family in Dublin in the 1920s. Even as an adult the Sheehan family always treated Annie as though she was a 'semi-grown-up' child and not really capable of properly looking after herself. In fact Annie was much smarter than anyone in that family thought. She had a much better comprehension of what was happening than she appeared to have. And she also had a wry sense of humour but this was carefully hidden except when she was sure that her comments would not get back to Maurice or Lily or even Paddy. As a child it was drummed into her that children should be seen and not heard and this marked her for the rest of her life. She was trapped in a life with no prospect of interesting or properly paid work. It's not known if any man had ever shown any interest in Annie – that was never mentioned, but marriage or going into a convent would have been the only ways out of having to spend all of her life in the Sheehans' household. As mentioned before Annie earned her living as an office cleaner. In between her cleaning jobs Annie was the Sheehan family gofer. In the language of Dublin, Annie did the messages. The last twenty years of her life were spent cleaning the offices of solicitors in the rather posh business part of Harcourt Street and looking after the recluse in the family - Paddy. She only stopped working a few years before she died. At that time she must have been already well into her seventies.

It is worth mentioning a little bit about Lizzie. Lizzie was a very strange figure indeed. Lizzie was already elderly when Maurice Senior went blind. She had come to work in service for Maurice Senior in his heyday when he had been a prosperous railway worker. She had no family of her own and she had stayed in the Sheehan household, unpaid but with no duties when Maurice Senior could no longer afford her services. In the later days of her life it appears that she had become a very grumpy old woman whose presence the family no longer appeared to enjoy but tolerated her due to the many years she had lived with them. She always wore black. All day long she sat by the fire place. She seemed to have very little interest of the outside world and just commented on what members of the family were doing. She was very old when she died in 1961. When anyone in the family complained about anything someone would say "You're becoming just like old Lizzie". This was considered to be a substantial insult. In a sense Lizzie was the Sheehan family's internal bog-eyman or should I say bogeywoman.

To help Maurice's father Maurice and Lily Sheehan gave up their own home and moved into an apartment on the second floor in an old tenement building in Cuffe Street. Tenements in Cuffe Street were dreadful. At that time it was a serious slum street at the edge of that part of Dublin known as the Liberties.

Overnight Maurice (Junior) became financially responsible for nine people. The income from the five additional people was virtually zero and this effectively plunged Maurice and Lily into poverty. This act of self-lessness of Maurice and Lily meant that they moved themselves from potentially the middle classes or at least the better to do end of the working class to the poor classes.

But the poverty then faced by the extended Sheehan family did not mean that they went hungry or that Patsy or Ted went without shoes. Maurice's job meant that his father's family was not destitute. But it did result in there not being a single penny to spare. There were a number of Catholic Church based welfare organisations from which the Sheehans could have obtained help but they were very proud and slow to accept any form of charity.

There is no question that the new found poverty adversely affected all of them. Cuffe Street was a dreadful place to have to live. Of course it can hardly have been the worst slum street in Dublin. In the 1930s an Irish newspaper declared that Dublin had the most dreadful slums in Europe. Subsequently it was established that in the 1939 to 1943 period about 112,000 people were living in 6,000 tenements in the city. By any standards conditions were said to be really extraordinary with, in the worst cases, up to 100 people living in a house with as many as twenty members of the same family in one room. These tenements would generally have little or no running water with a single toilet in the back yard. The Sheehan's tenement did not reach this level of deprivation.

In the early years the Sheehans would have had three rooms for nine people. However it is true to say that Cuffe Street was one of the most run down streets on the South side of the city. It was full of buildings which should really have been condemned. But that was where their home was. By the early 1940s Paddy and Annie were earning and the family had expanded into 5 rooms, two of which were on the third floor.

The tenement building dated back to Dublin's Regency or Georgian days. It had a typical Regency or Georgian door with a great fan light above the doorway. As is customary for this type of building, it had pseudo fluted classical pillars on either side of the door. There was a row of these buildings which ran along the East side of the street. All of these buildings were dark, shabby and dirty, not having had a coat of paint for years, maybe even decades. These tenements were all cold and damp and it was hard work for the occupants to keep them in a liveable state. The Sheehan building as was the case with the other ones in the street, had no modern facilities. It had one toilet in the back yard and no bath; nor had it had any basic maintenance for years. There was a zinc tub in which some sort of comprehensive wash was occasionally taken. Patsy occasionally went down to Tara Street where there were public baths.

As mentioned there were no in-door toilets. Everyone had a chamber pot, referred to as a potty or a 'po', under their bed. There was one cold lavatory without electricity in the back yard. But there was, however, cold running water in the main living room. For tea making, washing and other reasons water had to be boiled almost continuously. In turn this meant a fire fuelled mostly by coal but sometimes turf and sometimes in the form of briquettes was on the go most of the time. This made the whole house smell. There was no lighting on the stairs or on the landings in the building. This meant that a torch or more often some matches or a candle was used when you came in after dark. It was a trial to get up two floors in the dark. I recall how spooky the shadows seemed as we walked up the stairs with the shadows of the banisters moving on the walls as we moved upwards or downwards with a candle. It was a truly eerie place.

Cuffe Street was a tough location. On the opposite side of the road there were low income corporation flats. For some reason the Sheehans believed that it was worse to live in one of these corporation flats than in their tenement. At the North end of the street there were some shops which had slot machines and noisy people. During the end of the 1940s there was considerable unemployment in Dublin and Cuffe Street had plenty of unemployed youths hanging about, especially on the corners. The Sheehans referred to these young people as corner boys which was a seriously derogatory term. I guess that most of them were just kids with nothing to do. The Sheehan view would have been that "idle hands do the devil's work". This corner boy description was just one of the uncomplimentary terms used by the Sheehans to describe people in Cuffe Street. They believed that a lot of people around Cuffe Street were undesirable. The dismissive term, "they are common" was used by the Sheehans from time to time. This attitude might be described by the Irish aphorism 'Tuppence farthing looking down on Tuppence'.

The poverty of Cuffe Street was exaggerated by the street's proximity to one of the most expensive and fashionable Georgian squares or parks in Dublin. At the South end Cuffe Street ran into St Stephen's Green which was posh with a capital 'P'. Dublin's best hotel at that time, the Shelburne Hotel, was on the Green. Also there was the Government Department of Foreign Affairs. There were several exclusive gentlemen's clubs on the Green. Running off the Green was Grafton Street which was probably Dublin's premier shopping street.

So some of the corner boys hung around this intersection of Cuffe Street with St Stephen's Green and watched, what were to them no doubt, the well healed toffs, go by. There seemed to be corner boys on Cuffe Street any time of the day or night. However as undesirable as these youngsters may have been to the Sheehans, they did not seem to be involved in any sort of crime. Crime does not appear to have been an issue in Dublin during that period.

I cannot recall Steve ever using the term corner boy or the expression that they are 'common'. Steve was much more reconciled to the plight he found himself in and to the family he married into. I once heard the word 'common' described as the ultimate dismissive term. Once someone was classified as common they were of no further interest and the Sheehans used it that way.

Chapter Three

Backwards to go Forwards

Although at the time Steve and Patsy were married there was still 18 months to go before VE day, the course of the remainder of the war was pretty obvious. The Germans had been defeated in the desert. The Russians lifted the siege of Leningrad that January in 1944 when they were married and the Americans invaded Italy. Pressure was building up on the Germans on all fronts and Hitler was beginning to show himself for the ineffectual leader he was. It was now only a matter of time before the Third Reich would collapse and peace would be restored to Europe. At least a type of peace would descend on Europe.

The major impact of this on Steve and Patsy's life in Ireland was that Steve's business completely dried up. The charcoal business in Ireland was a wartime wonder and as the Germans were chased out of the Middle East, oil once again began to flow in volume into the British Isles.

It didn't take long for Steve's charcoal business to be wound up. According to Patsy, by the time Steve paid the business debts they had only one hundred pounds left. Although a hundred pounds was much more money then than it is today, maybe 20 or even 50 times more, this sum of money on its own didn't last very long.

Of course to make matters very much more complicated, on July 27 of that year Patsy produced a son. They decided to call their first-born Daniel Stephen Joseph. The name Stephen was used for continuity from one generation to the next; the name Joseph was used to show a link with Steve's elder and now dead brother and Daniel was the name that Steve liked. As Steve and Patsy had only been married six months at this stage, Patsy announced that she had had a premature baby. This is despite the fact that at birth the baby weighed over seven pounds. It did not occur to Patsy for many years that there was a fundamental contradiction inherent in the fact that she had given birth to a heavy baby and the declaration that it was nearly two months premature. She did not know about babies premature or otherwise. Patsy braved out this explanation of the fact that she had been married only 6 months before the birth for many years but by the time she was in her late forties she began to admit that she had, what she then began to refer to as, a 'love' child.

From time to time Patsy would describe how difficult the first years of her marriage were. Despite the large families which were customary in Ireland, Dublin was not child friendly. In fact, the sort of people who had property to let in Dublin in the 1940s were actually baby hostile. Many of the apartments or the digs which Steve and Patsy wanted to rent would just not take a baby at all. But they did get temporary digs although never for long and thus they moved again and again, living pretty well out of suitcases. They had very little money. Steve being a foreigner with a heavy accent couldn't get a regular job and picked up piecemeal work whenever he could get it. To be fair, jobs, any jobs were not easy to find in those days in Ireland. Ted, Patsy's brother, described Steve and Patsy as being the poorest people he had ever known. Of course, by 1944 the Sheehan family's fortunes had improved a bit with Paddy, Annie and Ted, all working now, albeit for low pay. Ted was working as a trainee baker. So Lily saw to it that Steve and Patsy got some help especially with the baby.

Steve and Patsy were also sustained in this period by the thought that a very comfortable life awaited Steve as soon as the war was over and they returned to Hungary. This was of course a pipe dream in several different ways. Patsy could never have coped, at that stage of her life, in such a different society. She had no talent for languages and she wasn't much good with understanding different peoples' customs. In any case the defeat of the Germans brought with it a whole new set of problems for Hungary. Having been 'liberated' by the Russians, Hungary was occupied by an ancient enemy. Furthermore Russian sponsored Hungarian communism at the end of the 1940s and well into the 1950s was very harsh and anyone who had property in Hungary lost it. The socialist ideal did not tolerate even the modest wealth of the Remenyis. This would have made Steve no better off in Hungary than he was in Ireland.

As soon as the war was over Steve decided that he should once again look for work as a seafarer. Although up to this time Steve himself had only been at sea for three short years, his brother Imre had spent more than a decade at sea from the early 1930s. And thus the idea of going back to sea came relatively naturally to the sons of the Remenyi family. His Irish citizenship didn't come through until 1949 but he had temporary travel documents, which were good enough to allow him to work on a ship. Thus he approached Irish Shipping, the state owned Irish marine transport company for a job. Irish Shipping was a state owned organisation which was set up in 1941 when the United Kingdom took the decision that it would not use its valuable fleet of merchant ships to supply Irish war time needs. The British argument was, "Why should we put our ships and our seamen at risk to supply a neutral country". The organisation had a number of problems in acquiring appropriate ships and also obtaining clearance to sail under a neutral flag. This was of course essential if the Irish ships were to avoid being sunk by the allies. The markings on the Irish Spruce in the photograph behind the cover of this book show how the seafarers tried to identify themselves as being from a neutral country. But finally this was all arranged and by the end of the war Irish Shipping had a substantial fleet of about thirteen deep sea vessels. However the post war fleet was a real rag tag bag of ships which would make anyone admire the men who were prepared to sail them into the blue yonder.

The job Steve was offered was that of a cabin boy. This was quite different to the work he had done before as a ship's radio officer but Steve was, not to put too fine a point on it, pretty desperate. Going to a job at sea in this capacity was certainly a backward step. Steve's duties included scrubbing the deck, washing the lavatories and all the other rotten jobs, which those at the bottom of the ladder have always had to suffer. Also the money was rotten but it was steady work, which was a great improvement on the past year of casual employment.

However, Steve was a hard working individual. He was both responsible and resourceful and within a short period of time he had escaped from that first painful job. According to Patsy, Steve moved up to be a kitchen hand, a steward, a cook and within a couple of years he held the post of Purser/Chief Steward. The Chief Steward was the equivalent of the hotel manager on board a ship. As Purser/Chief Steward he had at times up to a couple of dozen men working for him. In Irish Shipping the Chief Steward had the status of an officer. Steve had his own office and cabin on board the ships. It was always good fun to visit him on his ship. Climbing the gangplank was a thrill and the confined spaces in the ship corridors were always exciting. Steve always had a small library in his cabin which consisted of a collection of novels as well as a big dictionary. This book had been bought in America and was thus an American-English tome. This didn't always lead to exactly good, "received" spelling on the part of Steve but that didn't matter to him. There was also one of the largest cookbooks that were available in those days. He had taught himself to cook from this – no doubt experimenting on his captive audience, the crews on the ships. But he was naturally good with food and this was probably no hardship for the men. Steve genuinely appeared to enjoy his new role as Purser/Chief Steward and although the money was still not great it was much better than he had seen for quite a while. So Steve was now in a way beginning ever so slowly to move up the corporate ladder!

During the end of the 1940s and the beginning of the 1950s the Irish ships had a number of reasonably regular routes across the Atlantic.

These ships crossed the ocean in about ten or twelve days, off loaded their cargo in a few days at each of the ports they visited and took another nine or ten days to return. Thus Steve was usually away for about five or six weeks and then he was home for about one week before the next trip came up. This was not ideal for Patsy as a young wife and mother. In fact it was pretty awful. Being in the merchant navy does not really provide an opportunity for a reasonable family life. But she understood that necessity was the mother of invention and she made the most of the situation in which she and Steve found themselves.

Then Steve and Patsy had a minor lucky break. The tenants in the apartment at the back of the Sheehans' tenement house moved out. Steve and Patsy jumped at this place as, although it was in the dreaded Cuffe Street, it was a permanent abode and furthermore Lily was right nearby and this meant that Patsy would have help with the child. Also by this time Patsy was pregnant again and this would lead to the birth in 1948 of the second baby, a girl who they would call Jean Patricia.

In all, it was in some ways quite surprising how Patsy welcomed her return to Cuffe Street, a place which had been so damaging to her not many years before. But Cuffe Street was more permanent than short term digs. However these two years spent in Cuffe Street were still very difficult for her and money was still very tight.

At about this time Steve heard that his mother had been killed in the war. The Red Cross had done a great job in helping displaced people find their relatives and this had worked for Steve. He had already known that there would be nothing left of his family's business, house or estate. He took the news of his mother's death very badly. He went into a state of shock and was unable to talk to anyone for a week. He also learnt at about this time that his brother, Imre, had left Magda and settled in America, but he showed no great inclination to visit or even get in touch with Imre. Although it did not come out until much later, Steve actually had no interest in Imre. He knew that Magda had settled permanently in Sydney and she and he exchanged greetings every Christmas in the form of Christmas cards. In those days Australia was a world away and there was never any question of her visiting us.

My first memories as a little boy were of Cuffe Street and date back to 1948 or 1949. Some of these memories I have described in the previous chapter. By and large the Cuffe Street years were not too bad for a young child. I started attending school while I lived there and I always enjoyed my schooling. I was four years old and as was the custom then in Ireland

I was in a class of about 50 children and really enjoyed the hustle and bustle of being in a big crowd of noisy kids. It was at this time that I became aware that Lily had become the main mother figure in my life and remained so at least until the family left Ireland.

The circumstances which allowed Steve and Patsy to move out of Cuffe Street and to substantially improve their life style took place a couple of years after they moved there. By this stage Steve had established himself as one of the more well known Purser/Chief Stewards in Irish Shipping and his work had attracted the attention of some of the senior management in the company. This led to Steve being made an offer which he could not refuse. This actually happened in an interesting way. In 1948 Steve took ill and was eventually diagnosed as having gallstone problems. As a result he was hospitalised and operated on for their removal. He spent about a week in hospital and was then released and sent home for bed rest for another few weeks. He was not recovering very fast from the operation. He was very sore and feeling rather sorry for himself. However, about ten days later the head office at Irish Shipping sent a message by hand around to Cuffe Street that Steve should phone the office as soon as possible. This was a good couple of weeks before Steve's sick leave was to expire and thus this summons came as a surprise.

Anyway, Steve pulled himself out of bed and went around to the pub on the corner where there was a public telephone. He was told by the office that a certain gentleman, whom we shall call, for want of a better name, Mr Murphy, wanted to see him. Steve knew well who this Mr Murphy was, and the invitation to meet Mr Murphy was one of the most exciting things that ever happened to Steve. Just knowing that Mr Murphy had asked to see him made Steve feel very much better and the soreness of his operation immediately began to recede. What Mr Murphy had to offer Steve changed his life. By the way the offer that Steve was about to be made was to join a small group of Purser-Chief Stewards who were able to enhance their income substantially. Steve was always vague about how many people were actually involved in this circle but it is clear that although it was well known to the Irish Shipping seafarers, not that many people were part of it.

Mr Murphy was involved in the Irish Hospitals Sweepstakes Trust which may be thought of as the equivalent of the Irish national lottery. In its time the Irish Hospitals' Sweepstakes was one of the largest sporting based lottery type events promoted internationally anywhere in the world. It had been authorized by the Irish government in 1930 and it soon became a major contributor to the funding of the Irish hospital system.

Formally it was a government backed private trust created to run a lottery type of event and market tickets throughout the world. Tickets were sold as coupons from a book of tickets much like raffle tickets sometimes used at school fairs. The name and address of the ticket purchaser were written on the counterfoil or stub, which was kept in the book. Counterfoils of the tickets were sent back to Ballsbridge where the Irish Hospitals Sweepstakes headquarters was based and placed in a giant barrel. This lottery had two steps. First there was a draw to see who had won a 'title' to a horse. This was done by matching ticket holders' names with the name of a horse running in a major Irish or British race. Then the race took place. The prizes went to ticket holders whose horse won or was placed in the race. Thus Irish Hospitals Sweepstakes tried to combine some of the fun of going to the races with the excitement of drawing a lucky number at a lottery. The Irish Sweepstakes ended in 1987, when it was replaced by a state lottery. In the old days sweepstakes tickets were sold all over the world where there was and still is a considerable interest in horse racing.

Mr Murphy's job was related to the marketing and sales manager for Irish Hospital Sweepstakes ticket sales in the United States of America. This may not sound all that exciting a job until it is realised that all lotteries were, at that time illegal in the United States of America. This meant that Irish Hospital Sweepstakes tickets had to be brought into the United States under the noses and against the regulations of the US customs and they had to be sold and the stubs returned to Ireland without them falling into the hands of the American police. Money had also to be repatriated. Mr Murphy's success at his job has to be judged by the fact that money from Irish Americans constituted a large proportion of the income of Irish Hospital Sweepstakes. Mr Murphy ran a small group of chief stewards and other members of crew in Irish Shipping who made all the necessary transport arrangements for the tickets to arrive into the hands of the network of Irish publicans, barbers and others who sold the tickets in America for the Irish Hospital Sweepstakes.

Obviously this type of work carried a certain degree of risk. The chief stewards and others were effectively operating a smuggling ring into the United States of America for the Irish Government. Of course it was not heroine or cocaine which they were trafficking in and as was said by Irish Hospitals Sweepstakes Trust executives what they were doing was not illegal in Ballsbridge. But nonetheless it was illegal in America. Over the years the Americans caught one or two of these Irish Shipping crews. However, although they were fined and presumably Irish Shipping was also in trouble as a company in the United States of America, it was all regarded as being a relatively minor offence. In the final analysis the

American government could not really be seen as being too tough on an institution which was trying to raise the standard of health in 'poor old Ireland', a country from which so many of them, or their forefathers, had originally come.

Steve was perfect for this undercover job. Although he was a fairly gregarious fellow he was also very tight lipped. He operated on a strictly need to know basis and thus any confidences which came his way were safe. He was exceptionally thorough. He always crossed his "Ts" and dotted his "Is". He left nothing to chance. Then he was a very good chess player who could see four or five moves ahead. So he always thought carefully about what he was doing. He was well prepared and made sure that every avenue was covered. He once said, "The trick to smuggling is to arrange the contraband so that if it is found the finder will not know that he has found it". Finally Steve was also very affable. He was especially good at making functionaries, such as customs officers, feel really important. In a real sense they were very important indeed to him.

Risk brought with it profit and the payments made to the Irish Shipping staff were for them substantial. Steve had known about the ticket smuggling for some time and he had been hoping that he would be selected to join this small circle. So from his sick bed he went to see Mr Murphy and a few days later, still sore from his gallstones operation, he joined his first ship carrying Irish Hospital Sweepstakes tickets into the United States of America.

Of course, how the tickets found their way on board a ship was never discussed nor was how the tickets got into the hands of the individuals in America in the distribution channel, but what was always clear to me was that this Irish Hospital Sweepstakes tickets business was conducted on a large scale. Crates or pallets full of tickets were shipped out and suitcases of ticket stubs were brought back home. No doubt the crates were specially prepared and maybe they had Home Made Irish Butter plastered all over them. On the return leg the suitcases or boxes of ticket counterfoils would have simply passed out of America largely unquestioned.

As well as ticket stubs the return journeys brought with them quite a lot of other American goods. As a small child I was aware of having products in our home such as Campbell's Soups, Mrs Somebody's Devil Chocolate Cake Mix, O'Henrys, Hershey Bars of various sorts, Uncle Ben's Rice. All these everyday American products were generally not available in Irish shops. There were also quite a lot of nylon stockings and a variety of unusual beverages including root beer and big bottles of cola were always around as well.

There were quite a lot of different types of people in Irish Shipping, the lottery company and Dublin Castle involved in this Irish Hospital Sweep-stakes ticket endeavour and no doubt everyone shared in the additional prosperity which it brought in its wake. There were frequently men in grey suits hanging around who I was told were plain clothes policemen. These policemen accompanied the motor cars which went in and out of Dublin harbour carrying what I imagine were the ticket stubs as well as cases of whisky and gin. But as a general rule the ships' captains were not involved and neither were other bridge officers. Steve told an amusing story about who knew what which may well have been apocryphal. The story went that a newly employed rather young first officer was on watch one evening in a USA port when he became aware that strange men were on deck removing containers from the hold of the ship. The first officer knew that the captain was in his cabin and he decided to report this matter to his boss. When he entered the captain's cabin he found the captain having a glass of whiskey with a strange man. "Crates are being taken off the ship by strange men I have not seen before", said the first officer. "Don't worry about that", said the captain. "Shouldn't I report this to the customs?" replied the young first officer. "Half of those men are customs officers", retorted the captain. "Well then I had better report it to the po-lice", suggested the young officer. The stranger looked him straight in the eye saying in a cold clear voice, "We are the police! And by the way so that you know how serious this business is there are several million books of Sweepstake tickets coming off this ship tonight".

This ticket business required some socialising and there were many get-togethers especially at the North Star Hotel next to Amiens Street Station in the centre of Dublin and later on in The Goat, a well known pub in the southern suburbs. These were just two examples of the more favoured watering holes where these adventures were discussed and perhaps planned. Steve always paid for the drinks on these quasi-social occasions. I clearly recall Patsy saying more than once to Steve "Why do you always have to pay". Steve never answered this question. I guess he saw it as a rhetorical question. Recently it has come to light that Steve actually had Sweepstake money "to buy a drink for the boys" and clearly he enjoyed drinking with his ship mates. There is an interesting side story about drinking in Ireland during this period. Irish Publican Law had strict hours during which liquor could be sold. The opening times were 10.30 in the morning to shortly after lunch i.e. 3 pm when the pubs were required to close for one hour. This was commonly called the "Holy Hour" and it was designed to force day-long-drinkers to leave the pub and stretch their legs and take a breath full of fresh air. An hour later the pubs reopened until 10 pm when last orders were taken and then closing time was thirty minutes later. Like other parts of the world with closing times drinkers often wanted to stay a bit longer but Irish law formally prohibited this. There was however one way of circumventing the Law. There was an old rule in Ireland that a publican should not ever refuse a drink to a bone fide traveller. This Law went back to the days when it was a considerable hardship to travel and if you were caught out travelling late at night, no doubt you would have been cold and weary. The interesting point is that the definition of a traveller was someone who was 3 or 5 miles from home. And the evidence required to prove that you were a traveller was fairly slim. Patsy had her name and an old address engraved on her wrist watch with was all the evidence required by the Gardi. So the drinking could go on quite late.

Steve's new income completely changed the family's life. Within a year he had bought a new house four or five miles out of Dublin towards the Naas Road. The house was on the border of Crumlin, Driminagh and Walkinstown. None of these were exactly classy suburbs but they were miles ahead of Cuffe Street. It seems that Patsy and Steve thought that Crumlin was the area with the lowest status and that Walkinstown was the best of the three. So Steve would say that they lived in Crumlin and Patsy would always say Walkinstown. This was Steve's slightly perverse sense of humour coming out.

It was a small modern two up and two down semi-detached house on a brand new housing estate with a little garden to the front and a slightly larger one to the rear. Steve and Patsy bought the house before it was built off a set of blue print plans. They then visited the site several times to visualise where the rooms would be. They then made a number of trips to see the house rising up from the foundations. It was funny being taken out to a building site but these trips certainly gave Steve and Patsy quite a lot of pleasure. We moved into the house as soon as we could while the surrounds still had many of the characteristics of a building site. There was mud, heavy duty Irish mud everywhere and it took ages for the mud to be cleared up and a footpath put in and the grass to grow in the front and back gardens. There were big trucks coming and going as some of the other houses were still unfinished.

Being in a brand new house certainly felt funny. Its newness could be smelt in very room. It didn't have the familiar smells and noises of a tenement in Cuffe Street. And to us it was quite far out of the centre of the city. It seemed to be a long bus journey back into town and in those days the buses were crowded and they didn't move fast. However Patsy and Steve were very pleased to leave the Cuffe Street period of their lives behind.

Being in Crumlin was certainly a significant move up the housing and the social stakes. They had moved from a slum to a relatively upper working class area with all the 'mod cons' which one would expect to find in such a district. Patsy loved it. She had her own house at last. In addition to the new house she bought all new furnishing, carpets, curtains and so forth which she had not had the opportunity to do before.

Patsy was madly house-proud and spent an inordinate amount of time cleaning and polishing her lovely new home. Of course it was not easy to keep the house clean with a five year old boy and an eighteen month old baby girl. Nonetheless she tried and in doing so she created an unhappy home. It was from this house that I remember going with Patsy to the shops to buy groceries and using post war ration coupons or tickets which were shortly thereafter discontinued. But during this period many household items were still scarce and Steve was able to bring all sorts of interesting things into Ireland by virtue of his travelling job. I was moved to a nearby school that required me to walk about a mile each way every day. This seemed a very long way to me at the time. So I was bought a bicycle by Steve. The bicycle allowed me to get to school quickly and it also allowed me to have continual accidents like falling off the bike and crashing into neighbours' gates.

However living away from Cuffe Street had its drawbacks. Lily was not on hand in the same way as she had been before. Patsy found this difficult as looking after two kids was a challenge with which she could barely cope. When she was having a bad time she would say that she wished that she had thrown the baby off the end of the North Wall into the Sea. This idea of infanticide was voiced many times over the years. It wasn't that she was really serious in any literal sense and it's not certain that she would have had the courage – although who really knows? But what is clear is that she just didn't know how to cope with a child never mind two children and she didn't have a husband living at home in the normal way to support her. She, unlike Steve, never learnt how to deal with children even in her dying days. Patsy was proof that mothering does not come naturally to all women.

During the Cuffe Street years she had become reliant on having Lily to hand as a child minder and general house keeper and she really missed this unpaid help. At this time Patsy showed that she had picked up some of the worst habits of Maurice. When she was a school girl Maurice used to beat her with his leather belt. She did not have a leather belt with which to beat her children so she bought a bamboo cane instead from the local hardware shop. In fact she sent me down to the hardware shop to buy one. It is an interesting reflection that in the 1950s hardware shops in Dublin sold three foot lengths of bamboo the only purpose of which could have been beating children. They were of course also sold to schools where there was no shortage of beating going on.

There is no doubt that beating children was an important part of Irish life and in this respect Patsy was very Irish. 'Spare the rod and spoil the child' was quoted again and again. But for some reason she didn't believe in beating girls so she made up for that inadequacy in giving a double dose to her son. On the other hand I cannot remember Steve lifting a hand to strike any of his children. He was just not that sort of man.

Lily was greatly missed as now we saw her once a week instead of every day. It was at this time that I began to wish that I could have swapped Patsy for just about anyone else's mother but I was never to have any such luck. All my friends' mothers seemed to be better than Patsy and that impression which may well have been untrue stayed with me for a very long time. Steve of course didn't realise any of this as he always came home to an adoring wife, a spotlessly clean house and loving children. It took him many years to realise that Patsy had not been able to keep his small family emotionally together while he was away. It was all of twenty years later that the children were articulate enough for the resentment of the early years to come out and eventually Steve regretted the lack of attention the children had received from him in those years.

Steve knew how to arrive home after a trip. He always brought lots of presents. We ate a large number of O'Henry chocolate bars in those days. He also brought comics galore. So there were loads of Batman, Superman, Little Lulu and Richie Rich comics. When Steve was home he made sure that he gave some time to the children. He always pursued any opportunity to go to a circus or to a fun fair. In summer he would take us to the beach at the Sliver Strand or Brittas Bay or we would go to Dunlaoghaire to see the boats and the ships or climb Howth Head for the view over Dublin Bay. Going out and doing something as a family was very important to Steve.

Trips to the Dublin Zoo in Phoenix Park were other favourites of ours and Steve took us there often enough. Sometimes Lily would come too. She would dress up in her Sunday best for such an outing. Dublin Zoo had a big elephant, a rather ancient fellow who would take children on his back around the park and this was great fun for everyone. In the afternoon there was always a chimpanzees' tea party and we always delighted in that. Dublin Zoo had some big lions, which were caged, in the lion house. On one occasion while we were inspecting these fine specimens, the big male lion lifted up his leg and projected a large blast of urine all over Lily who was, as usual in her Sunday best. Everyone but Lily thought that was a grand joke.

At the time it was actually happening Steve's energy in entertaining his children, when he was home, was really great fun for us, but on reflection it was very superficial. There was no real closeness built up with him, in fact we really hardly knew him at all. But we didn't realise that then. It is not unfair to say that Steve had a closed personality who none of the children ever really got to know. It was not a question of our not knowing him well but rather we hardly knew him at all. But he was a generous man who when positioned next to Patsy who had a strong mean streak, became the hero of his children. On reflection it is truly surprising how little children can ask of their parents. In fact it is really amazing how little a father, and perhaps also a mother, has to do to win the love and admiration of their children.

At this time when Steve came back from trips he would enquire about my school work – I was the only child at school as at that time Jean would have been 2 or 3 years old. He was especially interested in encouraging numeracy. This was a short-lived attempt to encourage me academically as he actually lost interest in this fairly quickly. There was a big gap between how Steve had been taught in Hungarian schools and how the Irish schools operated and he was apparently not really able to help any of us with our homework. Patsy did not show any interest in any of our schooling. Patsy felt that her own schooling had been a great failure. She strongly blamed the nuns for that. Time and again Patsy claimed that she had been verbally and mentally abused by the nuns who had taught her and had beaten her for not reciting the Catholic catechism or learning her Irish verbs to their satisfaction. Like many other Irish people she resented having the Irish language imposed on her. There was no doubt quite a lot of truth in her assertions of abuse at the hands of the nuns. She had no self-esteem when it came to being able to write or to do any form of calculation, even the simplest arithmetic. It would appear that that's how many children were treated in Ireland at that time. As a result from the very start she resented any academic success achieved by any of her children.

Steve's work on the North Atlantic continued and he made more good steady money. The Irish Hospital Sweepstakes tickets deal looked as solid as a house. The extra money was very useful and Steve and Patsy really seemed to enjoy their new way of living.

After about three years Steve and Patsy decided to move house again. This time they moved considerably more up market buying a house in Mount Merion. Mount Merion was a considerably more expensive suburb than Crumlin or Walkinstown. It was well into the middle classes. It was a bigger house with a much bigger garden which was well established with a number of fruit trees. This time there was no mud about the house. In addition Steve bought a car. He actually bought a number of cars during this period but he never bought good cars. They were always pretty clapped out elderly vehicles. At least we now had some transport but it broke down time and again in the most inconvenient places. This all happened around about 1952 and thus it had taken Steve about six years to return to approximately the sort of social environment and financial comfort that he had enjoyed in his family home back in Hungary.

It was also decided that the children should go to private fee paying schools. Thus I was sent to Belvedere College on the North side of Dublin. Belvedere College was possibly the best or at least one of the best schools in Dublin. It was a Jesuit Fathers' school. The Jesuits, also known as the Society of Jesus were and perhaps still are the elite of the Catholic Church. As getting to school each day involved a long journey across the city, I was only at that school for about a year. Although the children did not appear to be beaten at Belvedere College by the Jesuit priests like they were beaten by the Christian and Marist Brothers, I was never more frightened. These apparently austere men in black knew how to control children. It is not clear precisely how they did this to the children but these men in black scared the living daylights out of most of the boys, especially the younger ones, who were unfortunate enough to go to that school. To get to Belvedere College I had to catch two buses – one into the Aston Quays on the Liffey and another bus up to Parnell Street.

It was soon realised that this travel was too much for a young child and I was moved to the Christian Brother's College which was called Oatlands, a relatively new school in Stillorgan, the suburb right next to Mount Merion. It was within walking distance from home. The Christian Brothers were famous for being tough, no nonsense teachers. They prided themselves in their ability to be in command of their pupils.

The Organisation of the Christian Brothers was started in Waterford in 1802, by Edmund Ignatius Rice with the aim of providing Catholic education to boys. For some time before it had been illegal to provide a Catholic education in Ireland and the establishment of the Christian Brothers was a major step to rectify this injustice. Initially a group of lay people, the Christian Brothers were only recognised as a religious order by the Holy See in 1820 when Rice's band of workers was constituted as a religious institute of the Church. The Order of the Christian Brothers grew rapidly, first in Ireland and then in various parts of the world including Canada, New Zealand, Australia, South Africa and the USA.

Some of the Christian Brothers, not all of them, were nothing less than brutal in their treatment of the boys in that school in Dublin in the 1950s. Every brother was equipped with a solid leather thong, which these holy men felt necessary to use regularly. The children sometimes wondered who manufactured these solid leather thongs and imagined a special division, staffed by little gnomes, in the Vatican, making tools with which to beat boys. Some of the worst beatings were doled out for not learning the Catechism as well as was required. Catechism had to be learnt off by heart – word perfect, and anyone who did not comply was in serious trouble. There was one particular Brother who revelled in telling the youngsters to learn impossibly large chunks of the Catechism overnight. The following day the whole class would be beaten – at least once for each article of the Catechism not perfectly known. There is something rather ironic about beating children for not knowing the Catholic code which is supposed to be one of "love thy neighbour as thyself".

Although the attitude of many of the Brothers was to beat first and ask questions later there was no sign at Oatlands College in Stillorgan of anything which approached paedophilia. Unfortunately this was not true in all the Christian Brothers' schools and over the past few years a number of very damaging court cases have been successfully brought against these Brothers. I wonder if the beatings which we suffered were a sort of trial maybe even subconsciously to see if the children's parents would complain. If the parents didn't care then the Brothers could proceed with more damaging physical activities. But this thought never entered the minds of 1950 Catholic parents in Ireland. They would simply say that the Brothers had it right and were basing their corporal punishment regime on the popular philosophy of spare the rod and spoil the child. Certainly the Brothers would also have been seen by someone like Lily as knowing that the harder the present life the better your chance was of going to the right place in the next life. Of course what was worse was the fact that the education delivered by these people was not necessarily all that good, especially in primary school, as far too much emphasis was placed on knowing your catechism and saying the Angelus and going to devotions, etc.

Steve was fairly enthusiastic about Catholic education. He believed that these church schools did a good job and certainly never queried the discipline regime in the school. By and large school life in Ireland in the 1950s was good. But having Steve as a father had some interesting side effects. It was clear that our family were different to other Irish families around us. I was told by Patsy that Steve's real name was István. That was certainly unusual. I once told another school boy this and he made fun of Steve's name and thus embarrassed me. Patsy always signed Remenyi with an accent on the second e and the i which was the way it was supposed to be spelt in Hungarian[6]. This was also a clear indication of being different. Steve was away much of the time and that was another difference. When he was home Steve cooked and that was unusual in Ireland in the early 1950s. Steve brought unusual foods from America. But also in cooking he used ingredients such as paprika and green and red bell peppers. He also cooked exotic dishes from different parts of the world such as curry and rice which was virtually unknown in 1950s Ireland.

Steve also had a different view on hygiene. From the time we moved into the little house in Crumlin and thus had our own bathroom, when he was at home Steve took a bath every day. He encouraged his family to do the same. The hygiene culture at Cuffe Street was a bath every now and again – maybe once a month or was it once a quarter. In a tenement a bath was a big deal. There was one of those big zinc bathtubs which are only seen today in cowboy films. It was taken out and placed before the fire in the living room. The bathtub was filled up with hot water which was heated on this fire. To supplement this Patsy did go to the public baths at Tara Street occasionally. I have several memories of being dragged off to be washed there. I don't really know how successful Steve was in his bathing suggestion to Patsy when she had her own bathroom. I do recall being in quite shallow baths of lukewarm water and feeling cold both in the bath and also on getting out of it.

Anyway the point of this story was that one day at Oatlands Christian Brother's School one of the Brothers decided to talk about personal hygiene and he asked various boys about their family bathing habits. This discussion went on for a while until he innocently enough asked me, "*So*

---

[6] This spelling used by Patsy was not correct as there is no accent on the i in Hungarian spelling of Remenyi

how often do you take a bath?" This question completely flummoxed me. I just couldn't produce any answer. My mind raced madly around the various things which I could have said. I knew that Steve wanted us to bath everyday. But I know that such a suggestion in an Irish classroom would be laughed at. Taking a bath a few times a year didn't sound right either. Once a week was not something I had specifically heard anyone in the family say before. It seemed to me like an age before the Brother spoke again. He realised that he had embarrassed me so he said, *"You like the rest of us all take a bath once a week on a Friday or Saturday night. That keeps you fresh for the whole week"*. Making sense of one's life with a foreign father was sometimes a challenge.

The problem of Patsy coping with the house and the children did not go away just because she now had a bigger and better home in a posh area. So Patsy again found help in the form of Lily who began to spend more and more time in Mount Merion. In the end Lily moved into our house and became a full time house keeper for Patsy and surrogate mother. This suited us very much as it was much easier to have Patsy as a mother when Lily was around. The only problem I ever had with Lily was the long, painful and excruciatingly boring periods on my knees saying rosaries. It was at least one rosary a day, sometimes two, and of course it was at least one mass on a Sunday. What a desperate waste of time it was to put a child through this. Otherwise I was much closer to my grandmother than I was to Patsy. In effect by the time we had settled in Mount Merion, Patsy had given up any pretence of playing the role of mother to her two children. Lily had completely taken over this function and Patsy was very pleased to allow this to happen.

It is not clear whether or not Steve knew how much Patsy had given up playing an active and caring role in the lives of her children. In later years he commented, perhaps not entirely fairly, that he had gone to sea to make a living and had come back to find the relationships in his family in a shambles. But the real shambles only began to evidence itself quite a few years later when the children grew into adulthood. And this happened long after Steve stopped working at sea.

However, with Lily living with us in Mount Merion, Patsy had very little to do. Lily got up in the morning, made breakfast and saw the children off to school. She then tidied the house and cooked meals for the children's return. Patsy stayed in bed until mid-day or later. Patsy found a local poker school where the stakes were not too high and here she could play from nine in the evening until three in the morning. To be fair the poker only happened two or three times a week. For the rest of the time it was the cinema and Patsy would take me along every now and again.

Lily returned to Cuffe Street no more than once a week and she went there to make sure that Annie was looking after Maurice and Paddy. In the six years we lived in Mount Merion, Maurice probably visited once or maybe twice but neither Annie nor Paddy were ever invited to our house. I don't know how often I was in Cuffe Street during this period but it was infrequent. At this stage Patsy effectively left her family behind, except for the fact that she used her mother as a servant. But there was to be one more coming together of the Sheehans, Steve, Patsy and the children.

In 1953 a third child arrived, who was a boy and was called Stephen Brendan. Patsy made it plain that it was Steve who believed that one should have quite a few children. Three kids were actually far too many for her, in fact so was two or even one. But not so for Steve. He had a greater capacity to relate to others in a relatively unselfish way and he was aware that children are in a way an investment for old age. But she was too immature and impatient to invest in her children in order to get a return in her old age. Thus this insurance against old age view of children was not the way things turned out for Patsy, or for that matter Steve.

Living in Mount Merion was great for all the children and especially for a 10 to 14 year old child. There were lots of kids in the area and we had a great amount of freedom especially when compared to children of today. When the Christian Brothers weren't beating us we all had a great time at school. We played Gaelic football and hurling, mostly in muddy fields and playgrounds. We had a sizeable piece of woodland not far from the house and this was a source of continual excitement for the kids in the area. In the woods a child could feel a thousand miles away. The woods themselves were magical and occasionally the excitement was enhanced by gypsies camping in the woods. We were almost exactly one mile from the sea side at Black Rock which had, for those days, a super swimming pool and we swam almost every day, even in the rain, from the months of June to September. Even in mid-summer the water from the Irish Sea was very cold and a lot of shivering was done when we were not actively swimming. Lily taught us the old Irish aphorism, "April and May stay away from the saay[7], June and July swim 'till you die". The Black Rock swimming pool had high diving boards and it was a great challenge to see how high you would dive from or even jump from. We had three month long summer holidays which we loved although, at the end of a three

---

[7] The word "saay" is the phonetical Dublin equivalent for sea.

month holiday, we were normally glad to get back to school to be with our greater circle of friends.

In the autumn months the kids enjoyed playing Halloween type games as ghosts and witches were always close to the Irish psyche. October and November were great months for boxing the fox which was a local term for getting into the gardens of private houses and stealing a few apples off their trees. Of course we all had apple trees of our own at home, but stolen fruit was much better and as it was only a venial sin it didn't really have to be mentioned in the confessional. And of course from early December onwards there was the preparing for Christmas.

In this period Steve's back injury started to give him problems again and he was diagnosed as having slipped a disk. Steve's back pain was very severe at times and after trying to improve his problem by wearing a plaster cast and going into hospital for traction treatment it was decided that only surgery would do. Apparently one of the better spinal surgeons of the day practised in Stoke-on-Trent and Steve was sent to the United Kingdom to be operated upon. There was some anxiety about his going to England for this operation and Patsy went along. With Lily in the house Patsy was not missed.

He was treated very well in the hospital in Stoke-on-Trent and made some good friends there. The operation was a success. For a number of years he was able to function normally but the problem did return and Steve went through surgery again a few years later. His back was never quite right but he handled this problem stoically.

The mid 1950s was generally a fairly miserable time in Ireland. The country was not doing well economically. Ireland had only been independent from the United Kingdom for about seven years. There was a tendency in Ireland to blame all its problems on the English who had after all occupied the country for about 800 years. No one seemed to know that the original invaders led by King Henry's knight Strongbow, were French speaking Normans and not Englishmen. As a child in school I had been taught slogans and rhymes such as God made the Irish, the devil made the Dutch and whoever made the English didn't make much. And what is the difference between a Chinaman and an Englishman? To which the reply was, the Chinaman is yellow outside and the Englishman is yellow inside.

One day Steve heard me repeat one of these rhymes. He did not create a great fuss but simply and quietly told me that these things which I had learnt were lies. He said that throughout the past few centuries the British, lead by the English had built the greatest empire the world had ever known and that the English Tommy had shown himself time and again to be among the bravest of soldiers. Steve went on to say that in all countries there were good and bad people and that the rhyme about the Dutch and the English was made up by people who thought that they were funny, but they were actually very ignorant and immature. Steve pointed out that the people who he had met in Stoke-on-Trent showed him more kindness than anyone else had ever done before.

There is no doubt that this talking to came at a very opportune moment for me and quashed the irrational and immature anti-English sentiment which was probably quite common in Ireland in the 1950s.

As well as anti-English sentiment there was also an anti-protestant attitude, which was primarily promulgated by the Christian Brothers but was also supported by many of the faithful. If you were not a good Catholic and if you did not die in "grace" you could not go to heaven. Admittedly there were two states of grace, one of which allowed you to go directly to heaven and another which provided a promise of heaven after a period in purgatory. Purgatory could be a long time for a repeated venial sinner. A venial sin was something like not saying one's daily prayers or telling a small lie or disobeying one's parents or as mentioned above stealing a neighbour's apples. A mortal sin sent you straight to hell. Missing mass on Sunday, eating meat on Fridays were among the big time mortal sins with which the Brothers frightened the children. Isn't it hard to believe that one could be dammed forever for eating meat on Friday? The first time I saw Steve eat meat on a Friday I was really shocked and puzzled. But in the case of Protestants and other 'infidels' if they lived a good sin free life they could only be rewarded by going to Limbo. Limbo is a state in which one is neither in heaven nor hell but somehow you are stuck in the middle. There was no time limit in Limbo a good Protestant was there forever. A bad Protestant of course went to hell.

This codswallop was doled out by religious men and women to impressionable young minds in the expectation of keeping them under control and stopping them from straying from the Holy Catholic Church, and, by and large it worked.

By this time Steve had been fully integrated into Irish life. He had been an Irish citizen since the end of the 1940s. He now spoke flawless English with, of course, not only an Irish accent but with Irish idioms. He was in fact sometimes confused for having come from County Clare in the south west of the country. Like all other Irish people he did not find it easy to pronounce the letters "th" and would say 'tree' instead of 'three'. He had acquired a taste for the Irish way of life and thus he from time to time took us to Leopardstown or Fairyhouse to the horse racing. He wasn't much of a gambler. Going to the races was a day out with a little excitement if you had a few shillings on a horse. He would go rabbit hunting with Ted. A jar in the pub was also an important cultural event. There is no doubt that we all perceived him to be fully Irish.

After three years in Mount Merion, in 1955, it was decided that we should move again and Steve and Patsy began to look at bigger houses outside of the city. They started to look around in the country side of county Dublin. The idea was that Steve and Patsy would establish a small boarding house or private hotel in a large country house in which we also would live. This was a recurring ambition of Steve's which he had most of his adult life. Of course the plan included Steve staying in his highly lucrative job in Irish Shipping, at least in the short run. The thinking behind this move was probably subconsciously motivated by Steve wanting to have some sort of estate like his family had in Hungary.

They found a suitable big old house dating back to the Georgian period. It was only six or seven miles outside of Dublin. It had really big rooms and really big windows. The hall and the stairway were enormous. It had a long drive way and was on 10 acres. They liked it and the price came within their budget. Whether they could have sustained a business based in this house in the mid-1950s is questionable. Cash flow forecasts were not a feature of that period and they would have needed much luck to have made a go of it. Anyway, they then put our house in Mount Merion on the market and to their surprise they received an offer almost immediately. Clearly Steve had under priced his house. Steve accepted the offer and the house was sold. A few days later Steve returned to the country house they had identified as being suitable for their prospective business and for some reason he decided to look at the wood work more closely. This resulted in his calling in a building surveyor. The survey did not go well. The surveyor declared the building to be riddled with dry rot. The cost of rectifying this was substantial and it explained why the old country house had been so reasonably priced. The owner was not prepared to negotiate on the price and thus the deal which Steve thought he had settled fell through.

Thus Steve and Patsy found themselves owning no home with the new owners of the old house wanting possession within a few weeks. This made Steve and Patsy very uncomfortable. It also frightened them away from the idea of buying the large house in the country.

After rushing around for about a week trying to find another house locally we heard that the father of our next door neighbours had been promoted to a new job which was located in Cork and that the family would move soon. Steve went in immediately to the neighbours and bought the house there and then. The deal was done even before the house went on the market officially. These were semi-detached houses and a few weeks later we moved houses by passing the furniture across the back fence. Some of the larger pieces of furniture were heavy and Steve and Patsy's brother Ted struggled to lift these over the fence. What a funny experience that was living in the house next door! Everything in the 'new' house was now the other way round. It was also difficult to explain to our friends why we should have done such an absurd thing as move next door. We spent another three years in that second house in Mount Merion before the family packed up and moved over six thousand miles away to a completely different life.

Those last three years in Mount Merion started off by being very good for Steve and Patsy. As Lily had moved in full time to look after the three kids Steve and Patsy could do a bit of travelling. For two years in a row Lily was packed off to Butlins Holiday Camp, which was on the coast a bit north of Dublin, with the children while they went abroad. Steve and Patsy went to London and somehow Steve re-discovered his uncle, Armand Kalmár who lived in Paris and they visited him there. Armand Kalmár was Mariska Reményi's brother. Armand had lived in Paris since 1900 when he had travelled from Budapest to Paris to see the Eiffel Tower. He had liked Paris so much that he had decided to settle there. By the time Steve found Armand he was long retired and living in a large apartment on the fashionable Quai d'Orsay next to the Ministère des Affaires étrangères – the French Foreign Office. He had a large three bed roomed arte nouveau apartment over looking the Seine. He had lived in this apartment for many years and was well known to the people who ran the shops and the cafés around the Gare d'Orsay. Armand had owned a carpet business which he had established and which had made for him some considerable amount of money. But his wife had died some years before and he was then a very lonely old man. He would continually say mostly to himself but just loud enough to be heard "C'est dur la vie". Armand Kalmár really welcomed re-establishing contact with his sister's son. Kalmár spoke only Hungarian and French and was thus never able to talk directly with Patsy. But she revelled in having a rich uncle in Paris. But by late 1956 or early 1957 problems began to set in with Steve's job with Irish Shipping which would force him to leave the company and this would lead to his emigrating and taking his family abroad.

In the ten years between the failure of his charcoal business and the mid 1950s Steve had turned considerable misfortune into a degree of success. This was no doubt due to the man's positive attitude towards life – he was a man who always saw the glass to be half full rather than half empty – and his preparedness to work hard and to take advantage of the opportunities which came his way.

Into Africa

Looking back on the Mount Merion years it is hard to say whether Steve and for that matter Patsy, felt that they had reached a new level of sustainable prosperity or whether they knew that it was simply a matter of Steve's lucky star being temporarily on the ascendant. They had moved into a middle class area, but it is not at all clear that they had joined the middle class itself. In those years fairly close to the memories of the Second World War, sustainability of their relatively prosperous life style probably wasn't even an issue that entered their heads. Life was just rather good at that time.

There is no doubt that they had broken whatever contacts they had with their Cuffe Street days. They hardly ever went to that part of Dublin – not that it was far away. No one would go to Cuffe Street willingly. Patsy had little interest in her family except for her mother, Lily. On the other hand, except for Patsy's poker playing friends, they hadn't made many friends among the Mount Merion crowd. It is interesting to reflect on the fact that they actually had few friends and hardly any among the residents of Mount Merion. Their social life was tied up with the people with whom Steve worked in Irish Shipping, and of course the Irish Shipping crowd was a mixed bunch of people from the middle and working classes. Steve was friendly with a few captains but he also had friends from the ships who were much more from a working class world than a middle class world. They were certainly a colourful lot. One special day when Steve took us to an event involving lots of different people stands out clearly in my memory. One of Steve's ship mates quit Irish Shipping to go fishing commercially. He joined in a sort of partnership with other fishermen who sailed out of Howth Harbour on what seemed to be a large trawler. It seemed they had bought this old fishing boat cheaply and had done it up and we all went out on its new maiden voyage around Ireland's Eye together with the priest who blessed the boat. It was a rip roaring party with lots of 'old salts' and their families. The man whose guest we were was a tough fellow whose name was Pearse McGloughlin. He had a chequered background and had been in prison for his political convictions. Well perhaps not quite for his political convictions, but for his political actions. He was a strongly ardent Irish nationalist. Apparently, he had been involved in the blowing up of a statue in one of the parks in the UK. Steve didn't know which statue it was. He thought it was King George, but he wasn't sure. Although there were those in Irish Shipping who thought highly of Pearse there were others who were weary of him. They would say, "Pearse has never been the same since he got out of prison". It seems to me that if Pearce had not been touched by the prison experience he would have been a very strange man indeed. After the prison sentence he joined Irish Shipping where he worked as a fireman. Fireman was Irish Shipping's name for a stoker. Thus Pearse worked in the belly of the ship below the water line and shovelled coal into the furnace that kept the ship going. This is one of the gutsiest jobs on a steamship requiring both strength and perseverance. Besides making his living literally by the sweat of his brow Pearce also wrote poetry. He had limited success in having his work published. However he wrote a poetic tribute to Steve which I have included later in the book.

But for now Pearse turned his hand to fishing. Of course some of the guests on the boat weren't fishermen, such as the Remenyis, and there was much queasiness all around and by the time we got back to dry land there were lots of 'thank you Father' to the priest that we had all been preserved from the sea. The Irish were not naturally a sea going people and they knew who to thank for getting back on dry land.

Whatever their view of the future at the time, the reality was that the circumstances which had allowed Steve to create their new-found prosperity were not to last that long and our lives were once again to be thrown into turmoil. But then the 1950s was a time of international turmoil and neither Steve nor Patsy ever gave the slightest impression that they could not cope with the change they had to face. The comfortable life in Mount Merion came to an end rather abruptly, not as a result of Steve having any problem with Irish Shipping or with Irish Hospital Sweepstakes ticket operation per se, but rather as a result of a high level decision made in Irish Shipping some years before. This decision was made in the early years of the 1950s which was to dramatically affect the company's traditional cargo and shipping routes and this in turn had a direct knock-on affect on Steve.

The Irish Shipping Company had been established in the early 1940s with the Irish government as a major shareholder. The company was the first Irish flag operator of deep sea vessels. It was difficult to buy ships during the war years and thus it owned a rag tag collection of old cargo ships. In the first few years of the 1950s it was apparent that Irish Shipping's fleet needed refitting and renewing and a decision was made to invest a substantial amount of money in the fleet. I do not know the technical basis of this decision but apparently it was not wisely made and by the mid 1950s Irish Shipping found itself with an uncompetitive fleet of ships which took longer to cross the Atlantic and were thus more expensive than other shipping lines on that route. The result of this was that, whereas in the early 1950s Irish Shipping had perhaps as many as six or seven ships regularly sailing to America, by 1956 they had far fewer, perhaps only two or three. The rest of the fleet was set to an activity known in the shipping world as tramping.

Tramping is one of the more unattractive modes of operating a shipping business and seafarers generally don't like it at all. It involves the ship sailing away with a cargo bound for a destination, from which there is no return cargo or consignment. When the ship reaches its destination it seeks out another cargo locally and takes that to whatever destination is required and then once again looks about to find its next consignment. In this way the ship works its way around the world in an uncertain manner or route not knowing where it will go to next and not being able to say just when the ship will get back to its home port. Sometimes ships are away on tramping voyages for years on end. In the 1950s crews were not flown home for holiday breaks.

The news that Irish Shipping would have to start sending its fleet away on extended tramping voyages was not received well by all the crews. There was some low level grumbling. But by the mid 1950s it was generally known that this was inevitable for a number of the ships. Initially Steve thought that he might be able to stay on the North Atlantic routes but this was not to be the case as there were more senior people in the company than Steve and they appeared to have the first choice of routes.

Steve's routine with Irish Shipping was broken in early 1957. In the aftermath of the Hungarian Revolution in October-November 1956 the Irish Government had accepted some 500 refugees[8]. Initially there was empathy in Ireland for the Hungarians who were seen as having been bullied

---

[8] The event which took place in Hungary and largely in Budapest during the end of October and the early part of November in 1956 is referred to as the Hungarian Revolution of 1956. It was not a revolution at all but rather a spontaneous uprising against the oppression of the Russian sponsored Hungarian Communist Regime. It began on October 23 with two government approved student marches attracting unusual support from people in the streets of Budapest. The marches turned into a protest and the protesters made demands for reforms. The exact sequence of events is not clear but shortly after the presentation of these demands the Hungarian Secret Police, commonly known as the AVO, fired on the crowd near the parliament building killing about 200 men, women and children. This converted the protest into an insurrection with rifles being supplied by workers from an armaments factory and Molotov cocktails being used against tanks. At the beginning the insurrection appeared successful with the Government promising reforms and the Russian tanks being withdrawn from Hungary. However in the early hours of November 4th the Red Army supported by the Russian Air Force invaded Hungary and suppressed the uprising and installed a hard line pro-Moscow Hungarian as Prime Minster. Approximately 10,000 Hungarians fought or directly supported the uprising. About 2,500 were either killed mostly in the streets fighting or were executed after the event. About 200,000 people decided to leave their country and seek a new life in the West. It is worthy of note that it took the Red Army 6 days to subdue Budapest and some more to bring the whole country under control.

by their big neighbour. As the Hungarians were staunchly Catholic they were considered to be worth helping. They were accommodated at Buckalisheen Camp. As can be easily imagined there were numerous language problems and the Irish Government's search for an interpreter lead them to Steve who was seconded from Irish Shipping to help with the situation. Both he and Patsy went down to the Camp which was situated near Limerick. Many of the Hungarian Refugees were unhappy to have landed up in Ireland. They wanted to proceed to Canada as quickly as possible, primarily because there were few job opportunities in Ireland. However the Canadians were not offering a carte-blanche to anyone who wanted to move there. The refugees had to have a family member or a close friend who was prepared to support their application. There was also some disagreement as to which government would pay for their transport across the Atlantic. Both Steve and Patsy spent some weeks working with the refugees. Patsy loved every minute of it. She picked up lots of stories about Hungary. She was told many times of how horrible the Russians were, both at the end of the Second World War, and after the recent invasion. There were plenty of people to tell her how much every Hungarian hated the Russians. Steve was anxious not to spend too long away from his job with Irish Shipping and they soon returned from Buckalisheen.

Steve had long before realised that he would not be returning to Hungary. He was unsympathetic to socialism in general but he was intensely suspicious of Russia and of Russians. Meeting and working with these refugees removed from his mind any prospect of returning to Hungary to live. In any event he would have known by now how near impossible it would have been for his family to settle in such a different environment.

A few weeks later Steve was sent away by Irish Shipping on his first long tramping voyage - I think about nine months. The ship sailed east visiting a large number of countries including Egypt, Aden, India, Australia and Japan. From the point of view of an eleven year boy, I enjoyed getting post from exotic countries to add to my international stamp collection. However from the point of view of family life, which hadn't been all that wonderful before, these new arrangements were quite devastating.

It was during this period that we used to play a trick on Jean who was then 7 or 8 years old. When friends came around we would ask Jean, "Where your daddy". She would then go to the wall in the dining room and to point to a picture of Steve. It was a handsome picture and the naivety of the child amused everyone for whom this show was put on. She obviously hadn't seen him much anyway and by the time he had been away for six months, he had just become a picture on the wall. It was rather a pathetic little joke indeed, which wasn't really funny. Steve's working on a ship that was engaged in long distance tramping was going to adversely affect all of us.

The impact of these long tramping trips on us was serious enough. But what also directly affected Steve and Patsy was the loss of the income from the Irish Hospital Sweepstakes ticket business. Being taken off the Atlantic route meant that Steve lost his second income that had taken the family out of the slums of Cuffe Street and had put them into the middle class in Mount Merion. There was no way in which Steve could replace this regular money. Either one of these issues alone were enough to precipitate a major change in Steve's working arrangements, but when one takes them together it becomes clear that Steve had to leave Irish Shipping and he had to leave it fairly quickly.

Of course, by this stage Steve had some capital and the house in Mount Merion was fully paid for, but he could not have sustained that middle class life style on just the salary of a chief steward. On his return from this first long voyage there was a lot of discussion about what else he could do. There was some half hearted discussion about his opening a restaurant or starting a bed and breakfast place, but Steve was never again to go into business for himself. None of these discussions resulted in any action being taken. It is not clear why Steve did not go back into business again for himself as he had some successful entrepreneurial experience, albeit for a short period of time. A few weeks later Steve returned to sea for another long trip.

This second tramping voyage did not last as long as the first one and he was home in about six months. This trip had also been to the East and on the way home the ship had stopped in the port city of Durban on the east coast of South Africa for a few days. Steve had never been to South Africa before and it appears that he quite liked what he saw there.

While in South Africa, Steve made contact with the South African Breweries Group which not only made millions of bottles of beer but also operated a chain of hotels throughout the country. While in Durban it appears that he had received an offer of employment, which was to manage one of the Group's hotels. Although this job offer was a long way away from Dublin, it was what Steve wanted as it would get him away from the sea and it would give him work at a managerial level. The details of the job on offer were vague but Steve was pleased to have a solution to his problems. A job as a hotel manager just fitted that bill as they matched the skills he had acquired as Purser/Chief Steward during the past ten years. Thus on his return to Dublin he immediately began the process of getting immigration to South Africa and selling up the house in Mount Merion.

The idea of emigrating was well established in Ireland. The Irish had been emigrating for hundreds of years but especially since the famine. At that time during the 1950s about 50,000 Irish people left their home country each year to find a new and more satisfactory life abroad. However, there were other places to have looked to besides South Africa which would have been more welcoming, but for some reason Steve never considered the USA, Canada or Australia. It was never really clear why South Africa was more attractive to him than these other countries. South African government were not in favour of Catholics. They were not all that sympathetic to English speaking people. They definitely preferred Protestants and Germans. The South African government required children to learn Afrikaans, a derivative of Dutch. South Africa was certainly the least stable of these ex-colonies of the British Empire. The three children have on more than a few occasions speculated why he chose South Africa but we have never been able to come up with an entirely satisfactory answer to this question.

Patsy was only moderately keen on this proposed move. She was now well settled into her relatively luxurious life style in Mount Merion. But it was clear to her that the sort of life which she had now become accustomed to could not be sustained on the enormously reduced income Steve was once again being forced to endure, and Patsy was realistic when it came to money. She expressed concern in leaving her mother and indeed the idea of losing the services of Lily must have been daunting as Lily was effectively an unpaid house-keeper and nanny to the three kids, but Patsy would be able to get 'help' – a euphemism for cheap labour - with the house and the family in a country like South Africa. Patsy had no other emotional attachments to friends or family in Ireland to speak of, except perhaps her poker playing chums. So leaving Dublin was at the end of the day not really such a big problem for her.

There was no question whatsoever of consulting the children about this move. We were a typical mid 1950 family where children were to be seen and not heard and their opinions were not asked. So the question of dialogue or consultation with the kids about radically changing their lives never arose. This is not to say that any of the three children could really have had a well formed opinion. But dialogue with the children just wasn't on the agenda.

In any case from my point of view I was pleased to be going on such a great adventure to the wild continent. I knew about Africa. After all the Christian Brothers had regularly collected money to 'buy a black baby'. Exactly what 'to buy a black baby' actually meant was not clear and on the occasion I asked one of the Brothers it was obvious that he didn't really know either. But there were charity boxes at school and in the church collection for this purpose. Of course I had a seen some Hollywood interpretations of Africa, including the African Queen and King Solomon's Mines. I had also been led to believe that there would be wild lions and tigers roaming the streets of the towns in Africa, including Durban, and so the whole idea of going abroad was terrific to me. I still have a clear image of what I expected to find when I arrived. I imagined the ship docking against a small quayside front with a luxuriant forest immediately behind the docks. This forest was alive with wonderful animals and wild people, like there were in the King Solomon's Mines film.

It was also going to get me out of a fairly dreary and oppressive school with wall-to-wall Christian Brothers. We only learnt after being in Africa for several months, if not a year, that there were no wild tigers on that continent. I, of course, learnt almost immediately on arrival that the Catholic Brothers had also gone out to Africa much earlier than us and were waiting for me to arrive.

There was a considerable delay in getting going on this new adventure which was frustrating to all of us. The business of obtaining immigration papers into South Africa was not trivial. The bureaucracy in South Africa House in London was substantial. In the mid 1950s the South Africa government, which had only relatively recently been taken over by Afrikaner Nationalists, was not all that welcoming to immigrants. There were endless forms to fill out, photographs to be taken and birth certificates to be copied and certified. A police report was required. We all had a variety of health checks as well as chest x-rays and so on. After that it was inoculations. The smallpox injections turned into wounds with big scabs and we wondered what we had done to ourselves. And the bureaucrats in South Africa House and Pretoria took their time in processing our immigration papers. It seemed to take for ever and a day. Steve realised that these governmental matters took lots of time and it fell to him to keep us from becoming frustrated and ratty about the delays. There was no assistance with the cost of getting to South Africa as there was to Australia at that time.

Before we left there was another hiccup with our accommodation arrangements. The house in Mount Merion was, of course, put on the market and again this house, like the last one, was sold almost immediately. Steve had mistimed the sale with the expectation of the immigration papers coming through in weeks rather than months. Steve must have under-priced both the houses which he sold in Mount Merion as they sold so quickly. Steve got the handsome sum of £1950 for number 59 The Rise. He sent all the furniture off to an auction for which he got the usual pittance. Our personal belongings were packed into tea cases and sent off for storage.

The sale of the house left the family homeless again. This resulted in our having to make a move to temporary accommodation in Dublin. As it happened this coincided with the Sheehans moving from Cuffe Street and this brought the five Remenyis back into contact with Maurice, Lily, Annie and Paddy in a direct way again.

Although the Sheehan's fortunes had turned up a little by the end of the war with Paddy, Annie, and Ted working Maurice refused to move from the slum which was Cuffe Street. Hard as it is to believe, Maurice's attitude was that what had been good enough for him in the bad years was good enough now. Also it was probably the fact that both his mother and father lived and died in Cuffe Street bound him in some way to the place. By that stage of his life he was also probably frightened of any change whatsoever. He had after all lived in the same place for more than 30 years.

However Paddy, Annie and Lily did not quite see it in the same way.

Eventually Paddy decided that he should move out of Cuffe Street and buy a house and he found a little place just off Cork Street not far from Dolphin's Barn. This area was in 1958 significantly better than where the family had spent the previous 30 years. It was, however a small terraced house with tiny rooms and no garden space at all. The Sheehans could well have afforded better. But Paddy made this purchase entirely on his own – in fact essentially against the will of Maurice. It was a big step for Paddy to do something so contrary to the wishes of his older brother.

Paddy wanted the rest of the Sheehan family to move with him. Maurice's whole emotional being was deeply dug into Cuffe Street. This difference of opinion resulted in there being a period of a few months during which Paddy had the 'new' house but the family did not move. This gave the five Remenyis a place to live for about four or five weeks while we waited for our immigration papers and Paddy waited for Maurice to warm up to the idea that he was moving which of course he eventually did.

Maurice lived more than twenty years in this little house and from the time that he retired he seldom left his armchair which was carefully placed in the corner of the front living room next to the fire place were he sat and watched his black and white television set.

In the end the South African papers did come through and in May 1958 we set sail for Durban. At this stage Steve would have had about £2,000 in his pocket with which to start a new life.

We, like many millions of Irish before us, sailed out across the Irish Sea from Dublin bound for Liverpool. We all sat at the back of the B&I ship as it sailed out of Dublin Bay and we watched Dublin city and then Howth Head recede into the horizon. At that point, although we were all excited about the bright adventure which lay ahead there was no doubt a degree of sadness about leaving the old country behind. It wasn't really a question of being scared of the unknown future; it was just a realisation that nothing would be the same again. I certainly knew that I was going to miss Lily. The B & I ferry was an overnight trip and we woke up the following morning in Liverpool. There we took a big fast train to London. It had a large steam engine with maybe twenty carriages. It was just simply amazing being on an inter-city express which was so completely different to the trains which we had been on in Ireland. We had been on Irish trains to Cork and of course to Knock as well as those that ran about the outskirts of Dublin. The Irish trains were just not in the same class as the English ones.

We had three nights in the English capital and Steve found a small hotel in Paddington. It was owned by an Irish woman who made us welcome and assisted us with suggestions of what to see in the big metropolis. What a mind blowing experience London was especially for three children from a small place like Dublin. We walked our feet off seeing the famous sights of the city. We queued for ages to go to Madame Tussauds and we asked one of the models for directions thinking it was a real person. We spent hours creeping around the British Museum looking at everything in sight especially the Egyptian Mummies. One of the real highlights of the stay in London was the Ceremony of the Keys at the Tower of London. To go to this you had to have a special invitation and Steve knew someone at the Irish Embassy who was able to organise us some tickets. Seeing the Beefeaters dressed up in their amazing garb was a great thrill which left a definite impression on us. But Patsy found all that culture a bit hard going. So when Steve took the children to the ceremony of the Keys at the Tower of London Patsy, now overloaded with history and culture, went to a west end cinema to see the latest Hollywood release, South Pacific.

It didn't take long for differences to start showing themselves between how the children had lived under the influence of Lily and how we would all live once we were out of Ireland. The first instance of how things were going to change showed itself on the second or third day after we had left Ireland. It was a Sunday and we did not go to mass. We didn't even make an attempt to so do. For me this was a mortal sin which meant that I would go to hell for all eternity. Patsy had no time for the church at all and although Steve would go to mass occasionally he certainly could not have been regarded as a devote attendee. This was a traumatic thing to happen as I had never missed a Sunday before and I had the most amazing bout of guilt to the point of being sick. When I look back on this I am quite amazed at the amount of indoctrination I had been put through by the system in Ireland. Lily, with the help of the Christian Brothers had inculcated in me a catholic conscience which was going to take years to shake off.

After London there was another great express ride on the boat train to Southampton. Waiting for us there was the Union Castle ship, the Pretoria Castle a 28,705 ton passenger liner. This was more than twice the size of the ships on which Steve had been sailing. Although this was not one of the world's great liners it was certainly an impressive ship. We set sail for the 14 day voyage to Cape Town. In its day this was a large modern passenger liner with every facility one could ask for and all three children really enjoyed every moment of the voyage. Steve had not skimped on the passage and we had two nice outside cabins. There were endless activities and entertainment ranging from deck games, to the swimming pool, to fancy dress parties and of course the daily bingo and guessing the number of miles travelled game. Just about every night there was dining and dancing, and a lot of inexpensive drinking for the adult voyagers which Steve and Patsy certainly enjoyed. It was truly a holiday camp for all ages being at sea in the most beautiful weather.

We had the inevitable one day of rough seas when we crossed the Bay of Biscay when the ship pitched and heaved but besides that dodgy 24 hours of feeling sea sick, the trip was magnificently smooth. Day after day there were blue skies and flat blue seas. There was hardly a puff of wind.

The Pretoria Castle was certainly the most luxurious thing the Remenyi family had ever experienced. All the public rooms were well appointed and the cabins were comfortable. We had bunks in our cabin and the

three children fought over who was going to sleep on top. We were presented with enormous multiple course meals three times a day and then in
between we had endless drinks and one sort of cake or cookie or another.
The stewards fussed over us all. I won the jackpot at bingo which was
£20 which was a truly vast sum of money in 1958. But Steve quickly took
it to put in a savings account for me – for safe keeping. We spent hours
and hours at the swimming pool at the back of the ship. All three children
especially enjoyed the pool but Brendan who was only 5 years old could
not yet swim. On one occasion he fell into the pool and swallowed several mouthfuls of water before being pulled out. This silly incident gave
him quite a fright and he didn't go near the water again for several days
and eventually had to be coaxed into the pool.

It was on this ship that I first heard racial comments. Some of the passen-
gers were South Africans going home after their grand tour of Europe.
Some of these people were enthusiastic about giving advice to the new
comers to Africa especially with regards to how to treat the locals. The
messages broadcast by these people were offensive. Even at my age their
prejudice was not really credible. The main gist of the prejudice was that
the blacks were just like children who needed white people to guide them
and teach them right from wrong. They admitted that the Zulus had been
great warriors. Great warriors they said need strong leaders. They said,
"The Zulus were never better than when they had Shaka looking after
them". The new South African Apartheid Government knew how to look
after them. They also spoke knowingly about the Indian in Natal. Indians
were especially awful people. Their religion taught them to lie, steal and
cheat, especially white people. These people were particularly awful
about Indians. These people on the ship were Natalians and they claimed
to be world authorities on Indians – well at least on all the negative things
about Indians. The closest that I had ever been to a black person was the
picture of a black baby on the Christian Brothers collection box. I had
never seen an Indian. But somehow none of this prejudice seemed to me
to be creditable or reasonable. Anyway the people who were saying this
were English and I had been taught not to trust English people. Despite
no knowledge of South Africa I was still able to tell that most of what
was being said was just plain wrong.

After two weeks of great fun in the sun, Steve and I got up one morning
to watch our arrival into Cape Town harbour. Cape Town is a remarkable
city. It is built under and around Table Mountain which is part of a mountain range that runs all the way down to the Cape of Good Hope. The
Cape of Good Hope was first encountered by European explorers in 1487
when Bartolomeu Dias set sail from Portugal to find a sea route to the

East. Although it was first called the "Cape of Storms" it was changed to Cape of Good Hope by the Portuguese. It has been described as the most beautiful cape in all the world. The next European to travel that way was Vasco da Gama some ten years later, but it was only in 1652 that the Cape was settled by the Dutchman, Jan van Riebeck who established a permanent settlement there. The Cape remained in Dutch hands until the end of the Napoleonic Wars when it was ceded to Britain in 1814. The British, and the Afrikaners who are the descendents of the Dutch settlers, have not ever been especially comfortable with each other. Today Cape Town, which is sometimes referred to as the Mother City of South Africa, is a fine combination of Cape Dutch and British architecture.

It was a bright cool morning towards the end of May 1958 as we approached the coast of South Africa and the view of the table mountain and the city was truly spectacular. It was an exceptionally clear day. There was a host of birds of different sorts following the ship. There were dolphins in the sea close to us. As there was no cloud on the mountain the enormousness and the majesty of Table Mountain really stood out. This was truly a different world to what we had left behind. Steve and I had got up especially early to see our arrival in Cape Town. As I stood on the deck with Steve appreciating the wonderful scenery he said that we were only coming to South Africa for a short while and that we would return home in a few years. This had not been said before and it came to me as a surprise. He went on to say that because of the temporary nature of our stay in South Africa I shouldn't get too involved with the country or its people. Steve made it clear that he was coming to South Africa to make his fortune and our sojourn there was to be as short as possible and we were then to go home.

It was in retrospect a classic statement of the English settlers' mentality. You come to the country to take what you can and then go back home. It was a mentality for which the Afrikaners bitterly resented the English speaking South Africans. Afrikaners would accuse English speakers of being settlers even when they were third of fourth generation born in South Africa. After all, many English speakers saw the United Kingdom as some sort of Home.

I didn't really understand what Steve was actually getting at and I guess if I had understood it wouldn't have made much difference to me. He was being unrealistic about the fortunes of the immigrant and about his ability or his family's ability to leave South Africa again. It was at that time he also told me that there were black people in South Africa and that although we would be sharing a country with them, they actually lived in a world, which we could never have any involvement with. I didn't understand this at all. He went on to say that we were not to speak to black people. We were to always keep our distance from them. Once again I didn't really comprehend what he was really trying to get at. I had lived in a protected society and I had no way of understanding these strange ideas.

It is virtually impossible to imagine Apartheid until you have actually experienced it[9]. Thinking about it years later it is indeed a mystery to me that Steve could have thought that he could bring his family, especially his children, to South Africa and have them live there without them becoming involved in the society and the country. I guess this was a little insight into how he was going to be able to stay remote from the goings-on in the country and which was to become apparent as the years unfolded.

Certainly, in retrospect Steve did not do a reasonable job in preparing his family for a new life in such a different world. We were basically just dumped into the deep end where the values were totally different to what we had ever experienced in Ireland. In due course this did lead to considerable confusion and discomfort.

But back to the ship, we had a wonderful day exploring Cape Town. The old narrow streets with little shops were exciting. We heard strange languages being spoken. We later learned that many people in Cape Town spoke Afrikaans. After a busy day rushing around the city we returned to the ship exhausted for the evening meal and a good night's sleep. The next morning the ship set off again. Sailing around the Cape of Good Hope on a clear day is one of the great joys of life and we were gobsmacked by the fabulous scenery as we moved from the Atlantic Ocean across False Bay and on towards the Indian Ocean.

The following exciting morning we woke up in Port Elizabeth which was a small city and relatively uninteresting and thus a great disappointment after the outstanding beauty of Cape Town. Nonetheless we went ashore on a tour as we were desperately keen to learn what we could about this new country. The tour took us to a nature sanctuary and for the first time we were to see wonderful animals. For years to come we were to spend

---

[9] Racial discrimination was not invented in South Africa. It seems to have existed all over the world. Wherever Europeans colonised it appears that they did not treat the indigenous people at all well. This ranges from the Spanish and Portuguese in South America, the British in Australia and India and all sorts of Europeans in North America and in Africa. I do not know if any other conquering races were any more benevolent to those they subdued.

quite a lot of time in various game parks having a variety of adventures, not all of which were desirable.

The next day, with our expectation a little lower now, we arrived in an even smaller town called East London which was one more step down the rung of interesting South African towns but the day after we docked in Durban on May 31. That was Union Day, a public holiday in South Africa which celebrated the bringing together of the two original countries (the Transvaal and the Orange Free State) and two colonies (Natal and the Cape of Good Hope) at the conclusion of the Second Boer War to form a so-called united country.

Of course South Africa was never a united country. The Afrikaners were never really able to forgive the British for what they had done during and at the end of the Second Boer war. Also the architects of South Africa in 1910 did not really have the rights of the other people of the country in mind. The rights of the blacks, Indians, people of mixed race and others were just not seen as being worth mentioning never mind enshrining in the constitution. It is now in the 21st century quite difficult for us to understand or imagine just how Eurocentric the world was then.

In 1958 Durban was simply magical for white children, especially white immigrant children. We had been transported into a type of wonderland. The difference between cold, wet and windy Ireland and the balmy climate of sub-tropical Durban was virtually unimaginable. We were in a Durban winter which was warm and sunny and dry. We had so much to see and do and learn that we just didn't have time to be homesick. The children did write post cards home as well as birthday cards but not much else. Patsy wrote a monthly letter to Lily. But despite Steve's cautions it took very little time for all the children to make South Africa their real home and for Ireland to become a relatively distant memory.

For Steve and Patsy, their life in Durban was to be different and much more difficult than they had imagined. None of their plans materialised and it took them a number of years before they were able to reach the level of comfort they had left behind in Ireland.

The New World in the South

Steve's arrival in South Africa was not easy. In fact it might well be described as a desperately awful one. He quickly ensconced his family in a small hotel in central Durban. This hotel was a come down from the luxury we had experienced on the Pretoria Castle and the kids complained that the rooms and the restaurant were not good. Steve remarked that it is surprising how quickly one can become used to 'the better things in life' and that we were already becoming spoiled. The next morning he went off to find the man who had offered him the job nine months earlier. However the man concerned no longer worked for South African Breweries and furthermore South African Breweries had no vacancies suitable for Steve. Steve did not have a letter of appointment and on reflection whoever Steve had met on his earlier trip to Durban probably only suggested to Steve that South African Breweries would have a job for him.

Steve did not show any disappointment to us. He appeared to accept this major let down stoically and he hardly commented on it. He just seemed to take this completely in his stride as though it was the most natural thing in the world to bring your family 6,000 miles across the world and to find the job he was expecting not to be there. Patsy was however different. Her immediate reaction was to wish the man who had made the 'promise' instant death. Steve had a different take on wishing evil for people. He said, "If you want to wish misfortune on anyone, don't wish they were dead. Rather wish that they live to be 101 years old and never have tuppence to jingle in their pocket". Such was Steve's practical outlook on life.

In the event Steve was resourceful and he immediately went to an employment agency and a few days later he started work as the Mâitre 'd in the restaurant come night club in Claridges Hotel, one of the more fashionable hotels on Durban's beachfront. This was a glitzy expensive restaurant and on the weekends it was a place especially known for dinner and dancing. It seemed a very exotic work place to the rest of us in the family.

Also within a day or two Steve and Patsy had located a modern house just off Berea Road about a mile and a half from the centre of town. Berea Road was the main thoroughfare out of the city and the road from Durban to Johannesburg. It was a busy road unlike anything we had seen in Dublin. Our house was fortunately a hundred yards off the busy thoroughfare and so it wasn't especially noisy. It was a maisonette and we had the upper floor. There was a huge palm tree in the front garden. We had known palm trees from Dublin but by our Irish standards this was a monster palm. The house was just big enough for the five of us. Our packing cases and tea-chests from the ship were delivered and we started to settle in.

The job in Claridges Hotel was hard and had long unsociable hours but even worse than that, it was paid poorly with Steve's gross salary was only £40 per month. To put this salary into perspective the rent of the maisonette was £30 per month so it was clear that there was going to be some short fall in the family budget. Patsy found a job in a small book-shop in an arcade within a large block of offices in the centre of the town. It was a little shop and it stocked a fine range of popular books and al-ways seemed to have plenty of people browsing in it. Popular books suited Patsy as she was a great reader and whenever she had a spare mo-ment in the shop she would be into another novel.

Patsy had not worked since being married and this was the first shock for her and generally she didn't like it at all. But she put up with it while let-ting the rest of her family know that she didn't get married to have to work. However Patsy's pay was £30 per month gross. So even putting their two pay packets together they were not able to make enough to sup-port the family. Of course, Steve had his capital with him but he wanted to go easy on that so that he would be able to buy a house and furnish it. As it turned out, he had to dig deep into those savings for some years be-fore he was able to earn enough to pay the family's way.

So the Remenyis' arrival in Durban was not exactly auspicious. But Steve and Patsy more or less kept the disappointments to themselves and got on with creating this new life. They were living together on a full time basis for the first time in twelve years and that was, perhaps, a major compen-sation for the hassles they were facing. There was never, at any stage, any discussion about going back to Ireland. In later years I asked Steve why, when his promised job fell through, he had not considered opening a res-taurant of his own instead of going to work for a pittance at the beach front hotel. He said that he felt that, with a wife and three kids, he could not take the risk of not having a pay cheque at the end of the month, even though it was a small pay package. The risk taking capacity which he showed in Ireland sixteen years before had been erased by family respon-sibility.

We were actually not used to living together and it took quite some ad-justment to come to terms with this. Lily had nearly always been there in Dublin to act as a buffer between Patsy and her kids and now we had to face Patsy head on. This often just meant facing her indifference. Patsy was bound up in her own misfortunes and really didn't have much time to think about how any other member of the family might be coping. On the other hand Steve appeared to be a caring father when he had the time, but, over the years, the type of jobs he had generally didn't give him much time for the kids. He was fundamentally generous with what little money he had and that counted for a lot with the kids. On reflection I think that what we settled into was nothing more than five people living together purporting to be a family.

Of course on a day-to-day basis, it was not all bad. Everyone just gets on with their own life. As far as the children were concerned Durban was magical because it was bright, warm and so colourful. Many of the people spoke English. There were very few Afrikaners. Durban was a beautiful clean and safe city in 1958. We had never seen beaches like those in Natal. We had never smelt the tropics. We had never really seen people other than the Irish.

The majority of people in Natal are Zulus. In 1958 they were seen by white South Africans as just another tribe which they had conquered at the turn of the last century. Part of the philosophy of Apartheid was to exaggerate the differences among people especially the black Africans. So Zulus were different to Xhosas to Tswanas to Vendas etc. Of course there is some truth in this but they also were South Africans. To us they were a colourful, helpful and often extremely polite people whom we encountered every day.

We enjoyed the hustle and the bustle of the two parallel main streets in Durban. West Street and Smith Street were always crowded with people of every type. Zulu women carrying enormous loads on their heads, often without using their hands to support the bundle were an amazing spectacle for us. Their sense of balance was truly superb and they were able to carry quite heavy bags or bundles this way. Seeing Zulus with pierced ears and huge earlobes made us stare with wonder. Once we saw a person with a toothbrush in his or her earlobe. Could this actually be attractive we thought? Zulu work gangs on the streets digging and chanting simultaneously were a great source of entertainment. You often saw twenty Zulus digging a hole with 3 or 4 white men who were their supervisors sitting or standing around smoking while watching them. We later learnt that some of these gangs were prisoners doing hard labour.

Durban city's transport was mostly served by trolley buses which we had not experienced in Dublin. We all loved the trolley buses. They were powered by electricity which they drew from overhead cables by means of two parallel poles. If a trolley bus went around a corner too quickly or if the driver mis-judged the angle of his turn, the parallel poles came away from the cables. This was a reasonably regular event and it required the bus driver to get out and reconnect to the electric current. We arrived in Durban just after the final segregation of the buses. Until shortly before we arrived buses carried people of all races. In the traditional manner of racist societies the white people sat in front so that all other races sat at the back of the bus. But this wasn't separate enough for Apartheid. Apartheid insisted on two types of buses - buses for whites and buses for everyone else. The buses for everyone else were colloquially known as Green Mambas as they were painted green. This meant that a white person might stand at a bus stop waiting for a bus while seeing several buses to the right destination, which were not allowed to pick the white person up, go trundling by.

Durban had a large number of people whose ancestors had been brought to South Africa from the Indian sub-continent. Some of these people were Hindus and some were Muslims. It was said that there were as many Indians as whites in the greater Durban metropolitan area. Indians had been brought to Durban at the end of the 19th Century to work in the sugar cane fields. The white land owners believed that the Zulu labourers would not work sufficiently hard to make their sugar plantations profitable, so Indians were brought as indentured labour. As was to have been expected these people were treated terribly.

The children and the grand children of these indentured labourers moved into the towns and into the city. They often spoke three or four languages and became an important part of the life of Durban. However as they were brown skinned they were not acceptable to white South Africa and Apartheid also discriminated against them.

We really liked going to Grey Street, the main Indian shopping road. Grey Street was a blitz of colour both on the pavements and in the shop windows. There was the continuous smell of curry and other spices. Women in saris were an eye opener for us. The Indian sweet meats of bright red, green, yellow and orange which were to be seen in the food shop windows were fascinating. The old Indian market in Durban was something really special with big open sacks of spices placed in front of the little shops and the owners standing at the front touting for business. The curry powders were all different colours and had extraordinary names. The hottest type of curry, mother-in-law curry powder was always being offered as a remedy for troublesome mothers-in-law as well as many other ailments. We discovered the Mosque in Grey Street which is the biggest mosque in the southern hemisphere[10]. We took our shoes off and went to visit it. What an interesting place and how welcoming the attendants were. Rickshaws pulled by powerful looking Zulu men were regularly used around the Grey Street area both for taking people and their shopping as well as for carrying goods. I never felt comfortable seeing people having to pull big heavy weights around in order to make a living. Seeing rickshaws with three or four people being pulled in them was especially awful. Besides these working rickshaws there were tourist rickshaws at the beach. In a way the rickshaws on the beach front were worse, as the men who pulled these had to dress up as Zulu warriors with big costumes and enormous headdresses as well as drag tourists around.

The Indian community was really quite welcoming to the whites. Although Indians would not be allowed into white restaurants the opposite was not true. One Indian restaurant in particular, named the Goodwill Lounge, was always available to white people although not many availed themselves of its excellent food. Apartheid inculcated a fear among the whites that if they went to an Indian restaurant they would somehow be ill. Besides being able to go to the Mosque, we were able to visit Hindu temples and on one occasion we went to a Deepavali festival as well as a Kavadi and a Theemathi festival. Here we saw fire walking as well as a variety of other amazing feats of what we regarded as self mutilation – fishhooks in the mouth, tongue and back. These were very strange rituals which even today mystify me.

For completeness it is important to mention the fourth 'racial' grouping used in Apartheid South Africa. There were people who were either of mixed race or who were descendents of Malay immigrants who were brought to South Africa in former times. All these people were grouped together and referred to as 'Coloureds'. It is inappropriate to attempt to assess which group of people were treated the worst under Apartheid, but it would be fair to say that these people were subjected to the most ferocious calumny. They were often described by whites as being degenerates, perpetual drunkards, promiscuous, thieves etc. These accusations like the ones made about Indians on the boat were simply lies. But it is

---

[10] The Juma Masjid or Grey Street Mosque was visited by very few whites. In fact few whites knew anything about it or about Muslims for that matter. I do not recall Muslims ever being referred to at school in South Africa, in any subject, history, geography or other wise. This is despite the fact that there were about 200,000 Muslins in that country at that time. In Natal most of the Muslims had come from South Asia while in the Cape Province they were mostly from Malaya and the islands of Indonesia. In Ireland we had been told about Islam by the Christian Brothers but only how the Muslims had conquered, by the sword, many parts of the world and how they believed that if they died while fighting for their faith they would directly go to heaven.

interesting to note that people from this group of mixed race who were employed in vineyards in the Western Cape were paid in part for their labour, by the white owners, with alcohol. It is hardly surprising that some of these workers became alcoholics and that there were many social problems among some of these people[11].

Back in Durban we discovered supermarkets which we had not seen before and enjoyed going to one of the biggest of them, the OK Bazaars and having our shopping delivered to our house within a few hours. Furthermore there seemed to be more department stores with more choice of things to buy than we had ever seen in Ireland. We discovered cola which was not generally available in Dublin especially in the small shop in Mount Merion from which we bought our groceries. But in Durban cola could be bought everywhere and in what was to us, huge family sized bottles (700 cl), as well.

Steve and the children quickly became swimming addicts. Patsy had never learned to swim and would have been typical of her generation and class in Ireland. Steve was especially keen on swimming as he felt that it was good for his bad back. We would go to the public swimming pool on the beach front in Durban which was called the Beach Baths nearly every day. It cost only a couple of pennies to go in. And of course in Durban in June the public's swimming pools were empty as it was the middle of winter and as far as the local whites were concerned it was too cold to swim. Only whites were admitted. We were of course very unaccustomed to the sub-tropical sun and we suffered greatly in the first few years from allowing ourselves to be over exposed to the sun. Many a night we sat round covered in camomile lotion to give us some relief from the pain of the sunburn. In retrospect it took far too long to learn how to live with tropical sun, i.e. cover up and keep out of the sun. In my case overexposure to the sun in those early years has inevitably led to skin cancer.

We really enjoyed being in a country where there was so much in the way of exotic animals. As well as visiting the national parks where the big game was we were enthusiastic observers of the animals which encroached on the city. One of our most favourite Sunday afternoon pass

---

[11] The system of paying part of the wages in alcohol was referred to as the DOP system and goes back centuries. It appears that it grew out of a maritime practice whereby wine was added to water on board ships to prevent it from going stale. This led to the issuing of an alcohol ration as part of the weekly pay. Though the Cape DOP system is no longer legal in South Africa, the effect of it remains a major problem – a vicious cycle of poverty and dependence on alcohol is still prevalent amongst some farm workers.

times was to go to the Athlone Gardens Hotel on the banks of the Umgeni river two miles out of town to have tea in the gardens. The main feature of afternoon tea there was that troops of monkeys would invariably come down from the trees and steal the cake and biscuits off the plates from which we were eating. They were bold and fast moving and invariably got your cake if you didn't eat it quickly. This was a guaranteed delight.

Was there a downside to our moving to Durban? Durban was very hot and very humid especially in the months of January to March. All we could do was to sit (or rather steam) it out. We often wished for a bit of cooler Irish weather. South Africa had strict laws with regards what one could do on Sundays. All forms of entertainment were closed. So for us it was swimming or not much else on the Lord's Day. The rest of the country went to church in their Sunday best. But there wasn't much else which we disliked. After film shows the National Anthem was played and this was not a Soldier's Song but rather God Save the Queen which I needed time to get used to. Durban was good to the children.

Neither Steve nor Patsy had anything much to say about the politics of the era in South Africa. Steve would later proclaim himself to be a liberal but he never really said or did anything which would support such a claim. Although I could not agree that he was a liberal, he had an unusually caring attitude to those who worked for him and which I have not quite seen in anyone else. More will be said about this later. All three children were too young to be properly politically aware. Of course we saw the whites living well and everyone else struggling, but everyone we met and everything about us told us that it was natural because whites were superior. But I knew how bad the English had been in Ireland for more than seven hundred years. Alas I didn't know anything else at all about politics. So it took a bit of time to become really aware of what was going on in South Africa.

In those days white people did not generally encounter other people in apartheid South Africa except in the role of servants. So there was always a big distance between the races and thus it was easy not to get involved with people who were of a different race. People we met in Durban told stories like those we had heard on the ships about the other races. There was, for example, the story we were told about how to treat our servant. The maisonette had a woman living in a tiny room in the back yard and we were encouraged by the owners to employ her. The first thing that struck me was her pay. I no longer remember the amount she was paid but I have an impression that it was a few shillings per month and not pounds. The second thing was the accommodation she lived in and the food she ate. The room and the facilities which were offered with it were truly dreadful. The room could hardly take a small single bed. The toilet was a hole in the ground. The woman was supposed to be fed by the family employing her. This meant that they bought her a sack of mealie meal, a sort of porridge made from maize, each month. They also supplied a couple of pounds of the cheapest cut of meat that could be bought. For the rest the woman was given tea and bread and jam. We were specifically told that it was wrong to give her more than this and that especially we should not supply any more meat because the eating of meat made black people ill. "They are just not used to meat, it will make them really sick", said the estate agent confidently. It is amazing how often one heard this lie about black people - their supposed inability to eat meat being used to justify the meanness of white employers.

Another incident which helped to create political awareness for us was to do with the fact that there was some activity among the Irish Catholic community in Durban. We soon met two Irish families who had also emigrated from Dublin a few years before us. It was through one of these families that I experienced my first tinge of political awareness. One of these families, whom I will call the Moores, as I have forgotten their real name, came to have lunch with us one Sunday. They had a young daughter about the same age as me. Our maisonette had a balcony which overlooked a small garden, with a big palm tree, and the pavement outside the front gate. On arriving at our house the daughter strayed out onto the balcony, to see the view, on her own, while the rest of us were chatting in the living room and the kitchen. She came running back inside shouting that there was a boy at the gate. Straight away I went out to the balcony with her to see what she was on about. I could not see a boy anywhere. In a very irritated tone she asked what was wrong with me as the boy was right in front of us at the gate. Standing at the gate was a very old black man. He was so old that all his hair was snow white. He was holding a large drum, which he was beating gently with his hand, and chanting some Zulu song and asking for pennies.

In South Africa this was a boy!

I never forgot the insensitivity of that young Irish girl who had bought so completely into apartheid thinking, in such a short time after getting to South Africa. It took a while to realise that immigrants to South Africa were, by and large, prepared to comprehensively accept apartheid perhaps even more so than the local whites. This incident also reminded me about stories told by the Christian Brothers in Dublin as to how the English treated Irishmen with a similar sort of contempt.

Steve and Patsy were typical immigrants. Steve had spelled out his settler mentality to me on the ship as we approached Cape Town. They made virtually no comment on the way other people were treated. They just accepted the political status quo as if it were the most natural way of living. It is probably true to say that if they were capable of questioning the political situation then they would never have brought their family to such a morally deficient country. So the children had to find their own political awareness somewhere other than in the family.

The question of schools was postponed for two months as the South African one month long July holidays was said to be just around the corner and it was thought that the three kids would like a break before starting their new schooling. In reality this was simply Steve and Patsy not wanting to make a decision about which school to send the children. The Christian Brothers had made it clear that to go to non-Catholic schools was a mortal sin and although Steve and Patsy didn't care a jot about this, the kids did and they wanted to allow us to settle in before making this type of decision.

The catholic schools in Durban were private and the fees were substantial. But the local priest made an arrangement for the fees to be waived temporarily. A second hand school uniform was also supplied. So I went to the Marist Brothers' College who were in some respects a little more humane than the Christian Brothers I had gladly left behind. Interestingly neither Steve nor Patsy went to see the school. I was picked up by the priest and taken to be interviewed by the head brother who agreed to accept me into the school. Jean and Brendan were sent to a local convent for a short while but were moved to government schools sometime before I was. By the end of July 1958 seven weeks after we arrived in Durban, we all three had settled into school life again.

The maisonette just off the Berea Road was just too expensive and so we moved after three months. First we moved to a much smaller modern flat near the beach but Steve was not happy with having the family in a one roomed flat and so we moved again, quite quickly to a substantially bigger but much older apartment – in a state of what might be euphemistically called graceful deterioration - right opposite the Beach Baths.

After about a year Steve found a better job as the manager of the Merchant Navy Officers' Memorial Club in central Durban. This job came with an £80 per month salary and a free flat and food for the family. He enjoyed his new position and tackled it with a lot of energy and enthusiasm. Steve now had a staff of about 40 people which included cooks, waiters, cleaners and security personnel. The club was close to Durban harbour and we enjoyed being able to walk around the corner and watch the ships and the yachts in the bay. By this time Steve had bought a car. Like he had done in Ireland Steve during this period of his life continued to buy old bangers. He was keen on big American cars on the questionable grounds that the wear and tear on big cars was less than that on small ones. But Steve's car continued to break down in the most inconvenient places.

We started exploring the north and the south coast and one of Steve's favourite haunts was the Game Park in Zululand about 70 miles away called Hluhluwe (pronounced shushlui) and we went wild game spotting there fairly regularly. Steve also discovered the mountains. The Drakensberg Mountains begin about 100 miles from Durban and there are several nature parks and hotels in this area of exceptional natural beauty. Steve took us to Giant's Castle nature park several times. On one occasion we had a special adventure in these mountains on the way to Giant's Castle nature park. We set out late. It began to rain as we approached the mountains. The last 20 miles was a poor dirt road which should not have been travelled in anything other than a 4 wheel drive vehicle. Steve got half way up a hill before the car began to completely lose its grip on the road and simply skid. As he couldn't get the car up the hill he tried to turn it around. This required Patsy and the three kids to try to push the car around. It was now pouring with rain and mist had settled in. The attempted turning got us nowhere. The car just slid off the road into a ditch. It was now an hour before dark. It was about a 10 mile walk back to the last village or a 10 mile walk to the nature park gates. It was an unwritten rule that whites should not be out at night on foot in the country side which was only populated by blacks. It was pretty scary out in the back of beyond in the dark and in the pouring rain. There was nothing to do but wait for the next day or to see if we would be rescued. There was no rescue service as such but Steve had booked a cottage in the nature park and so we would eventually be missed. True enough the rangers came out to look for us. We had sat in the car for four or five hours before we were found.

The Nature Park Rangers were not impressed by the predicament Steve had got us into. They were on the verge of being grumpy with us. Of course it was late; it was wet; and it was cold. But more profoundly South Africans in general were not sympathetic to anyone who stranded themselves out in the 'bush' especially at night. They came in a large Land Rover, took us and some of our belongings but refused to help get the car out of the ditch. Steve had to call a breakdown service the following day and have the car pulled out.

The Merchant Navy Officers' Memorial Club attracted a mixed group of people not all of whom were too genteel. One of the reasons for joining a club in South Africa in those days was that South African law prohibited the sale of alcohol on Sundays except as an accompaniment to a meal or on the premises of a club. So it was a Sunday 'watering hole' for those who had some connection with seafaring. But the club was also there to provide a place for officers from the ships which visited Durban. And Durban was a busy port. So the job kept Steve on the go. Steve's style of management was participative; he spent many long hours on the job personally directing or working along side some of the staff. He was always keen to ensure that the food which came out of the kitchen was up to scratch. There were probably 40 or 50 people in all working for the club which was situated on two large floors of a building close to the harbour. There were maybe 12 Zulu cleaners who had an Induna, which is Zulu for a supervisor to look after them. They were extremely good workers and the whole club was kept spick and span. There were cooks, waiters, barmen, wine stewards and billiard room staff. These jobs were all done by Indians. And then there was the white office staff. Job reservation was an important pillar on which apartheid was built. Not only were people racially categorised, but so were jobs and different types of work had to be done by different races. There were a number of laws which defined the work different people could or could not do, but as well as this many jobs during this period were so called reserved by custom.

Steve was quite a stickler for the rules of the club and insisted on the appropriate dress code etc. The South African liquor laws were quite strict then and Steve was keen to see that no one disobeyed them while at the club. The hours during which alcohol could be sold were short and there were often situations which arose due to closing the bar at the prescribed time. But large orders for drinks could be placed before the bar closed and so late drinking occurred this way. Another aspect of the law was that no alcoholic drinks bought in the club could be taken off the premises. On one occasion it was brought to Steve's attention that one of the visiting officers had put a bottle of beer in his pocket and was on his way to walk out of the club with it. Steve challenged him at the door asking him to leave the bottle of beer behind. The man, who no doubt had already had more than a few drinks, took the bottle out of his jacket and proceeded to whack Steve's head with it. Steve collapsed and in falling bashed his face on the floor. The sailor walked off quickly and no doubt made his way back to his ship. Steve was taken to the Casualty Department of the Hospital. He spent most of the night having glass picked out of his head. I learnt about this the following morning when I got up for breakfast and found Steve with a bandage all around his head like some war wounded casualty. Fortunately no serious damage was done to Steve's skull.

However, Steve did have one other quite different exciting evening at the club. After being in this job for a few months Steve and Patsy invited a small group of Irish people around for some drinks and snacks. After a few hours of moderately heavy drinking one particular Irishman began to wax eloquently about the hypocrisy of the Catholic Church. This was not a subject which was discussed among Catholics in 1960. The detail of the argument is irrelevant other than to say that he eventually made a comment which suggested a degree of improprieties in behaviour between catholic priests and nuns in Ireland. It may have been initially intended to be in jest as much as anything else, but to make such a generalisation under any circumstance is unfortunate, and to make it in a group of Irish people after a degree of heavy drinking was just plain stupid. The whole mood of the group changed. After a few seconds of silence the other Irishman sitting opposite him challenged the loud mouth fellow to a fight, there and then in the club. The one man jumped up, took off his jacket and started to roll up his sleeves. Everyone looked in amazement, shock and then embarrassment. Steve stood up and said, "You two get out of here. I will not tolerate any such nonsense in my home". Steve immediately escorted these two Irish gentlemen off the premises, suggesting that they go to the boxing ring in the YMCA which was around the corner from the club. In a way there was some irony in this incident. Steve always maintained that the Hungarian Catholic Church tolerated their parish priests having what might be described as common law wives. According to Steve the Hungarian parish priest would often end up living a married life style with his housekeeper as a bed partner and sometimes even having children with her. If Steve had said that sort of thing at his little get together he might also have been challenged to a fist fight in his own sitting room. Such was the inability of some Irish Catholics to see beyond their rather particular view of Catholicism.

Steve stayed in this job for about a year, leaving it not only because he was required to be on duty from early morning to late at night, but especially because of the need to work on weekends. The next job was with another club, this time for ex-servicemen, not far away in the centre of Durban. This was the South African Air force Club. This job came with a little more money but no flat. The main advantage was that it did not require work on Sundays. There was also a short day on Saturday and the club closed relatively early, six o'clock in the evening. Steve was certainly financially no better off through this move. Steve needed some more leisure time than the previous job allowed. Steve and Patsy's joint salary did not cover the family expenses yet but they still had a reasonable amount left of the capital which they brought from Ireland so they were able to get by.

So we were back in the accommodation market again. We moved home several more times, at least six times, in the next few years or so. Some of the flats or houses were big and others small. At one time we lived over a shop on a noisy corner. We were just unable to find a place that really suited us. It was unsettling and had a detrimental effect on all the three children. The house moving meant that Jean and Brendan changed schools a couple of times as well, but for some reason I stayed on with the Marist Brothers while the others moved. About the time that Steve moved jobs to the South African Air Force Club, Patsy decided that she would look for another job too. As mentioned she had left school very early, her educational qualifications were nonexistent. Furthermore Patsy could neither spell nor do arithmetic at all well. There is no doubt that she was severely dyslexic. However she had been through school at a time when this was not recognised and she was simply regarded as educationally backward. Consequently her job opportunities were limited. One day she saw a job advertised in the newspaper for a production supervisor in a clothing factory and she decided to apply for this position. Patsy went to the job interview, spinning a complete yarn about the experiences she had had in Ireland in the clothing industry and as a result she landed the job. It was sheer bluff. She had worked out that there wouldn't be much to supervising a team of ladies sewing shirts in a clothing factory and she was right. By doing this she more than doubled her pay. The family was now at a break even with respect to income and expenditure. Patsy had sufficient imagination and creativity to re-invent herself as she went along and she stayed with that firm for several years and was by all accounts well thought of. She was especially pleased that she had doubled her salary.

The Marist Brothers was a French order of teaching brothers dating back to 1817. They were not as ready to beat the boys as the Christian Brothers were. Nonetheless they used a cane and the boys were beaten on the rear end rather than the hands. The Marists in Durban also had a particularly nasty little man who specialised in what would be today regarded as verbal abuse which I had not encountered in the Brothers in Ireland.

The school was located on the top of a ridge above Durban from which it directly overlooked a large black housing area. This big sprawling housing settlement was called Cato Manor and was a slum area with old dilapidated houses and many people living in shanties. In 1960 South Africa experienced one of its worst periods of unrest leading to the murder of some 69 people at Sharpeville on 21 March, many of hundreds of miles away from Durban. On that morning about 4,000 people assembled in the centre of Sharpeville at the police station to protest against the obligation imposed upon black people to carry an identity document called the pass-book. The pass-book was a hated symbol of the control imposed by apartheid. Every black person had to have his or her pass-book on them at all times. If he or she was challenged by a policeman to produce a pass-book and he or she failed to so do then an arrest was made and this frequently resulted in a prison sentence for the offence of being without a pass-book. It was a highly objectionable aspect of Apartheid.

The South African Police's first reaction at Sharpeville that day was to call out the air force, but the low level flights of jet fighters did not disperse the crowd. As the day progressed the police became more and more jittery and reinforcements were called for and eventually there were about 300 police facing the crowd. In the early afternoon a scuffle broke out and part of the police station fence was pulled down and a police officer was knocked over. The crowd pushed forward being propelled by curious onlookers from behind. This was hardly unfettered violence. It appears that the police misinterpreted this and opened fire. The people in the front turned around but were unable to run away because of the crowds behind them. Bodies lay scattered around. When the dead were collected it was found that many had been shot in the back. They were running away from the police. It was certainly a black day in South African history and it is now remembered by a public holiday.

However the killings at Sharpeville had both national and international repercussions and some of these directly impacted on our life in Durban. Durban had its own post-Sharpeville riots, burning vehicles and loud protests made by the people of Cato Manor. At one stage hundreds if not thousands of Zulu workers carrying sticks and chanting what appeared to be war cries streamed out of Cato Manor and made for central Durban. One of the important routes from Cato Manor to central Durban went directly past the Marist Brothers' College. The whole school came to a halt. All the children ran to the windows to see the excited hoards of colourful and noisy Zulus march by. No one was allowed to leave the premises. The Brothers contacted the police who sent a contingent of soldiers to guard the school. The soldiers, looking like they were ready for battle, arrived with armoured cars. They parked one armoured car at the school gate and another in the assembly area. There was a public bus which ran below the school into town and which many of us caught. On that day the bus service was suspended and a special bus driven by solders and police came and picked us up. When we got to the centre of Durban there were solders and police all over the place and armoured cars located at strategic points in the main streets. It was indeed an exciting time. Some people thought that the 'revolution' had started and that a brand new world awaited us all. The housing property market crashed as did the stock market. This state of emergency lasted several days with police and soldiers staying on the school grounds all day. Peculiarly enough there was no sense of fear among the boys. It was the Brothers and the lay teachers who were frightened.

There was unrest all over South Africa as the black people struggled to be treated like citizens of their own country but it was still another thirty years before they were to get their independence from apartheid. However Sharpeville caused a lot of white people to leave South Africa and settle abroad. The events at Sharpeville and Cato Manor were exciting to kids in Durban and it was another small step in creating political awareness.

Steve and Patsy took this all in their stride. They just didn't discuss Sharpeville. They never mentioned the idea of going back to Ireland. Steve moved jobs again. All was normal.

The Remenyis lived in Durban for nearly four years before moving first to an adjacent suburb called Westville and then to Gilletts which was a bit further away in the hinterland behind Durban. By these moves Steve and Patsy substantially improved our living conditions, but we were now living in houses with large gardens in relatively less populated suburbs. It was perhaps for this reason that Steve decided to purchase a gun. It was already quite common for white men in South Africa to own a fire arm. After looking around various gun shops Steve decided that he wanted a revolver. He was of the view that automatic pistols jammed when they were most needed. So a particular revolver, relatively small – the sort that you could put in your pocket was chosen and the shopkeeper gave Steve the necessary forms with which to obtain a gun licence. Obtaining a gun licence in South Africa at that time was not a trivial matter and required an appearance before a magistrate. Steve completed the form and despatched me to the magistrates' court. I had been sitting in a queue for about an hour when a clerk came to me and asked if I was really 18 years of age as that was required to be eligible for a gun licence. I replied that I was in fact only 16 and I had come to get a gun licence for my father. I was sent away with a flea in my ear. Steve had to do this himself which he did the following day. As far as I know Steve used the revolver twice in 30 years. On both occasions it was used to shoot snakes. But he did keep the revolver and it was specifically left in his will to his younger son Brendan.

It was about this time that a dreadful accident occurred resulting in Brendan losing one of his eyes. This accident was brought about by my recklessly playing with fireworks. At that stage Brendan was not quite seven and he should never have been near any fireworks at all, but during that period both Steve and Patsy were working all day and so we were left to our own devices. We were in effect latch key kids even before the term was invented. This accident drew the five of us more closely together for a while, but it didn't last. There was no real driver of cohesion in the family. It is a great credit to Brendan that he has never allowed this accident to enter into the equation of his relationships with any of the members of the family. He has also done just about everything any person could do who had not been through the loss of an eye. This painful incident did not really change the family in any way. Like the Sheehans before, this incident is something which was and is still mostly just not talked about. Whether that is a good or a bad thing is by no means obvious.

During this time Steve and Patsy's attitude was slowly changing from being temporary settlers in South Africa, thinking that one day they would return to Ireland their true home, to seeing South Africa as a long term place to live. Steve did not make an instant success in his New World and would not return home soon with riches. Although having stayed this while in Africa Steve always saw himself as an Irishman and always kept his Irish passport up to date and never for a moment considered the possibility of acquiring South African nationality. He was perfectly comfortable being an Irish long term settler in Africa. Putting this in context there were people in Durban whose grandfathers and grandmothers came from England and they also thought of themselves as English.

Steve took a fifth job in Durban which was different to the others he had held. He was appointed to the role of catering manager for the canteens and dining rooms of the Dunlop Tyre Company in South Africa. This was a challenging job in which Steve had to arrange the delivery of three meals a day to several thousand people. It brought more money and he seemed to obtain quite a lot of satisfaction from it. However it did require quite a lot of travelling to and from the Dunlop industrial site and in retrospect it was not a position which would lead Steve to the sort of job he really wanted.

On a few occasions we met Hungarians who had left their homes during the 1956 revolution. Steve was not especially comfortable with these people but he offered no reason for this. They had told us that Steve's ability in the Hungarian language was definitely on the decline. Although it is said that one never loses entirely one's mother tongue, by now Steve would have been away from Hungary for going on 25 years and he would hardly have had any opportunity to speak his original tongue. Steve never sought out Hungarians and hardly ever spoke to the children about any aspect of his past before he arrived in Ireland. In the early years in South Africa, Hungary was effectively written out of the family consciousness.

There is no doubt that these were busy and exciting years for all of us. Steve and Patsy both worked hard and were also emotionally stretched by the fact that they were living such a different type of life to that which they had left behind. Of course one of the major differences was the fact that they were actually living together every day, which they hadn't done since the end of the war. But looking back on those days, there was perhaps little closeness between them and the children and also among the children. The children were sort of dragged behind them in their jet stream as they moved from house to house – about ten moves in six years - and job to job – four jobs for Steve and two for Patsy. There was little if any real reflection on how we were living or even coping. Steve clearly felt under a lot of pressure as he did not have the type of job he felt he could handle and it took him quite a few more years before he achieved this.

From South to North and back again

From the 21st century it is hard to write about South African Apartheid. It seems so unreal. The sort of things which were done and the sort of comments that were made by relatively ordinary, rational people were so off the wall to be almost unbelievable now. Much of Apartheid's propaganda about blacks, Indians and people of mixed race was just ridiculous. But no one laughed and the system persisted from the coming to power of the Nationalist Party in 1948 until they handed over power to the ANC in 1994. It is however fair to say that Apartheid had already begun to collapse during the 1980s.

In 1958 Durban was not an uncomfortable place for Steve or the Remenyi family. In these years of high apartheid it was a safe city for white people to live. In the white areas at any rate, there was a low crime incidence. Mugging of whites was just about unheard of, unless one went down into the harbour late on a Saturday night or perhaps if one frequented the Smugglers' Inn in the red light area. Car high jacking had not yet been invented. It was perfectly safe to let white children come and go on their own around the city. Of course, white children were generally speaking not allowed to go near to black areas where there was much higher incidences of various sorts of crime. Blacks generally lived in slums away from the whites. They had poor housing – sometimes only shanty dwellings. Hunger was rampant. One of the main sources of entertainment was in shabeens. At this time it was illegal for a black person to purchase normal alcohol in South Africa. Black people were only allowed to purchase what was known as "kafir beer" or in more polite circles "Bantu beer" which was a sour brew of cereal usually sold in a milk carton type container. It looked and smelled revolting. It had a low alcoholic content. Another one of the ubiquitous lies told by Apartheid was that normal alcohol drove black people mad.

Shabeens also sold, in contravention of the law, normal alcohol to the black population in the townships. But they also made their own booze. This was fermented from anything they could get their hands on and sometimes it was no better than poison. As Zulu labourers generally lived in barrack-type buildings without their families, shabeens were often used as dens of iniquity where other vices were to be found as well. Shabeens were regularly being closed down by the police and had to be moved around to new locations. But these places persisted because, as said before, they were one of the few locations where black people could relax and enjoy themselves.

The Remenyi family had one brush up against the law with regard to illegal brewing. One morning at about 2 am we were awakened by loud voices in our back yard and a dog barking its head off. Steve got out of bed as best he could and hurried out the back door to see what was going on. There were several cops who were questioning some black people in high pitched voices. It appeared that the domestic lady who worked for us had been selling illegal booze. It was not clear to us as to whether she was actually making it in her room or whether she was just a distributor. In the event she and her clients were taken away and the following day Steve had to pay a fine in order to have our domestic returned to us. If the fine had not been paid, and few black people had the money to pay such fines, she would certainly have gone to jail.

At that time, South Africa was characterised by the two very separate worlds of which it consisted. The whites' world might as well have been in Europe or the safer parts of America. Our world was relatively prosperous and comparatively secure. The other African world was desperately underprivileged and it was a world in which neither of these desirable states of prosperity and security existed. Furthermore there was relatively little information available to whites about the detailed lives of the black people. For example there was a high rate of crime in the black townships but this was seldom reported in the white press.

Apartheid was nothing more than segregation which had been the basis of the way of life in the Southern States of the USA ever since slaves had been brought in from Africa. It was also how the British had run India before it was independent and partitioned. But the Nationalist Government needed to have an underpinning rationale to justify Apartheid. There were two major streams to their rationale. The first one was that when white people originally arrived at the Cape of Good Hope there were few indigenous people already there. Two small groups of people populated this area and these were the Khoikhoi who were referred to generally by the offensive word, Hottentot, and the San who were called Bushmen. The Khoikhoi are now thought to have lived in Southern Africa since 500 CE.

It had been known that the arrival of the whites resulted in the Khoikhoi being contaminated with diseases for which they had no immunity and thus caused them to perish. The San also picked up some of these diseases but as many of them lived in remote areas some survived.

The Nationalist Government argued that there were no other indigenous people in the Cape in 1652. What we today think of as traditional black

African peoples were moving down from central Africa at that time. The whites and these peoples, who are technically called Bantu by anthropologists, only met in the Eastern Cape Province many hundreds of miles from the Cape itself. This fact, asserted the Nationalist Government proved that the blacks have no superior right to the land of South Africa. Blacks were every bit as much invaders as the whites – but the whites had ultimately been more successful. There is also a reference in the Old Testament which says that the "Children of Ham shall be cursed". It was said that Ham was black and that the victory of the Afrikaner over the blacks was in someway the realisation of what was said in the Old Testament. I never really understood how these issues could be used to justify the bad treatment of people.

The second rationale which underpinned apartheid was the notion that groups of people were fundamentally different and that different peoples do not get on with each other and therefore they must be kept apart. When you think like this then you need to be able to classify people and this lead to the necessity to have a vocabulary to describe the different groups. The need to have official classifications seems to have been deeply entrenched in the psyche of the Afrikaner. And when the classification is sorted out and people carry identity cards saying which group they are in, then public facilities may be labelled. In the case of South Africa the labelling was either White or Non-White. It is worth mentioning that pre-1948 the largely English speaking backed United Party operated a degree of segregation. They did not want an integrated country. But they were more subtle than the Afrikaners. They did not mark facilities "Whites Only". Much like in India and also in former times in Ireland, local people were much more subtly informed where they were not welcome.

The way that people of South Africa were referred to by the Government during the apartheid years changed a number of times. When we arrived in 1958 the official language used by the Government was that the country was populated by Europeans and non-Europeans. There were a few English speaking South Africans, mostly from Natal, who still talked about natives, instead of non-Europeans, but this was on its way out. The people who talked about natives were normally second, third or fourth generation English and they still referred to England as home.

The terms Europeans and non-Europeans presented a problem as some of the whites especially the Afrikaners, had ancestors who had been in South Africa for three or four hundred years. Their connection to Europe was remote. They were certainly better described as a white tribe in Africa rather than as Europeans. So in the mid-1960s the language was changed by the Government and the official way of talking about the population was Whites and Non-Whites. Bearing in mind the national psyche which underpinned Apartheid this was probably a fairly inevitable way of talking about people. But even the apartheid Government could see that it was fundamentally objectionable to refer to anybody as a "non" something such as a Non-White.

So this particular nomenclature or classification of people did not last long. At some point the word Bantu was introduced to describe black African people. There was a Department of Bantu Affairs which was the Government Department which controlled Black people. But this was not a popular word either and was again changed. At one point this Government Department's name was changed to the Department of Plural Relations. There is no doubt about the fact that it was difficult to find an acceptable set of words to camouflage the realities of apartheid.

This manipulation of vocabulary was worthy of a Gilbert and Sullivan comic operetta but, as said before, no one laughed – it was simply too tragic.

As well as blacks, whites, Indians and so called 'Coloureds' there were also a small number of Chinese people around. They had come to South Africa to work primarily on the mines in the Transvaal and it was the fear of competition from the Chinese which had initiated the restrictive labour laws of Job Reservation. As the South African Government was intensely anti-communist, many of the Chinese people tended to say that they were originally from Taiwan, which may or may not have been correct. Thus South Africa was and still is a country with an enormously rich blend of cultures. Instead of celebrating diversity as an asset, the apartheid mentality saw this diversity as a liability and initially tried to sweep everyone who wasn't white into one big category – Non-European or Non-White. Later the Government perceived the opportunity of confusing the issues underpinning apartheid by converting the tribal nature of the black people into an idea of nationhood. If the black people were classified by nations then there was no nation with a population bigger than the Afrikaners or the English speaking South Africans. So we were told how many Zulus, Xhosa, Tswana, Sotho, Shangaan, Venda etc there were and as their individual numbers were smaller they should have less influence.

At every turn the Government encouraged suspicion and distrust if not downright phobia. And it is surprising just how easy it is to get people to distrust and be suspicious of each other. Dislike, if not animosity, easily followed and then the Government said that the different peoples had to be kept apart because of the hostile feeling which the Government themselves had created. Underpinning this pathological need to find differences there was the unspoken belief that people whose skins were not white were inferior and thus they could be, at best, second class citizen and that they should be made to develop themselves separately. Separate development then went on to say that 80% of the population, i.e. black people, could have 13% of the land mass of South Africa as their own in which they could be full citizens. The 13 % offered was in underdeveloped areas and black people could use this land to develop themselves. Blacks living in white areas were then considered foreigners and need not be given much in the way of facilities nor treated with the courtesies which white people could claim in their own 87% of the land mass of South Africa. All of this was double-think and double-talk but the apartheid Government saw one of its tasks to invent a philosophy and a mythology to justify its awful treatment of people.

In its 45 years of existence apartheid was responsible for the deaths of tens of thousands or possibly hundreds of thousands of people. Apartheid wrecked the lives of millions or tens of millions. Time and again apartheid affronted the dignity of black people in just about every way one can imagine. There were daily examples of this attitude which are now well documented and do not require repeating here. But in addition to this callous attitude towards black people apartheid also propagated malicious lies about black people as individuals which were destructive not only to their relationship with whites and other people but seriously damaged their own self esteem. Apartheid propaganda said that blacks were stupid; blacks were uncivilizable; blacks were lazy; blacks were dirty; blacks were thieves; blacks were cruel; blacks smelled; blacks wanted to rape white women. Apartheid went on to assert that black people don't trust each other. If left alone blacks would murder each other. And so on and so on. The problem about these lies was that the different population groups believed some of them to some extent. It appears that even some of the blacks began to believe these lies about themselves.

Apartheid also encouraged animosity between blacks and Indians and blacks and people of mixed race etc. An incident occurred in Durban in January 1949 during which Zulus attacked members of the Indian community. Over one hundred people were killed and more than a thousand injured. The South African Navy were called in to quell the fighting. This incident was used time and again to "prove" that blacks and Indians needed whites to keep them apart. Meanwhile many less racially prejudiced people tried to suggest that apartheid had created the environment in which this incident could take place – but alas to no avail.

In contrast apartheid's propaganda about white people said that they upheld Christian values while black people didn't. Apartheid asserted that white people understood the need for law and order. White people believed that they implemented the rule of law. White people were the source of civilisation in Africa. Perhaps most important white people were the bulwark against Communism which was atheistic and ungodly. Also it was regularly said that black people didn't want to have anything to do with governing themselves. Black people liked the apartheid system – they didn't want to be ruled by their own. When black people did rule themselves chaos descended like that which happened in Nigeria, Ghana, The Congo, Uganda and other parts of Africa. South African black people, it was said, wanted the law and order that the whites provided. The ability of white South Africans to be self deceptive was truly phenomenal.

But there was a much more profound way in which Apartheid undermined life in South Africa. Apartheid did not just harm the blacks, Indians and people of mixed race. Apartheid also damaged the whites. In the Merchant of Venice, Shakespeare says that "The quality of mercy ... blesseth him that gives and him that takes". Apartheid harmed both "him that gives and him that takes". It led to the whites unnecessarily fearing anyone who was different. Contact with other groups could only be on what the South African law called a Master and Servant basis. Any other contact would lead to trouble. It was commonly said that, "If they didn't mug you or steal from you then you would pick up some sort of disease from these people". Although fear is not always a bad emotion, unnecessary fear is debilitating. It was responsible for a host of draconian laws which controlled people – sometimes even white people. The Immorality Act and the Prohibition of Mixed Marriages Act were examples of such laws. There was also a fear of how black people might take their revenge on whites. This was seldom articulated but a joke going around in the 1970's focused on this deeply held dread. The joke went as follows: "What do you call a black man with an AK 47?". The answer to this was "Sir". Perhaps many a true word is spoken in jest! And this fear was fuelled by the Nationalists continually pointing to countries north of the border where there were highly unsatisfactory Governments.

But besides this problem of fear, Apartheid hurt whites in a more profound way. One of the reasonable expectations many people have for themselves is that as they grow older they will develop. Development is reflected in a fuller appreciation of the world and its peoples. Mature people would generally agree that contact with different races, colours and creeds opened up awareness of the different dimensions in the world and helped them towards a fuller appreciation and enjoyment of life. Apartheid completely discouraged this. It wanted white people to be cocooned from the other cultures in South Africa. It saw multi-culturism as a pernicious virus which could only lead to destruction - the destruction of the traditional Afrikaner way of life which was Christian, capitalist and democratic (as long as you didn't count the masses of people disenfranchised by the system). This attitude was reflected in the refusal to allow television to be broadcast in South Africa until 1976. It led to the banning of the book by Anna Sewell about a horse called "Black Beauty". It was at the root of the objection of allowing South Africans to hold two passports – to mention only a few issues. But the real harm came not so much from what was forbidden by law but rather from the lost opportunities to live a much richer life by engaging with the other cultures which were right in front of us.

It was into this remarkable political climate that Steve Remenyi brought his family in 1958. The Remenyis lived in South Africa as a family of 5 for 6 years. The political awareness of the children did not happen over night. It took 3 or 4 years for me to understand what Apartheid was really about. My original discomfort with it was due to my relating what I saw being done to people to what I was told had been done by the English to the Irish. But this did not produce in me any animosity towards the English speaking South African who appeared to sympathise to some extent with those subjected to Apartheid. By the time I reached university I had the need to discuss politics with Steve, but by and large this was a futile exercise. Although he described himself as a liberal and he was clearly always very considerate towards the people who worked for him regardless of race, colour or creed, he never brought himself to say anything about Apartheid. He certainly did not openly support Apartheid. He would say that black people and Indians are treated very badly all over the world. He would point to the Congo or Nigeria to illustrate hopeless black governments on the African continent. He was very concerned that I might come to the attention of the Government as a number of students had. Some students were detained without trial or placed under house arrest. This did not happen.

These years were not good for Steve's health. Steve's back problem always haunted the family. We all knew that it was serious and that it had the potential to totally disable him. Steve was philosophical about this and stoical about the pain and discomfort which accompanied the perpetual back pain. On the issue of stoicism Patsy was the exact opposite. She was frequently ill with aches and pains of various sorts. In later life she claimed that her menopause started at about the age of 30 and that from that date on she was sick.

Steve's back problem caused him to spend time in hospital in Durban on several occasions and eventually he had another operation on his spine. The Dunlop Company were quite generous with regards to sick leave and also they had Steve covered with a comprehensive medical insurance policy. There was no national health system in South Africa. A serious surgical procedure was performed whereby a 'disc' was removed and replaced by a ball bearing. This was cutting edge hi-tech medicine at that time. We were all intrigued by the X-rays of his spine which showed a sphere where there should have been his tissue. The result of this operation was that Steve no longer had much pain or discomfort in his leg or back but he was left with a distinct limp which he had for the rest of his life.

During this time Steve applied for many jobs. The commuting to Dunlops was tiring and it often had to be done through peak traffic. Also as the factory worked three shifts for seven days a week Steve would often feel obliged to go into the industrial site a number of times over weekends. He had a large number of people working for him and as such he was faced with people difficulties every day. It took Steve a year to be allowed an assistant. During his Merchant Navy Officers' Memorial Club days Steve employed a general handy man named Freddy Govender. He and Steve got on well. But as a handy man Freddy was paid a pittance. When Steve was given the go ahead to employ an assistant he proposed Freddy to Dunlops and he was immediately appointed. What neither Steve nor Dunlops knew at that time was that Freddy had a golfing history. He had been a caddy in his youth and he had a nearly scratch handicap. It did not take the bosses in Dunlops long to realise that Freddy could be an asset to their golf ball business and Steve lost much of Freddy's time as his assistant.

Steve had an old typewriter bought for a fiver and he would, with two fingers, type letters of application and curriculum vitas probably once every other month or so. This was in the days before liquid Tippex. As an amateur typist he would make typing mistakes and either start again or try to rub out the errors with abrasive rubbers. It was a long hard slog to find a better job. Considering the fact that he was good at what he did, the lack of job offers now puzzles me. The first half of the 1960s in South Africa was characterised by a high degree of uncertainty based on the unrest which followed Sharpeville. This meant that there was minimal growth for some years in the type of jobs that Steve could do. Also Steve didn't look good on paper. He had no formal qualifications in the field in which he worked. He had not been to an established catering school and he had no specific management training. And he had an unusual surname. The importance of the surname has only recently occurred to me when I remembered a funny incident which occurred when he was working for Dunlops. As catering manager for a company that fed thousands of people Steve was responsible for the purchasing of large quantities of food. To have the canteens and dining rooms operate effectively Steve was always on the look out for new suppliers of quality food at good prices. On one occasion when he made first contact with a new potential supplier he was asked his name and he said Remenyi. The person on the other end of the telephone call said abruptly, "We don't do business with Indians", and hung up. The name Remenyi exists in several different cultures. It is used in India and in a number of different parts of Africa. It is a Luo name in Kenya and it's a Sotho name in South Africa. I have on two separate occasions been told by black people that they were surprised to find that I was not black.

In apartheid South Africa during a time when photographs were not routinely attached to CVs, the name Remenyi was probably not an asset and his application for a job may have just been rejected out of hand. But who knows?

It took until the end of 1964 for an interesting job to turn up and it was not in South Africa.

Finally Steve was made an offer of the position of catering manager of the Salisbury Club in the northern neighbouring country which had just changed its name from Southern Rhodesia to Rhodesia. This meant a move from a major seaside resort city to a much smaller city in a land locked country nearly a thousand miles away.

This job in Salisbury was better paid and the hours were shorter than the Dunlop's job in Durban and Steve sold up lock stock and barrel again, as he had done in Dublin, and moved the family north. This decision was made quite quickly. Once again there was no family discussion about the impact of the move on the other family members. There was no major delay in obtaining immigration papers as the white Rhodesian Government was nowhere near as difficult about immigrants as the South African Government had been six years before. It is interesting to note that the South African Government had also by this time become much easier on immigration as they had begun to realise that they needed more white people, even English speaking Catholics, to try to counter balance the numbers between whites and the other racial groups. The South African Government had even begun to pay for the passage to the country for immigrants.

This move did not have the air of excitement which we had when we transposed ourselves from Dublin to Durban. Moving further up into what was relatively speaking unknown darkest Africa seemed more of a chore than an adventure. There had been quite a lot of young Rhodesians in Durban either studying or on holiday and they did not make any great impression on us or make us feel that there was any special reason why Rhodesia would be interesting.

Except for Steve, none of us really wanted to go to live in Rhodesia. By now we were well settled in Durban with a circle of friends. Patsy had a reasonably good job, but she was prepared to go to Salisbury so that she would not have to work. For my part, Steve made it clear that I was expected to stay with the family. I had already left school and I was struggling to figure out what type of career I wished to follow. Steve wanted me to be an accountant but I knew that the work of an accountant would not suit me at all. I thought that I might like to be a teacher but Steve was strongly against this referring to teaching as a life of relative poverty. There was quite a lot of tension concerning this matter and this was to be repeated in the family when Brendan left school and was trying to find out what work would suit him.

To add to this it was no easy job leaving home which I only finally managed to do some years later. Steve believed that children should stay at home until they married and quoted examples in Ireland where the sons and daughters only moved out at the age of 40. At this stage none of the children realised that he, himself, had actually left home by the age of 19. There was no discussion about how long we would stay in Rhodesia. Steve wasn't prepared to speculate where his next move might be to. The family was growing up and he realised that he had only just managed to talk me into going with them.

Our large furnishings were once again shipped off to an auction for which very little was received. Packing the car carefully Steve piled ourselves and everything else we owned into an old Wolseley and we set out on this voyage of discovery. We took three days to travel the thousand miles in the cramped little car. We spent the first night in Pretoria, the second night in a village in a remote part of Rhodesia. The village was West

Nicholson and the third evening we reached Salisbury. We were certainly glad when at last our great trek was over.

Rhodesia then and Zimbabwe now is a much smaller and far less wealthy country than South Africa. The economy of Rhodesia would have been hardly one tenth of that of South Africa. Thus everything was on a smaller scale. It was essentially an agricultural economy based largely on tobacco. The second main industry was cattle and it was regarded as producing some of the best beef in the world. It also had a few minerals and a small amount of tourism as its main source of employment for its people.

Salisbury was a carefully laid out city based on a grid patterns. It had a modest central business district and large sprawling suburbs. It was a clean city with reasonable parks and gardens. It was too small to have a rush hour. Many of the streets were lined with Jacaranda trees and in October the city was a blast of the most beautiful colour.

Rhodesia was in some respects quite different to South Africa and in other respects not that much different. Whites ran the country and the blacks did what they were told. Rhodesia had its own version of apartheid – a very British version. South African apartheid was based on deeply felt principles of racial difference as well as superiority and how these principles needed to be expressed in terms of separate development. Rhodesian apartheid thinking did not have the same depth. It was based simply on the fact outlined by Julius Caesar 2000 years before i.e. veni, vidi, vici – I came, I saw, I conquered. There were no principles behind this except for the patently obvious fact that God was an Englishman or perhaps more correctly God is an Englishman.

There was a small amount of cultural diversity in Rhodesia. There was a few thousand Afrikaners and a small number of people of South Asian descent. There were two major tribal groups – the Shona and the maNdebele; also some mixed race people but few others. Unlike South Africa which could trace the roots of colonial settlement back to Jan Van Riebeck when he arrived in the Cape on 6 April 1652, Southern Rhodesia had only been established since 1889 when Lobengula, King of Matabeleland, entered into a treaty with Great Britain[12].

---

[12] King Lobengula granted the British South Africa Company the right to search for gold in the extreme south-west of Matabeleland for a period of 25 years. This treaty, called the Rudd Concession, was signed by Lobengula on October 3, 1888 and by Queen Victoria on October 20, 1889. It specifically stated that Lobengula would not offer any similar rights to either the Boer Republics or the Portuguese. Lobengula was paid in money and weapons for these rights and given

The English speaking settlers were the bosses, just as they had been in India and Ireland and elsewhere around the world and that was that. Black people were frequently referred to by whites as muntus or munts which was a highly pejorative term. The whites were indifferent to the offence this caused. As English speakers had problems in pronouncing the word maNdebele, they renamed the tribe the Matebele and they were related to the Zulus in South Africa.

Of course, in general terms Rhodesian apartheid was much more subtle than South African apartheid. There were even black parliamentarians and members of the civil service. But these were few and far between. There were no signs on park benches or on door ways or on public toilets proclaiming Europeans or Whites Only. In fact all facilities were officially multi-racial. Mixed marriages were allowed in Rhodesia, although few occurred. There was no official job reservation. In Rhodesian apartheid all the Government had to do was to control the expenditure on education. The franchise was based on education so if blacks were uneducated they were not eligible to vote. To be fair the Rhodesians spent a much larger proportion of their education budget on black children than the South Africans did and the quality of its education was better than what was offered in South Africa. But alas it wasn't enough and also the idea of a qualified franchise was a 19th century idea. With little or no education most people couldn't get reasonable jobs and thus except for very few well-to-do blacks, they had no money to go to the cinemas or restaurants or pubs. They simply could not afford to live anywhere other than in low cost black areas. And furthermore people living like this cannot get their families out of this poverty cycle. This formula has been used all over the world by Governments who couldn't care less about the poorer classes. The Anglican Church was the primary religious community and from time to time it spoke out loudly in favour of better conditions for black people. The Methodists were also important with the

---

assurances that his Kingdom would not be occupied. Lobengula had been promised that the British only wanted mining rights and that they had no ambitions to settle in his kingdom. It is said that the British promised that whites would surrender their weapons when they entered the Lobengula Kingdom. However despite assurances that these conditions were clearly stipulated in the Rudd Concession document this did not happen. Shortly after the British arrived in substantial numbers with arms and it became clear to Lobengula that the foreigners had come as settlers and wanted much more than just mining rights. Lobengula appealed to Queen Victoria but to no avail. The Matebele War began in November 1893. The British machine guns devastated the Matebele warriors and by 1897 much of what eventually became Rhodesia was occupied by the white settlers. Before he died Lobengula told his few remaining warriors to seek the protection of Cecil John Rhodes.

Methodist Bishop Abel Muzorewa eventually playing an important role in Rhodesian politics.

The whites had a virtually limitless pool of cheap labour which they treated just like any other commodity or factor of production. There were no trade unions to speak of and there was no protective labour legislation. People were hired and fired at the whim of the employer. Pay was miserable. And when the "natives" got restless there was of course the British South African Police to remind them who the bosses were. The British South African Police were run more like the British police than the South African. They were not gun toting cops. But they were not to be trifled with either. Anyone who stepped out of line quickly learnt who was in charge. Rhodesian apartheid or British apartheid created a tight vicious circle and essentially was little or no better from the point of view of those discriminated against than South African apartheid. Paternalism was the key driver behind Rhodesian apartheid. And if anything Rhodesian blacks were materially less well off than the equivalent people in South Africa.

The Remenyi family drove into Salisbury in mid January 1965 eleven months almost exactly to the day, before Ian Smith took the step to unilaterally declare independence which was generally referred to as UDI, from the United Kingdom. Many white Rhodesians saw this as an act of political lunacy. It was the hardliners in the Rhodesian Front who wanted to show the UK that they were in power in Rhodesia. The first reaction to this was to lead to economic sanctions against the country and ultimately to a civil war in which many people were killed and the country was brought to the verge of economic collapse. Fortunately for the Remenyis the civil war was only to start later in about 1970 by which time the Remenyi siblings were out of the country. This was just as well as we could have been called upon to fight for the Rhodesian vision of Western Christian Civilisation in Africa. None of us could have stomached that.

Just like his attitude to politics in South Africa, Steve was impervious to the politics of Rhodesia but as he did before he took considerable care in looking after the people who worked for him.

The Salisbury Club was a gentleman's club which modelled itself on the well established clubs of Pall Mall in London. As a gentleman's club in Rhodesia this meant that The Salisbury Club was mostly used by businessmen, civil servants and white politicians as well as senior officers in the Rhodesian Forces. The Club was located on Cecil Square – the square was named after Cecil John Rhodes who was one of the main architects of British imperialism in Africa. The Club was within a two minute walk of the parliament building.

It was not easy to join this club as a proposer and seconder was needed as well as a vote by the membership. These were also times when it was possible to be 'black-balled'. In addition the entrance fee was expensive. The Club also had procedures for excluding people who they thought were unsuitable. It was a well appointed club and it attracted many of the big names in Rhodesia including many leading members of the ruling Government political party, The Rhodesian Front. The Club espoused old fashioned values. Women were not allowed to become members. In fact it had only recently opened a ladies' restaurant with a separate entrance in the street around the corner. Women could not enter the Club by the front door. Jews were not generally welcomed, but as with many such organisations there was a token Jewish member or two.

Steve was in charge of all the catering and he appeared to enjoy this job. He had a real flair for food and had he been born 40 or 50 years later and been sent to a cordon bleu school instead of a radio operator college there is no doubt he could easily have been one of those famous chefs with his own TV programme and chain of restaurants etc. He clearly enjoyed working for a prestigious or elite institution. As part of his job he had been introduced to many of the leaders in the country. Both his pay and conditions of work were better than he had before. He also had more holiday entitlement. The job included accommodation in the club. The family had a three bedroomed flat with a living room and two bathrooms, but no kitchen as the club supplied all the food. In effect we were fed from one of the best kitchens in the country. But on the downside we could not make a cup of coffee for ourselves. It had to be made in the club kitchen and brought to us. It was a bizarre way to live indeed.

Steve had much more personal time than he ever had before and thus he was able to spend time getting to know a bit of the country. Zimbabwe is a spectacularly beautiful country with many tourist attractions. We visited Kariba Dam, the Victoria Falls, the Vumba and the Zimbabwe Ruins. It is interesting to reflect on the Zimbabwe Ruins. Great Zimbabwe is a stone built city in the southern central part of the country. In Rhodesian times it was said that they were built by King Solomon or the Queen of Sheba or some such famous monarch. The idea was never entertained that these ruins could have been built by Africans. To Rhodesians, the local blacks could never have developed this level of technology. The best that blacks could do was to build mud huts.

In Rhodesia Steve also speculated in property, in a small way, buying a house or two, fixing it up and reselling it. This was a hobby out of which he made some money and gave him an additional interest to his work at the Salisbury Club. But unlike the jobs he had held at the Merchant Navy Officers' Memorial Club and the Air Force Club in Durban, Steve was not the club manager and thus he was rather limited in how much he was able to achieve work wise in Salisbury.

None of the other members of the family settled all that well in Rhodesia. Patsy complained bitterly for just about the entire duration of his stay at the Club that she missed Durban and all her friends. She did not have to work during her stay in Salisbury and thus she had time on her hands. She never really found a niche for herself. She tried to write a novel and became pretentious about her limited literary abilities. Although neither she nor Steve could be regarded as practising Catholics, Patsy made contact with a number of priests and nuns. These priests and nuns were of course Irish and it made her feel more connected to her roots.

It was here at the Salisbury Club that some of the facts about Steve and Patsy's early life came out. One evening over dinner the five of us started talking about anniversaries and Patsy said that no one ever remembered her wedding anniversary which was sometime in January. During this discussion it became apparent that I was born a mere six months after Steve and Patsy's wedding day. It was well known that I had been a big baby weighing considerably above the average. All of a sudden it became blindingly obvious. Steve just went silent and Patsy simply shrugged it off with the comment that I was a love child. All three children had a good laugh at Steve's and Patsy's discomfort.

Rhodesia had television in 1965 which was not available in South Africa. As already mentioned the South African Government had refused to allow television broadcasting due to its corrupting influence. After all, television had programmes which showed blacks and whites living contentedly together. Rhodesian television was monochrome. There was only one channel and it broadcast for five to six hours per day. The programming was dreadful but it did help to pass some of the time for Patsy. As well as travelling around Rhodesia Steve and Patsy took a holiday each year in Durban to keep up with old friends. The sanctions imposed after UDI made various commodities hard to find in Salisbury but Steve's attitude to customs which he had picked up during his Irish Shipping days, were put to good use in bringing some of the Club's requirements back to Salisbury undetected by the customs officers at the border.

Salisbury was not an intrinsically exciting city to live in. It was a small town with a parochial attitude and little entertainment. It claimed to have a couple of night clubs where some of the local white women sometimes doubled as the cashier and striptease artists. Beer drinking was the national preoccupation especially when it was done in conjunction with watching rugby or cricket. As UDI was declared only a matter of months after the Remenyis arrived. Salisbury became a great hive of sanctions busters. The Rhodesians certainly did not lack enterprise. Within a month or two after economic sanctions all sort of goods were being produced locally which had previously been imported. However not all of these were great successes. The local cornflakes were initially not fit for consumption and the first batch of tomato sauce was thick, almost black in colour and tasted nothing like the original thing. So the country was not entirely without interest. Watching the UDI struggle unfold was sometimes entertaining.

While Steve and the rest of the family lived in Salisbury I went to attend University in Durban. This was between 1966 and 1968. While at the university an unfortunate incident occurred which disturbed Steve. I stood for election to the Students' Representative Council of the University in 1966 and I was duly elected. The Principal and Vice-Chancellor was a certain Professor Owen Pieter Faure Horwood. Professor Horwood had recently been appointed to this high office. He was conservative in his political outlook and especially in his attitude towards the students. With regard to his qualifications for the job of university principal he held only one degree which was a bachelor of commerce. He was married to the sister of Ian Smith, the then Prime Minister of Rhodesia. He was well connected in conservative circles in Southern Africa. It didn't take long for a row to breakout between him and the Student's Representative Council. The detail of the row is quite irrelevant and I have forgotten most of it but it is worth mentioning that one of the things which offended the Vice-Chancellor was a cartoon which appeared in the student newspaper for which the Students Representative Council was responsible. The cartoon showed Horwood as a big bulk of a man holding a very small degree in his closed hand.

In 1967 Horwood suspended the Students Representative Council and banned a number of its members including me from being on the campus except to attend lectures. For the banned students all extra-curricular activities were suspended. We were expected to come onto the campus only to journey to a lecture theatre and then leave immediately once the lecture was over. If anyone of us had an hour's break between lectures we were expected to walk off the campus and wait on the street until the hour passed and then return for the next lecture. This was an over reaction to a situation which did not merit this level of punishment. But Horwood appeared to have bullying tendencies and he wanted to stamp out any suggestion that he was not in complete control of every aspect of university life.

Horwood then charged these students with a series of misdemeanours, the most important of which was that we had brought the good name of the University into disrepute. He made comments to the press in which he insinuated that some of these renegade students were *pinko liberals* if not actually communists or fellow travellers and similar comments appeared in the newspapers. This was serious as it was at that time in South Africa a criminal offence to be a communist. However this accusation was so outrageous that no one took the communist slander seriously.

Horwood appointed a tribunal to hear his charges against the students. He carefully chose conservative Professors who were prepared to hear his case. Some of the students were represented by either their fathers or by some sort of legal counsel. Steve was in Salisbury and I didn't have the money for a lawyer. It was a fairly anxious time for us all.

The row had occurred in June and we had a winter vacation break in July. The University hearing was to be held in August. I spent the holiday in Salisbury. The news of the row with the Principal had, as mentioned above, made the newspapers so Steve had read the public side of this fracas. When I explained the details of what actually happened Steve did not show much sympathy for my position. He wasn't concerned in the rights and wrongs of the fight with the Principal. He was very concerned that I might be brought to the attention of the authorities and by this he meant the police - especially the Special Branch[13]. Being known to the Special Branch could have been a first step in being punished for your political views. I had already become a South Africa citizen which I had done so that I would qualify for financial assistance at university. Steve felt that despite my new nationality I could easily be deported back to Ireland. I

---

[13] I had a number of friends who had come to the attention of the Special Branch and as a result had either lost their job or had some sort of restriction placed on them. I had one incident with the Special Branch myself. I was staying with a family not far from the University when I was called to the phone. A man who introduced himself as an officer in the Special Branch asked me if I knew certain students. They were friends and I said that I did. He asked me if I would assist him with his enquiries into these people. I told him that I knew that they had not been involved in anything that would be of interest to the Special Branch. I was then told that I might be called upon by the State in the future for assistance. Of course nothing further happened. I saw this as simply a strategy to make people worry. It was a Big Brother approach. I didn't tell Steve about this incident as it would not have helped his peace of mind.

did not think that this was a serious possibility. Anyway this situation made Steve uncomfortable and nervous.

I returned to Durban to face the music. Despite Horwood's attempts to bully the students in his role of prosecutor at the hearings he did not succeed. Even his hand picked conservative Professors did not believe that any of the students had committed an offence or had done anything improper. Eventually it was agreed that if we signed a document which said something to the effect that if we offended anyone it was unintentional we could get back to normal university life. Horwood was not impressed as he wanted the students severely punished.

Steve was delighted that peace had returned.

By the way, Horwood did not stay in the position of Principal and Vice-Chancellor of the University of Natal for long. Within a few years he was appointed by the National Party to the South African Senate. Shortly after that he was invited by the Prime Minister to join the Cabinet. He then became the only English speaking cabinet member at that time. His portfolio was Minister of Finance.

It was from Salisbury in 1968 that Steve and Patsy made their first trip back to Ireland for a holiday. They had now been away for 10 years. Steve was 49. When we first arrived in Durban we had been told by other immigrant families both English and Irish that it was the norm for immigrants to have enough money to pay a visit to the homeland after about 20 years and then those who did well would probably have a second visit when they retired. No empirical evidence was ever suggested for this. By the time Steve and Patsy made their trip fly-now-and-pay-later had been invented so they could travel and face the main bill on their return. Also in those days both the South African and the Rhodesian currencies were relatively strong.

By all accounts this trip went well as a holiday and Steve and Patsy were warmly received by the Sheehans. Steve caught up with many of his old ship mates. Some were still working but others had retired to the country. Irish Shipping appeared to be doing well. Steve and Patsy treated themselves to a round Ireland trip taking in the Blarney Stone, the Ring of Kerry and other favourite haunts.

Life in Ireland had moved on and so had Steve and they returned to Rhodesia knowing for certain that he would never go back to Ireland to live. Africa had rubbed off onto them and they realised that even if Steve could have found an interesting job in Ireland, the re-adjustment to that way of living in that country would be too much for them. Up until this time he had sort of felt that maybe one day he might get lucky and make enough money to resettle in the sense of retire back in Ireland but now that dream was finally over. This didn't mean that Steve felt any less Irish but now the talk was about how he and Patsy would retire back to South Africa, perhaps back to Durban. The dream he had revealed to me on the ship as we approached Cape Town ten years before was now put to rest – permanently.

After visiting Ireland Steve and Patsy went on to Paris to see Armand Kalmár who was now in his eighties. He was in the same large apartment on his own. He stayed there because his wife had died in the apartment and he wanted to be physically close to the memories of her. This apart-ment was far too big for him but he refused to move to a smaller place. He appeared to have been fully alienated from his adopted son, Jacques and he made it clear that he was going to leave his money to his only liv-ing blood relatives who were Steve and Imre, if Imre was still alive - and of course if Imre could be found.

Armand's son Jacques was a medical practitioner and a homoeopath and lived between two homes in France at St Raphael and Grenoble. He was successful in his professions. Jacques' sons had moved into publishing and had their own business. Jacques' problems with Armand, which were apparently due to some political ideas, did not interfere in Jacques estab-lishing a positive relationship with Steve and Patsy. They all enjoyed a few days together in the South of France. Armand was to live for quite a few more years and Steve did not inherit much from him as there was a twist in that tale. The trip to Paris was not exactly routine as Steve arrived just as the student/worker mini revolution began in the spring of 1968 and the cobblestones of Paris were being ripped up and thrown at the police. The photographs which Steve took showed Paris in turmoil. The photo-graphs also reflected the concern which Steve and Patsy felt for their own and Armand's safety during their visit. There were no smiles on anyone's face but rather serious frowns. It was not a good time to be in Paris. Steve certainly had a tendency for arriving in a place at the wrong time. So they spent the minimum period which was respectable with Armand and they rushed home to where it was, at that time, relatively safe.

In about 1971 Steve invited Imre's ex-wife Magda to come to Rhodesia and spend a holiday with him and Patsy. Magda travelled all the way from Australia and spent a few weeks with them in Salisbury and travel-ling around the country visiting the main tourist attractions of Rhodesia.

This was the first real contact that Steve had with any member of his Hungarian family for more than 30 years. From Steve's point of view Magda's visit was a success but Patsy didn't really warm to Magda. Magda was already getting old and she spoke with a heavy Hungarian accent and was not always that easy to understand. This one visit did not lead to any further contact with Magda and the whereabouts of Steve's brother Imre seems to have been completely left off the agenda. It is not clear whether or not either Steve or Magda knew at this point if Imre was actually alive. In any case they didn't appear to be interested.

Steve stayed in this job in Salisbury for some seven years only leaving for a significant promotion to the manager's job in a similar club in Port Elizabeth back in South Africa in the Cape Province. This was the St George's Club where Steve took over the position of Club Secretary or as they tried to call him in later years, general manager. No sooner had Steve and Patsy arrived in Port Elizabeth than Patsy complained that she missed Salisbury and her friends who she had left behind. This time her inability to settle and the fact that her last child had left home caused her a lot of difficulty and her medical doctor advised her to seek psychiatric help. Steve had always suggested that there was something unwholesome about people who needed psychiatric help and the suggestion that Patsy seek this sort of treatment did not rest well with him. It is not easy to know why he was so opposed to psychiatry which, together with suicide, he regarded as unspeakably awful subjects. Steve's leaving of Rhodesia was well timed with regards the inevitable civil war. At his age and with his back problem he would not have been eligible to have been called up to serve in the Rhodesian Army. Nonetheless the war was a painful time to be in that country and he was better off out of it. At the time Steve left, the Rhodesians used to laugh at how inexperienced the guerrillas were and how they used to blow themselves up more than damage the Rhodesian Army. In the event it did not take the guerrillas very long to become an effective fighting force.

There is no doubt that his time in Rhodesia consolidated Steve from a professional point of view. The status of the Salisbury Club put him in a position from which he would be considered for a much better job. He had also made some money while in Rhodesia through his property acquisitions and improvements. His second immigration to South Africa saw him, at least in some respects, much better placed. But there was one catch. When UDI was declared money flooded out of Rhodesia. Both private and industrial investors perceived UDI to be a wrong move which would have substantial adverse economic consequences for the country. To stem this financial flood the Rhodesian Reserve Bank imposed a draconian regime of exchange control. The sum of fifty pounds was the limit of the funds which could be taken out of the country. Many people felt trapped by these regulations while others just took off leaving whatever property they had behind. It was well known that there were queues of emigrants at Beit Bridge which was the border with South Africa, with a car load of belongings getting out of the country as soon as they could. Sometimes Rhodesian dollars were deeply packed inside their belongings as these dollars could be converted to South African Rands down South. Occasionally such people were caught and everything was confiscated and even prison sentences were handed out to these currency smugglers. A high level of discouragement was in place to try to keep people from fleeing the nascent war which had already started on the Northern border. Steve was never clear on how he got his money out of Rhodesia. I always assumed that he had given up his smuggling ways. In any case he did not have a large sum of money to move. It took time for the money to come out of the country but he did get it into South Africa in the end.

The end of the story?

When Steve and Patsy returned to South Africa in 1974 apartheid was still holding its own but to do so it was becoming tougher and tougher. There was a veil of fear over the country which didn't exist when they had moved to Rhodesia. Any real opposition was put down with an iron fist. There were rumours about police brutality and about torturing in police cells[14]. But it was only in 1977 when the Black Consciousness Movement leader Steve Biko was beaten in a police cell and die in a police van while being transported to a hospital about 1,000 km away, that the real extent of what the police were doing come into public view[15].

Furthermore from a conceptual or philosophical point of view the apartheid system seems to be like a leaking boat. It could no longer be justified only on white superiority and Swart Gevaar (black threat). To keep it floating there was a need for more and more political devices. There were the so-called independent Bantustans. These had their own parliaments; their own prime minister; their own cabinet members; their own civil servants and other institutions. The cost of this political ruse was enormous. Of course these pretend countries were not recognised by any other country besides South Africa. Later in the 1980s Apartheid introduced Tricameralism which refers to having three parliamentary chambers which were introduced as a concession to Indians and people of mixed ancestor referred to as Coloureds. Complexity and money were no obstacles to propping up the leaky boat of Apartheid.

In the 1970s in the hope of putting in place a pro-South African government, South Africa was being drawn into the "civil" war in Angola and there was a surprise in store for the young inexperienced South African troops. As far as I know there has never been a full accounting of the fatalities or the casualties caused by that unfortunate episode but it was believed that the numbers killed or injured were substantial. In order to place some pressure on the internal industrial scene black trade unions were beginning to become established. Ten years before the existence of a black trade union was unthinkable. Change was on its way and daily life in South Africa was becoming more challenging.

---

[14] What were rumours in the white community were regarded as fact in the other racial communities.

[15] The extent of the governments' complicity in Biko's death was marked by the comment made by the Minister of Justice and Police at the time, Jimmy Kruger whi said – speaking of Biko's death - "It leaves me cold" - a literal translation of the Afrikaans "Dit laat my koud".

Returning to Steve, the St George's Club was a well appointed Club in a new building set on the verge of a park just above the city of Port Elizabeth. Like the Salisbury Club it was set up by businessmen and other well to do members of the community as a place to meet at lunch time when most of the club's business took place. He was really in his element there both in terms of his work and also the social contacts which he made through the job. Steve was in charge and this meant that he frequently dealt directly with the members on a range of issues and he got to know some of them quite well. He turned the Club round from being a loss maker to being a good business. Steve had a special touch for food and really knew how to make a restaurant work both in terms of the quality of the dining experience for the members and the profit for the club. Steve settled into the St George's Club in a big way enjoying the culture of both the Club and the city and, in fact, mostly stayed there until he retired which was shortly before he died. He made many friends and acquaintances from wide strata of people in Port Elizabeth and he really felt that he had found his niche.

After a while, and as far as I know, without psychiatric help Patsy stopped complaining about Port Elizabeth and started to enjoy life there. Once again she used her increasingly precarious connections with the Catholic Church to befriend Irish priests and nuns some of whom became regular callers to their flat within the club. She got involved in the local dramatic society. However her involvement with the theatrical crowd in Port Elizabeth, modest as it was, gave Patsy even more encouragement to develop a pretentious tone and outlook towards life. Her humble beginnings in Cuffe Street were certainly completely forgotten. She was capable of passing herself off in a variety of ways. Her previously dark red hair had become a yellowy flame colour and she began to wear green eye shade. Her rather bizarre look could be seen coming yards away.

Steve was a popular manager and the Club named one of their public rooms The Steve Remenyi Room after he left. However although Steve's salary was better than it had previously been, it was actually not all that great and furthermore he had little by way of a pension fund. As mentioned the trips which they did overseas were always on a fly-now-pay-later basis.

The second son Brendan left home, if one could really regard the manager's flat in the St George's Club as ever having been a home, in about 1973. He first went to Durban where he studied accountancy at the insistence of Steve. Steve had strongly believed that the best thing a young man could do was to become an accountant and specifically a Chartered

Accountant. But Brendan had little or no aptitude for this and after four or five years and little success he eventually gave up accounting. Brendan went on successfully to study electronics in Johannesburg and eventually had his own computer business in Canada. There was an interesting incident regarding Brendan, Steve and Steve's acquaintances a few years after Brendan settled in Johannesburg. In the 1970s it was common for young people to share houses as a way of spreading the cost of rent. This Brendan did with a group of people his own age, in their twenties. They had a large house in a posh area in the suburbs of Johannesburg. As is the wont of such young people they had from time to time relatively large parties accompanied by loud music. One particular Saturday night the music was so loud that one of the neighbours came around to the party to ask for the volume of the music to be turned down. He was an elderly man in his dressing gown and it was 1 am. Whoever he spoke to was unsympathetic to his request and the man returned home. Some 30 minutes later four or five police wagons turned up at the house and every one who couldn't run away was placed in custody and taken to the local police station. As it happened Brendan and a friend were the last to be so arrested and were placed in a police wagon on their own. On the way to the police station the policeman received an urgent call on the radio to go immediately to another location where there was an emergency. While the police man was attending to the emergency, Brendan and his friend escaped from the vehicle by breaking a catch on the back door. They were now on the run from the police but it didn't take much effort to re-arrest them.

All the other party goers were cautioned at the police station and turned loose to walk the two miles back to the party house or just go home. However Brendan and his friend were charged with resisting arrest, escaping from police custody and criminal damage to police property. All of these matters were sufficiently serious that the accused had to appear before a magistrate and this meant Brendan sitting in police cells for the rest of the weekend. Of course, Brendan was given his phone call and he informed me and I called Steve to give him the 'good' news. Now it so happened that one of Steve's acquaintances was General Van Den Berg, a member of the St George's Club and one of the top cops in South Africa. Steve phoned General Van Den Berg and told him about Brendan's plight and asked if he could help his son. General Van Den Berg was good enough to phone the police station in Johannesburg and enquire about the incident. The result of the General's call was that Brendan was taken from the cell to see the duty sergeant who told him, "You are in enough trouble as it is. As a result of the bogus telephone call I have just received from someone pretending to be General Van Den Berg, do you realise that I can now charge you with conspiracy to impersonate a senior police officer?"

On the Monday morning Brendan was remanded for trial and bailed. The police wanted this matter to be taken seriously but the courts saw this for what it was – youthful exuberance. In the end Brendan was required to attend court several times during which the matter was deferred and re-deferred until eventually the court dismissed it. Steve's influential acquaintance only had the effect of potentially making matters worse.

After being in Port Elizabeth for a couple of years, Steve and Patsy made another trip to Ireland, Hungary and France. The Irish trip went off routinely as was expected and the Sheehan family, who except for Lily were all still alive and well at that time, welcomed them back for their holiday. Once again they also spent time with their old friends from Irish Shipping days.

The Hungarian trip was interesting. Steve reported on this trip without showing any emotion. He said that he could not find any living relatives. I am sure that he didn't try hard. He was on holiday after all. He did find some family friends and neighbours and he reported that they were living in abject poverty – he actually used the word penury[16]. The issues of poverty and property was much closer to Steve's heart than any other political consideration and thus seeing people he had known living on the bread line was what touched Steve and he commented strongly on this. He referred to a family doctor he had known as a child living in a hovel and not having enough money to feed himself properly. He said that Budapest was looking dowdy and still had many bullet and shell scars from the 1956 uprising. In Budapest Steve found it necessary to offer a policeman some packets of cigarettes in order not to receive what Steve regarded as an unfair parking fine. Steve felt that this was not unexpected and made the point that the Hungarians were not communists at heart and that they were past masters at making the most out of any situation in which they found themselves, even if this meant taking bribes.

However, in general he did not seem to be particularly elated or depressed by the trip to his original home country. It appeared that he was able to go back to Hungary and to be no more than just another tourist

---

[16] Steve mentioned that he had met a very old man who had been the village pharmacist. This had no meaning for me at the time. But now having read Máriska's story (see Chapter Nine) this man had to have been the friend of the Jews who smuggles parcels to them after they had been detained and before they were transported to Auschwitz.

there. Of course who knows how he actually felt about this experience. He was an expert in not showing any emotion. I expect that he had really gone there just to take Patsy to see Budapest in order to fulfil a promise he had made to her nearly 40 years before. But Patsy did not see Steve's family home on this trip. In fact she was never to have any real insight to how the Remenyi family lived in the 'old' country.

Their trip to France was more eventful. Steve and Patsy saw Armand who was well enough considering his advanced age. But while in France Steve and Patsy had a falling out with Armand's son Jacques. Steve had planned to meet Jacques in the South of France but after the row the plan was changed and Steve and Patsy toured Normandy instead. Hard as we tried, Steve could not be drawn on any of the detail about the row. He said that Patsy had precipitated an argument on the phone which, although believable at the time, I now regard to have been a smoke screen. The cause of the fight with Jacques I believe to have been far more profound and personal to Steve and I will return to this issue in a later chapter. In all they came home relatively pleased with this holiday trip.

Not long after this visit to Europe in 1975 Armand Kalmár died. By this time he was well into his 90s. Armand's lawyers got in touch with Steve and invited him to come over to Paris as he was mentioned in the old man's will. The lawyers also said that they had located Imre in New York and that he was mentioned in Armand's will too. Steve was truly surprised that Imre was still alive and that it had been possible to find him.

Patsy more than Steve, was excited by this turn of events. She expected Armand Kalmár's estate to be worth a material amount of money. Her thinking was that if he could have afforded the large apartment on the Quai d'Orsay then he must have had bags of money. She was also keen to meet Steve's brother. As mentioned above, Patsy had not much liked Magda and she thought that she might get on better with Imre. It is worth mentioning that Imre had changed his name. According to Steve, when one becomes an American citizen one is apparently asked the question, "By what name do you want to be known?" and Imre answered John Remy as he felt that Americans would not do justice to his original name but that they could grasp John and the relatively simple and abbreviated name of Remy. In fact this choice of name was quite indicative of Imre's state of mind in which he had lost any sense of what he was and where he had come from. At the time of Armand Kalmár's death, Imre had spent his life in the American merchant marine and was now in retirement in a modest home for seafarers in down town New York.

Imre, Steve and Patsy met up in Paris for a reunion. Although expectations were high the meeting turned out to be one of the biggest flops of their lives. First, Imre who was now about 75 years old was a loud, objectionable cranky old man. He was highly opinionated. He had some sort of persistent chronic illness which did much to make him ill tempered. He didn't like Patsy and she didn't like him – and they confided this in each other in a rather loud way. Imre apparently felt quite guilty about the fact that as a young man he had squandered so much of Ödön and Mariska's money. He believed that Steve had not had his fair share of the original Remenyi family wealth. Steve regarded all this as ancient history and wanted no part of Imre's guilt or the money Imre was trying to offer him in compensation. Patsy returned home saying that Imre was truly dreadful and Steve simply commented that the years had pushed them apart.

Secondly, as it turned out Armand Kalmár's estate was actually worth much less than any of them had thought. Both Steve and Patsy believed that Jacques may have had Armand give him whatever valuables he had in the last months or weeks of the old man's life. Also Steve recalled that Armand had placed certain investments in Germany and these could not be found by the Trustees of Armand's estate.

In the end Steve and Patsy got enough out of Armand's estate to pay all their expenses on the overseas trip. Steve who really did not expect anything from Armand's estate was not as disappointed as Patsy was. Patsy had always thought that somewhere in her life she would be made rich by someone else and never really came to terms with the fact that this wasn't going to happen until Steve died and she got his insurance money, but there wasn't all that much money involved with the insurance payouts either. But the trip to Paris gave Patsy something else to talk to her Port Elizabeth friends about in her now acquired pretentious manner.

Although Steve had really found his niche at the St George's Club in Port Elizabeth, his pension arrangements began to worry him. This was a time of great inflation in South Africa, as it was in many other countries, and his pension was not inflation proof. Steve had held extensive talks with the governing body in the Club but by and large they were not particularly sympathetic to his pension position. He had not been with the Club long enough. The governing body knew that Steve enjoyed his job and that at his stage in life it would be difficult for him to move. Anyway, to everyone's amazement in 1977, when he was 58 years old, Steve applied for and was appointed to a position as manager of a sports club in Westville, near Durban. On a month's notice he and Patsy packed up and moved off to Natal were we had spent those early years in South Africa.

This left everyone in the Club in a state of shock. It also came as a great surprise to the rest of the family.

Patsy was initially pleased to be moving back near Durban but it didn't take long for her to realise that her old friends of 12 years before were either no longer around or no longer interested in her. Steve didn't much like the sports club. The club was new, its facilities were not yet established and it had a rather small membership. So Steve and Patsy braced themselves to grin and bear it in Natal. However despite several attempts the St George's Club were unable to replace Steve. Furthermore they actually seemed to miss him as even in the few short years he had been there, he had become a real personality in the Club. The result of this was that they approached Steve to come back. Despite the fact that both he and Patsy really wanted to return, he didn't jump at the opportunity but took his time to be wooed by the Club. He also told the Club that they would have to convince Patsy that it would be in his best interests to come back. In the end he received both a substantial salary increase and a major capital contribution to his pension fund. This helped Steve feel that his work was really appreciated and it allowed him to retire comparatively early at 62.

So Steve and Patsy returned to live in Port Elizabeth.

About a year later the family met in Durban while Steve and Patsy were on a short break there. However just before I left to drive back to Johannesburg where I was then living Steve, while talking to me alone dropped his emotional portcullis for a few minutes and said how he wished the family had been able to live together more harmoniously. He started off by saying that as a young man he had faced enormous difficulties and that he was very fortunate to have been able to live with them and or to handle them. At that time I was not sure exactly what he was talking about and I did not feel that I should interrupt his outpourings. He said that he knew what the problems were. He knew that the family barely hung together. He knew how destructive Patsy really was. He said that he went to sea for 10 years and when he got back home the family had already been wrecked. He couldn't actually bring himself to say that this had been Patsy's handiwork but as the kids were 13, 10 and 4 when we moved to South Africa the damage to the family could hardly have been done by anyone else. He went on to say that he was sorry for the sexist thinking behind the fact that he did nothing to encourage Jean to get a university education. Jean had trained as a radiographer which she did not enjoy sufficiently to continue in that job but at the end of school this training got her away from home and gave her a qualification. He also said that his great enthusiasm for both his sons to become accountants was mis-placed. He realised that Brendan had spent four or five years of his life trying to get a qualification for which he was entirely unsuited. He real-ised that the short term settler mentality he had displayed on our arrival in Cape Town was misguided. But he also said that he had by and large achieved what he wanted to and that he had been able to give his family a reasonable standard of living and that they received a fair amount of schooling. This was the one and only time that Steve ever discussed these matters in such a personal way. Unfortunately all this was said in what was only for a few minutes outside a beach front hotel in Durban while I was standing by my motor car as I was about to drive away to Johannes-burg.. After that evening he never raised these matters again.

In 1976, Jean got married and after a year or so she moved overseas with her Rhodesian husband. Jean continued to look like a younger version of Patsy. On one occasion Jean told me that I could not distinguish her from her mother and although I did not agree with that at that time, I subse-quently began to understand that this remark was largely accurate.

I packed up my bags and moved to London in 1978. While on my way to settle in London I took a trip to New York. I wanted to meet Imre or John Remy as he now was. I found the seamen's home in Manhattan easily enough and the reception called John down to see me. The way the recep-tionist referred to John in a very slightly condescending way made me realise that he was tolerated rather than welcomed in this home for eld-erly seamen. He took me up to his room for a few minutes. It was a very basic room with few personal possessions. It was more like a monk's cell rather than an ex-seafarer's home. He then decided that we should go out to a local diner.

John wasn't as bad as Steve and Patsy had claimed. He was much worse. It was hard to describe how I felt after being with him for just a couple of hours. I was simply dazed by what this man was or had turned into. He had become an embittered old man who hated the blacks, the Jews, the Muslims, the Catholics and the Democrats to mention only a few, and of course above all else the Russians. He spoke in a heavy central European accent. We had the regular American breakfast. He covered his eggs, ba-con and hash brownies with tons of golden syrup as he emitted abuse about the city he lived in. He told me that his health was not good and because he had little money he had to use the public health system which was terrible. In fact nothing in America seemed to please him. As we were leaving the cashier in the restaurant asked Imre where he was from and he replied, "I'm a Russian. Can't you hear my accent? I'm a Russian". My surprise at this was considerable. When I asked him why he had said that he was a Russian he replied in a most derogatory tone that, "The bloody Americans are thick and ignorant and they wouldn't know what Hungary was never mind where it is". He went on. "But every American knows where Russia is. That's all they ever think about is how the Russians are trying to get them". I wasn't a stranger to Russophobia but I had never heard it expressed quite like this before. Furthermore although like Steve I am not a great fan of the USA but the intense dislike John was showing for the people of his adopted country was, as the Irish would say, gob smacking. I was glad that his name was no longer Remenyi. I was pleased that I was only able to spend a couple of hours with him and basically I felt that perhaps Steve had been right not to involve us in his original family. I left New York wondering what the rest of Steve's family used to be like. I hope that there was no one else like John in the family tree. But the thought didn't last long as my life was full with my move to London.

In 1980 while living in London I received a telephone call from New York. A Manhattan policeman wanted to know if I was Dan Remenyi and if I was related in John Remy. This was more than a little surprising. I replied hesitantly that I was. I could feel the policeman's relief over the 3000 mile telephone line. He told me that John Remy had committed suicide. He had jumped out of the window in his room in the seamen's home. It was on the sixth floor. I felt no sense of remorse as Imre had been one of the most awful bigots whom I had had the misfortune to meet.

The New York cop said that Imre could not be buried until he was identified by a member of the family. This seemed mighty strange to me as there must be many down and outs who die on the streets of New York every day of every year. Anyway I certainly wasn't going to identify him. So I called Steve.

That phone call resulted in Steve and Patsy visiting New York in order to comply with the New York cop's request to identify the body. Then Imre's remains could be cremated. The New York Police Department were extremely pleased to see Steve. He was welcomed into an office and given a cup of coffee. He was then taken to the morgue. He saw his dead brother and he then signed the necessary papers of identification. Having signed off as requested, Steve asked if they had any of Imre's belongings from the seaman's home. However having signed for the body, Steve was then amazed to be asked to prove that he and Imre were brothers in order to be able to obtain his few remaining, and virtually valueless possessions. In all, this trip to New York was a pretty awful experience for Steve and Patsy and I wonder why they bothered to go through all this trouble.

To add to this trauma, all his life Steve had believed that a suicide in the family was in some way a great slur. I am not actually sure what his logic for this was. But whenever he mentioned suicide he would always do so in a lowered voice as though he was saying that the person concerned was some sort of outcast, like a leper in olden times. Thus it was not easy for Steve to accept or admit that his own brother had done this dreadful thing. Steve claimed that Imre had fallen out of his window accidentally. Having seen Imre's window it was clear to me that Imre had to have jumped. Imre took his own life because he was old, he was lonely and his health was failing. He had little money left. This seemed to me to be a perfectly respectable and probably responsible choice for him to have made. I felt that Steve's judgement of Imre's exit from this life was basically unfair. But I felt that Steve's prejudice was hardly worth a second thought.

On their way back from New York Steve and Patsy spent a few days in London. This was no doubt a bad time for them. Seeing that her children had left home and knowing that they had little time for her, she became emotionally destructive. But by this stage Patsy's credibility was non existent and all she achieved was to further damage herself. Months later she tried to recover by writing long letters which pleaded that she had to be understood and forgiven for her conduct because she had been abused, i.e. beaten with a leather belt as a child by her father, Maurice. She recognised how much of a dismal failure as a mother she had been and that she desperately wanted to be forgiven. By now this was all twenty or more years too late. The incident in London was just another event in a life long bad relationship. There is no doubt that Patsy was a victim of a very unsatisfactory childhood and a very severe father but at the end of the day her life was her own responsibility and she had plenty of opportunities to put her house in order - and she didn't.

Steve and Patsy returned to Port Elizabeth and lived there without leaving South Africa again. Steve wanted to retire as early as possible. Eventually he was able to retire a few years ahead of what was customary in those days.

In 1981 when he was 62 Steve retired. He had been a popular Secretary of the Club and was regarded by the club members as a fellow member rather than as a club employee. When he left there was a collection among the members to buy him a retirement present. I do not recall the amount collected but it was much larger than anybody expected and caused some resentment among a few members who had never seen such a large amount of money collected for anyone before. However that resentment was short lived.

Although now retired Steve was a reasonably healthy and fairly energetic 62 year old. Even at this age Steve still walked, with a limp, as fast as many people ran. So Steve and Patsy bought a small holding or little farm some distance away in an attractive mountainous area known as the Hog's Back. It was a beautiful place located in a special part of the country at an altitude of some thousands of feet. The area is surrounded with indigenous forests and is known for its bird life and for its flora. They intended to convert the house and adjacent cottages into guestrooms and to operate a small country retreat or resort. For a short time this appeared to be going well. They restored some of the farmhouse and the cottages.

However within a few months of moving to the country Steve was diagnosed as having cancer. It was cancer of the oesophagus. Clearly this was devastating to the whole family. He had trouble swallowing and in the next few months he lost a lot of weight. When I saw him he had been reduced to something like half his original weight before he got ill. I would hardly have recognised him had I passed him in the street. He looked so tiny. I was amazed at how I hardly recognised him.

He needed an entirely new wardrobe of clothes.

But I was also taken back at how energetic he still was and how he appeared to believe that the cancer was beatable. By this he made his condition bearable for himself and the others around him. In fact his attitude to his illness was simply exemplary. Steve had various forms of treatment over a 15 month period including surgery. They acquired a small flat in Port Elizabeth and they shared their time between the farm in the country and living in the flat while Steve had cancer treatment. There is no doubt that some of this treatment was helpful. He and Patsy kept up the illusion that he would be cured right up to the last time he was admitted to the hospital about a week before he died.

Steve had always been a stoical person. He lived with bad back pain most of his life and he took the same attitude towards his death. Whatever he felt inside he kept a brave face right up to the every end. Steve told me that he didn't want his family sitting around his death bed and that he would prefer it if I didn't come down from London to Port Elizabeth.

I telephoned him virtually every day for the last few weeks of his life. He didn't lose interest in his environment. The day before he died, although he was very ill indeed, we were still discussing what I was doing in London as well as life in general. Steve's last words to me were a request to try to be nice to Patsy. I replied that I would try but in fact I found that to be just too difficult and I had nothing to do with her, which I felt was a better alternative to fighting with her.

I don't know whether Jean didn't get the message that Steve did not want to be crowded in by his family at his death bed but she went down to spend a few weeks with him as he was dying. Jean was not able to leave his side as it was so clear he was dying. But Steve just wouldn't die with Jean at his bed side and eventually she had to give up and go home to her husband in London. Steve died a couple of days later. I have no proof whatsoever but I have always suspected that in those last hours he talked the doctors into giving him a large shot of morphine. Of course, Steve's not wanting his children at his death bed was just another symptom of his inability to allow his family to be really close to him.

This was 1984 and Steve had just, a few months before, celebrated his 65th birthday. Steve Remenyi's death certificate had shown him to be a citizen of the Republic of Ireland and a Roman Catholic. He received the last rites of the Catholic Church.

As mentioned before during his Irish Shipping days Steve regularly brought home with him American comics. They were normally Superman type comics. However on one occasion the bundle of comics included one which was a ghost story. One of the illustrations in this comic showed a head stone in a grave yard with the letters RIP on it. I had been reading this with the help of my grandfather Maurice Sheehan and I asked him. "What does RIP mean?" He immediately replied, "Rise If Possible". When I mentioned that I knew what RIP meant to my grandmother, Lily she was really annoyed with Maurice and said, "Don't be putting ridiculous ideas into the boy's head". Well the RIP on Steve's memorial stone could well have meant Rise If Possible as the real story of Steve, which I can only assume he intended to go to the grave with him, was to reach out and to touch the lives of all his children years later. It is not even clear today if his memory has rested in peace. What happened next none of us were prepared for. The three siblings were completely oblivious to what was in Steve's pre-Ireland background. What was to come made a different impact on each of us. What is certain is that Steve reached out from beyond the grave and changed our lives.

When is the end not the end?

Steve's funeral was held in the little Catholic Church near the St George's Club. It was attended by more than two hundred people, many of whom were associated directly or indirectly with the St George's Club. Patsy was gratified by the turnout which she saw as an important tribute to Steve and in a sense it was. He was cremated and his ashes were scattered out at sea. With his ashes there must have been a small ball-bearing which had replaced the disc in his spine for all those years ago and I always wondered if that got thrown out to sea as well. It is not clear if Steve wanted this form of being put to rest and certainly none of the other members of the family were consulted. Patsy's justification for the cremation and the scattering of the ashes at sea was that he had come from the sea in 1941 so he should go back to the sea in 1984. None of his children attended his funeral but Brendan went out to South Africa shortly thereafter to spend some time with Patsy as she settled into widowhood. Our primary thoughts about Steve now were may he rest in peace.

As far as the three children were concerned Steve was a good enough father who was now dead and although we knew not much about his early life, there probably wasn't that much to know anyway. We had our own lives to get on with. Steve's life in Hungary was and, as far as we were concerned at that time, would always be, a closed book. He had always played down any enquiry we had made about pre-war Hungary and, at this stage of our lives, none of us had that much interest in his past.

However, events were afoot which would change all that and these happenings had a rather strange origin and worked themselves out in a peculiar way.

Over the years whenever Steve was asked where he had been born he had always replied by stating Budapest. This was the capital city of Hungary and no one ever questioned that statement or asked for a qualification such as "What part of Budapest did you live in?" However, when Brendan was applying for Canadian immigration in the early 1980s, the official form which he was required to complete asked the question "where was your father born". Instead of just writing down Budapest, as I would have done without giving it a second thought, Brendan actually went to the trouble of asking Steve this question. On this occasion Steve did not reply Budapest but rather he told Brendan that he had been born in Rácalmás which is a village some 60 kilometres south west of Budapest on the banks of the Danube. Brendan wrote the name of this village into his immigration form and never thought any more of it. However before submitting this form to the Canadian authorities Brendan copied the form and filed his copy away.

In due course Brendan obtained landed immigrant status into Canada and moved to Montreal. He initially worked with large computer vendors but after a few years he set up in business on his own. During his 15 years as an entrepreneur he had a couple of different business partners one of which was a Hungarian born man called Geza.

By 1986 Brendan, with his business partner at the time Geza had set up their own business dealing in computers and offering a bureau service for garment design to the clothing industry. Geza was a few years older than Brendan and, like many Hungarians his age, had fled Budapest as a refugee during the 1956 uprising against their Soviet over lords. After crossing the Adriatic in a rubber raft Geza ended up in Montreal via an internment camp in Italy. In the early 90s things were changing rapidly in Eastern Europe. Hungary in particular was opening up to the West and so Geza and Brendan (with the financial backing of another Hungarian expatriate) decided to open a personal computer wholesale & retail business in Budapest. Brendan had a bit of spare cash at the time and thought that it might be fun to have a business interest in the land of his forefathers. He thus agreed to invest in Hungary and shortly thereafter Geza moved to Budapest and opened up an office. This business did not turn out to be great but it was good enough to survive for a few years.

After about a year of being involved in this business venture in Hungary, Brendan decided that he should visit the office in Budapest in which he was a partner and he and his wife Camille set out for a trip to central Europe. Before leaving Brendan having remembered that he had the name of his father's birth town in his immigration file, dug out the papers and wrote down the word Rácalmás. I had been to Budapest before but I had not been aware of the name Rácalmás nor of Steve's association with it. I had enjoyed Budapest as a tourist, as it is a remarkably beautiful city. After a few days in Budapest, when Brendan's business affairs were finished, Brendan asked Geza to take him to Rácalmás and they set out on the journey one afternoon.

The road to Rácalmás is not a great one as it is both narrow and windy and has too much traffic on it; it can take a good hour or more to drive the 60 kilometres there, even if you know the way. Rácalmás is a tiny, dusty village of maybe a 100 homes or less. It is close to the Danube in a fertile part of the country. On arrival Brendan was surprised that they were easily able to find the Remenyi family house. It appears that the Remenyi family was well known in Rácalmás as they owned and operated a general merchandise shop. This shop was regarded as the best shop in the village and for quite a long distance around.

Geza found several people in Rácalmás who remembered the Remenyis quite well and who spoke highly of them. That was a bit strange, as Mariska had already been dead more than 40 years at that time. Brendan was shown the shop and the Remenyi family house. It is a sizable house which is today rather run down. However Brendan was unable to find where the wine and the charcoal were made. After spending an hour or so in this village they prepared to leave. It then occurred to Brendan that it would be useful to try to find the Remenyi tomb stone in the Rácalmás grave yard. Rácalmás has a large church and a considerable grave yard so Brendan and his wife Camille and Geza proceeded to scour the grave yard for a tomb stone with the name Remenyi on it.

After about an hour the three investigators had found nothing and, as it was now beginning to get dark, they wanted to get back to Budapest. They started to leave the grave yard. At the gate they met a little old man who had been riding past on his bike and who had seen them searching the grave yard and had decided to stop to see if he could help. Geza asked him if he knew the Remenyi family. He replied that everyone knew the Remenyis if they were old enough and even many of the young had heard of them. Geza then said they were looking for the Remenyi tomb stone and did he know where it was. Again the little old man said yes. He knew where the Remenyi tomb stones were but that they would not find them in that grave yard. The little old man said "only Christians are buried in this graveyard". I guess Geza was taken aback as it took a while for him to translate this to Brendan. It was said in such a round-about way. Fifty years later this old man was still sensitive to the treatment meted out by the villagers to the Jews during the war. The message was that the Remenyis weren't Christians. They were Jews and Christians and Jews don't get buried in the same graveyard in Hungary. It was getting dark and although a brief search was conducted for the Jewish cemetery it could not be found. On a subsequent visit to Rácalmás the grave stones were found in the Jewish graveyard which was badly desecrated and Ödön's and Joseph's head stones had been over turned.

We had no inkling of Steve's Jewish background and it certainly came as a complete surprise. In fact when Brendan first told me this story I thought that he was pulling my leg with a tall story to see how gullible I was. But he was able to show me a photograph of a tombstone with the name Reményi and with half the words in Hebrew. That was enough evidence to stop me in my tracks.

Before telling me about this discovery Brendan had earlier informed Jean and she began an investigation which eventually lead to her finding a first cousin of Steve who was still living in Budapest. Her maiden name had been Ibi Reményi and she was the daughter of Ödön's older brother Lajos.

I decided that I would like to talk to Magda in Sydney who I had met before and with whom I had got on rather well. I didn't think that this issue justified my hopping on the first plane to Australia. But I had business reasons for going to Australia and within a few months I was able to obtain a lot more information from a source close to the Remenyi family, Imre's second wife.

Basically Magda confirmed that the Remenyis were Jewish, as she was. They were not especially religious but they did keep some of the Jewish festivals. Mariska had seen the war coming and knew that Hungary was pro-Germany and would get drawn into the war. Furthermore Magda told me that there had always been a strong anti-Semitic feeling among certain Hungarians dating back hundreds of years. So Mariska, already with Imre living abroad, sent her other son Steve away to avoid the forthcoming conflagration. Mariska had no idea of how serious the war was going to be, especially for Jews. Something like 80% of Hungarian Jews were in the end murdered by Hungarian or German Nazis.

Magda knew that Mariska had died in Auschwitz. When I asked what evidence she had of that she said everyone knew that for the fact it was. Magda knew that all the other Remenyis and the Kalmárs who had been alive at the time of the war had ended up being victims of Auschwitz except for Ibi who, although she had been initially taken there, had subsequently been moved by the Nazis to another camp at Allendorf where she was used as slave labour in the making of armaments. Ibi got out of Auschwitz because she was young enough and strong enough to make guns for the Nazi war machine. She was fortunate enough to have survived that experience as she was liberated by the Americans shortly after she arrived at Allendorf. But neither Ibi's father Lajos nor her husband Ladislas survived Auschwitz. On being liberated from the Allendorf camp, Ibi had been asked where she wanted to go. She could have chosen anywhere in the world but she went home to try to find her father and her husband who were in fact both dead. Going back to Hungary meant that she fell into the hands of the communist regime which did not treat her particularly well either.

The little village of Rácalmás has published a small book of its recent history in which there is a list of the Jews who were taken away to the concentration camps and Mariska is listed in that book. Against her name is the word 'burnt'. That is how the citizens of Rácalmás know what happened to the Remenyis and that is why they are still remembered there today.

Magda put me in touch with the Szende family. Klára Szende and Magda were cousins whose maiden names were Fitz and the Fitzs were the next door neighbours of the Remenyis and they were also Jewish. Klára was the same age as Steve and these two children had spent their childhood together. In fact as little kids Steve and Klára were virtually inseparable. Klára Fitz married Michael Szende and they moved into the Jewish ghetto in Budapest and were therefore not rounded up by the Nazis and taken away to the concentration camp like Mariska. Klára told me about a book written by a woman who had lived with Mariska during the war. It appears that Mariska had taken in a lodger and this lady had written a book after the war in which she describes Rácalmás in the final months of the war and also how the Nazis took Mariska away to the concentration camp.

I went to Rácalmás twice; the first time with Ibi. That was a bad mistake. Ibi who was well into her 80s couldn't find the way out of Budapest and we struggled for quite a while with that. We drove around in circles in the suburbs of the city for about a half hour before I could find the right road. Ibi had not been out of town for years and although she was brave enough to say she would come with me she was not comfortable. When we got to Rácalmás she wouldn't get out of the car, not so much due to her age but rather due to her emotional state. She couldn't remember where the Remenyi house was. However, we did find people who showed us the way to the Remenyi family home. It had not been well looked after and had a distinct feel of being run down.

The shop which is attached to the end of the house is still there and operates to this day, but was closed that spring morning. No one knew why it was closed but we were told that the owner lived in Budapest.

We tried to find the Jewish cemetery but no one would show us the way. It was not the thing to do in Rácalmás to ask about Jews. Various people told Ibi that the cemetery had been moved away or that it had been turned into a sewage or waste dump or something. As it transpired, these were lies but we were not going to find the Jewish graveyard that day. Ibi was showing a lot of distress by this stage and I realised that the trip to this desolate little village was not a good thing for her as it brought back the wrong set of memories. I recall feeling silly and rather insensitive to her emotional state. This was compounded by her lack of English and my lack of Hungarian. But of course, she had offered to accompany me to Rácalmás although it was really a disastrous trip. We spent only 25 or 30 minutes in Rácalmás and then I went back to Budapest.

The second trip to Rácalmás was a bit better. This time I went with Klára Szende and her son Andrew. The Remenyi family shop was open and I bought a few bits and pieces there, including a locally made tea towel and a jar of honey. The Szendes told the people in the shop that I was Mariska's grandson and they asked her if I had come to take the shop and the house back. The descendants of the Hungarian Jews murdered in the holocaust are now able to reclaim their family property. In fact they do not necessarily get their actual property back but maybe paid money in compensation for their loss. On a previous trip made by Klára to Rácalmás, she had been approached by people in the street who had come up to her and said that the holocaust was not their fault and that they had not killed any Jews. No doubt guilt still runs high in this little village.

The Remenyi house was locked up on that day. It was obvious that it had been empty for a while. Its current owner had moved to Budapest and the house was now for sale. Walking around the house it was easy to see that it was quite substantial and was probably an important house in the village in its day. The Szendes managed to get into their old house which was across the street from the Remenyi house. The current owner had no problem in letting them in and showing them around. It was the first time that Klára had been in her original family home for more than 50 years. Klára's parents had also been rounded up for transportation to Auschwitz and had been murdered there along with Mariska. The old house was now really run down. This was clearly an emotional experience for her. Later Klára said that it was a mistake to have gone into that house again. I was glad that Klára and Andrew had taken me to Rácalmás but I could see how it would be a painful experience for Klára.

We went to Rácalmás' village office. It is too modest to be called a town hall. There we got a copy of the village's history book, in Hungarian of course. As mentioned before, Mariska Reményi's name is listed in the village's history book and perhaps this is one of the reasons why she is remembered as one of the villagers who was deported and murdered in

Auschwitz. Against Mariska's name in the village's history book is the Hungarian word for burnt.

Then there was our hunt for the Jewish graveyard. We had nothing to work with other than Klára's memory. After a lot of difficulty we eventually found it. Clearly it had not actually been destroyed or moved. It was basically hidden behind a big overgrown hedge. Although it had not been attended to for years it was only partially overgrown and many of the tombstones were still visible. But it was actually in a poor state of repair. I saw that Ödön Reményi's tombstone had been over turned and Joseph's tombstone was lying on its side. But there they were at least hard evidence of their existence.

The tombstones looked much like they had been pushed over and partially up rooted perhaps by vandals. These were big and heavy marble tombstones engraved in Hungarian and in Hebrew. The Jewish graveyard was old and quite substantial with many tombstones in Hebrew only. In 1939, there had been more than 20 Jewish families living in this tiny village of Rácalmás. In 1998 however there was only one family who had returned to the village after the war. In all, we spent about an hour and a half in Rácalmás before we drove rather sombrely back to Budapest. It is not a place that I would ever feel the need to return to.

But why had Steve been so enthusiastic about forgetting his family background? According to Magda and Klára it is not that unusual for refugees to want to completely wipe out their past and live their lives completely anew. Clearly this is what Steve wanted and in fact managed to achieve. What is not clear is whether Steve wanted to do this because of a fear of anti-Semitism in Ireland and South Africa or whether he actually wanted, in a positive way, to leave behind his roots.

As a result of discussions with Magda, Ibi and Klára it is now possible to put together a glimpse of the Remenyi family and of Steve's childhood in Hungary. Ödön had one brother, Lajos and one sister Ilona. Ödön's father had not actually been born a Remenyi but had changed his family name. Originally the family name had been Hoffer but in the middle of the nineteenth century they had changed the name to Remenyi. In Hungarian the word Remenyi means something like the word "hope" does in English. About the same time Mariska's family had also changed their name to Kalmár. Originally her family name had been Cohen. There seems to have been an offer by the Austrian-Hungarian administration at that time that if Jews changed their names to Hungarian ones they would in some way be less discriminated against.

When Lajos finished school he decided that he wanted to be a teacher so his father sent him to university and he obtained the necessary qualifications. However by the time Ödön finished school just a few years later new anti-Semitic laws had been enacted which prevented Jews from attending university in Hungary. At that time old man Remenyi, né Hoffer, did not have the resources to send Ödön to Italy, which was where the more wealthy Hungarian Jews went for higher education after they were barred from Hungarian 'Universities'. So there was no question of further studies for Ödön. However his father did have enough money to set Ödön up in business with a shop. Rácalmás was the location chosen for this and Ödön turned out to be a good shop keeper and so was his wife Mariska. Their shop was regarded as having the best range of merchandise for many kilometres. On the side they had a small holding in which, like many others who lived in that area, they grew grapes from which they made their own wine. They also made charcoal. Together they built a prosperous life for themselves in Rácalmás.

On the other hand Lajos became a teacher and lived on the humble salary which was paid to his profession. Lajos obtained a post in a school in Tapolca which is a medium sized town a few hundred kilometres from Budapest. Ibi, his only child told me that it was a great treat for her to visit her rich relations in Rácalmás which she did from time to time.

Ödön and Mariska were happy enough in Rácalmás and the village was indeed quite good to them. However it did have the draw back which all tiny villages have and that was that it had limited educational opportunities in that it only had an elementary school. So when Steve reached the age of about eleven he had to go to live with Lajos in Tapolca to attend middle school. Ibi really enjoyed having Steve live with them. She felt that she had a special relationship with her cousin. It is not clear that Steve enjoyed the friendship of Ibi. It seems that she was rather possessive of him and that he did not enjoy that relationship. However Ibi spoke highly of Steve. On the other hand Ibi did not appear to have much time for either Imre or Magda. When I met Ibi in 1997 it was clear that she had been hurt by the fact that Steve had never contacted her after the war.

Steve did not spend all that long living with Lajos as the school in which he had taught did not cater for older children. Thus in due course when Steve was ready for high school he was sent to Budapest where he attended the school which allowed him to specialise in business or commercial subjects before he was sent off to be a radio operator.

Whereas Steve was attached to his mother and father, Imre seems to have been very much the opposite. When he finished his schooling Ödön set him up in business with a shop of his own. It didn't last long as he was neither interested in having a shop or in living in Rácalmás. Ibi described Imre's early life as being one long series of wine, women, song and gambling. In the end, Imre left his wife and went to sea to get far away from his family and his life in Hungary.

Mariska knew just how anti-Semitic Hungarian society was and it wasn't hard for her to see the war coming. She knew that this was going to be very bad indeed for her sons. Of course, like so many other European Jews she did not anticipate Hitler's final solution. If she had then maybe she would have left Hungary too, although it is not clear how easy that was to do, even if she had been able to sell the house and liquidate the business. So she decided to hang on to the house and the business in the hope that the war would blow over. In the event, when the Germans finally "invaded" Hungary the treatment of the Jews, by the Hungarian Nazis, was certainly the most brutal outside of Germany itself.

We do not know much about Mariska's final years in Rácalmás. A letter from her to Magda shows that even towards the end of the war, she was still hoping that Steve and Imre might return home again. This is also confirmed by an amazing document which came to light. Magda or her cousin Klára Szende found a book written in Hungarian which includes a chapter which describes Mariska's last days in her home before she was taken away by the Nazis. Andrew Szende, Klára's son, has translated this chapter and it has been reproduced here in the next chapter. I believe that we have been extraordinarily fortunate that we have been able to get a glimpse of and hear the voice of Mariska and have a record of how she bravely faced her last days before she was taken away by the Nazis.

But perhaps more important than being aware of the characters and the events of the family history, knowing a bit about Steve's family background helps explain some of his behaviour and much of his attitude to life.

For example, Steve's view of Irish Catholicism and how he compared it to Hungarian Catholicism was probably based on the fact that he didn't know that much about Hungarian Catholicism. What he appeared to know about Catholicism must have largely been from books or from people whom he knew.

It is probably the case that Steve would not emigrate to Australia or Canada because Magda was in Australia and Klára was in Canada and he knew that his Jewish background would leak out if his family were living near by his friends from the old country.

Knowing that Steve was Jewish helps at least partly to explain how he had managed to live with Patsy for so many years. Patsy was the classical strong, in fact dominant wife/mother and he was the passive husband/father which seems to be quite a common pattern or model among Jews.

Maybe Steve's apolitical stance in Southern Africa is more understandable when you know that his mother was murdered in a gas chamber. On the other hand maybe it's not. Steve must have known just how unstable the political system in South Africa was likely to be in the long term and that sooner or later his children would feel it necessary to have to leave that country. As he had done that sort of thing himself he must have known how disruptive this type of experience actually is. Steve must have thought that the Remenyi family sojourn in South Africa was only going to be a few years.

But perhaps the most important aspect of Steve's story is that being a Jew in Hungary meant that you didn't trust too many people and that you kept things to yourself and Steve certainly became a past master at that.

But at the end of the day what the discoveries in Rácalmás did for us more than anything was to bring home the fact that we did not really know Steve at all. Of course I kind of knew that all along but finding out about Rácalmás really put what had only been a suspicion right up in our faces as an indisputable fact. And it is indeed quite sad that Steve did not want his family to know anything about his past and to some extent about him at all. It would be somewhat of an understatement to say that Steve was a private man.

Mariska's Story

After discovering Rácalmás we were left with a feeling of a gaping hole in our knowledge of Steve's family. It's true that Magda, Ibi and Klára told us facts about the Remenyi family's life and how it came to an end. But it is very insightful if you ask someone to describe another person. It isn't easy and Magda, Ibi and Klára are of advanced age and it was hard to press them for details.

But I did have a little luck when Klára pointed me to a chapter in a book written about Rácalmás and Mariska. As will be seen later I also found something written about Steve by a seafaring friend.

The following chapter was written after the war by a Hungarian woman, Margit Izsáky, and published in Budapest in a Hungarian book the name of which when translated into English is *A Country on the Cross*. As can be seen Margit lived with Mariska during her last months in Rácalmás. I have not been able to find Margit Izsáky but at this stage if she were alive she would be well into her 90s. I am grateful to her for providing this insight into the life of my grandmother. Margit called this chapter in her book *A Simple Tale* and indeed it is.

The translation was made by Andrew Szende and I have made no attempt to edit it in any way.

It is just past Easter. The radio is always turned on in the apartment; British bombers have made their first appearance over Hungary.

Rácalmás is an angelic little village on the shores of the Danube, with blooming lilac trees, crooked hillside-hugging houses, buzzing bogs, a lot of puddles and frogs. In the evening, on the goose grazing fields, there's an entire army of frogs holding field exercises and the fishermen catch the fattest fish at night, at the island's nose. Because Rácalmás has its own island, too. It is surrounded by two channels of the Danube; one is good for swimming and fishing; in the other, the boats float. The island is the village's fruit orchard; it produces the reddest apples in the region.

My younger sister, her little baby and I are living with Aunt Reményi, who has had a general store in the village for the past forty years.

Aunt Reményi is a tiny, shrivelled old woman. She is as speedy as a squirrel. She works from morning to night. She's no longer in the store, since they closed the only general store, as a Jewish store, a few days ago. Aunt Reményi now is taking inventory, from morning to night: shoelaces, whips, wicks, stockings, hazelnuts, "klöpli" lace, steam iron, there is everything here.

She checks each item two or three times, to make sure nothing is left out. She scurries down to the cellar, up to the attic, she revises her list, then into the kitchen to prepare dinner. Her older sister is tired and suffering from heart disease, so after the inventory is done, Aunt Reményi washes the floor.

She is not allowed to employ a maid. Her former washer woman secretly comes by and takes the laundry home to wash.

In vain both my younger sister and I plead with her to let us help her, since we would not be paid for it, we would be permitted to do so. Her answer is always the same. "How could you think that, my sweet soul? It could lead to trouble. For you and for us."

The two little children spend the whole day hanging onto grandma Reményi's skirt. No matter where she goes, they follow her. Grandma. They stretch their little arms and tug at her apron.

They are used to an older person with white hair, who will take them in her lap, play with them, spank the floor on their behalf, if the floor hurt them, put tasty food in their always hungry beaks, read stories to them. And it is so nice to fall asleep in her lap ¬that's grandma. Of course, grandma. Grandma Reményi. Sometimes a gendarme appears.

"Good evening, madam," he says politely.
"Good evening, my son. Have a seat. Well, what would you like?"
"Well, I just came over to see if you have a bicycle, binoculars, or camera?"
"You borrowed the bicycle a month ago. You are still using it now. You will find an old broken down pair of opera glasses in the drawer under the wardrobe with the mirror. But my son took the camera with him."
"Mr. Steve?"
"Yes, Steve."
"Have you heard any news about him recently?"

They sit on the porch. The gendarme is eating a piece of cheese strudel. Then he lights up a cigar. He clicks his heels, politely says good-bye, takes his bicycle - Aunt Reményi's bicycle - and rides away.

Of Aunt Reményi's three bedroom home, now only one bedroom belongs to the family. "It's smarter, dear, if you live in two of them," she told me. "This way perhaps they will leave us one. I just hope we can stay in our home!"

What can one say?

The papers say: The ghetto is ready in Kolozsvár and Vásárhely. Endre Laszlo expressed his appreciation for the humanitarian treatment.

Many people gather at Aunt Reményi's. Here is Farkas, the former chief clerk, whose father was also chief clerk in Rácalmás. Mrs. Weisz, the doctor's young wife and daughter, the other Weisz, who had always been farmers, and the Frankels. They discuss things. "It's important to obey the regulations," they say.

But slowly, our acquaintances stop coming. The district doctor and the pharmacist still sneak over to us at dusk, but other acquaintances will walk us only to the gate and then turn back.

"Please excuse me, my dear," says the widow of the chief clerk, "we cannot come in. We can return the visit later. You know, you live with Jews and we don't want anyone to say that we are taking away Jewish property. We don't want even a single nail!"

An evil genie could have shown me in a magical mirror that four weeks later I would be picking up a broken doll from the dust in front of Dr. Weisz' house. In the yard there was a heap of children's toys. The little girl's doll was thrown out through the window by the wife of the chief clerk, who didn't even want a single nail from a Jewish house. Just the whole house, as it was.

And rumours fly: the village is full of spies, the director's family, the supervisor's family, such and such is designated to watch who is friendly with the Jews, who is taking something from them, who visits them...And then will come the gendarmes, they'll be interviewed, any friends of the Jews will be deported and their fate will be worse than that of the Jews.

Don't trust anyone, because the person who is the nicest to you will be the one to betray you - so whispers the voice of the village.

And women who for decades used to call each other my sweet, my dear, my angel, with whom they used to exchange their baking recipes, with whom they used to share their secret recipes for making preserves and liqueurs, turn their heads, so they don't have to greet someone, or perhaps to stop to talk under the watchful eyes of a window.

Because the windows are watching. Behind the geranium pots, the corner of the curtain carefully rises, women in kerchiefs with the eyesight of a pointer, are guarding the street.

Now the local intelligentsia is being tested. It is failing the test. None dares to stop in front of the windows.

In church they exchange one or two hurried sentences - since to the Farkas family, the Fränkel family have been Catholics from way back - they reassure them about their solidarity, and how painful and unfair these things are; how sorry we are for you my dears; they sigh as they raise their eyes to the sky; but when they step out of the church, they say good-bye and they scurry along with hurried steps.

Because church is one thing, life another. The wife of the district doctor fears for her husband. There is need for the whole extended family apparatus to air brush certain birth defects in the doctor; God will punish us for tolerating what is being done to these people, he says, but then he thinks of his children and what will happen if his children are also...

So he speaks, sometimes carefully, other times less carefully, bitterly...

But to do something? A revolutionary movement in a small Hungarian village? Everyone fears for the pension, the job, the children's education, the good winter coat. They didn't raise us to be martyrs.

In the evening after dinner, we are having a conversation with Aunt Reményi at the table.

"Where were you, Aunt Reményi? Because you weren't at home."

"We were in Adony to turn in our jewellery. We didn't have much: a gold necklace, a brooch, all family pieces. Some were worn by my dear mother. The bank manager asked me, why would I bother with these, at best, their value is that of gold by weight. I was sorry only about my husband's watch. But I couldn't keep it in any case. I know it well. It's a fat old clunker. It has no brand name, but I believe it can ring. It has a thick golden lid, with initials. It is kept in a leather case.

"What do you think? Will we get them back? We got a receipt for them. We have it all in writing."
"If they get here soon..."

Our eyes meet. The perpetual refrain. But it all looks so hopeless. The German army is already in the village. Aunt Reményi is pensive. In her soft voice, she says:
"I am always thinking about what will my son say, if he comes home and doesn't find me here? I would at least like to know that he will receive what I leave here for him.

Aunt Reményi's two sons are sailors. One is a radio-operator, the other a steersman. They served on an ocean-going Hungarian commercial ship, which developed some problem. The mother usually corresponds with them through Sweden. They exchange a few indifferent lines: we are well, we are alive.

"I don't even know where they are. Perhaps in Sweden...or perhaps they have been interned in another country. I wonder what their life may be like in such a camp?
"But dear auntie...your two sons are just about prisoners of war. One could interpret it that way. Couldn't an exception be made for you? The mother of two Hungarian sailors, whose sons were taken prisoner while serving the Hungarian state? Couldn't this be done with a little good will?"
"But there is no good will. 'An old Jewish woman should die.' That's what they told me in one place. 'And you are lucky that your two sons are not at home, or else we would take care of them, too'."

One evening, someone secretly whispers to us:
"Tomorrow morning, at 10 am, they are going to take Aunt Reményi and all the Jews. The order is that they must not know in advance; they will be told an hour ahead of time."
"Jesus. Poor dears."
"And you will be better off to take care of yourselves. There will be a big search at your house.

They will look at every pillow case to see whether it belongs to you or the Reményis."

In other words, if there is something, we should hide it, right? Thanks for alerting us."

"Oh no. That's not what I meant. But they're going to look at your clothes, too, to see if they're really yours. And do you have a piece of paper to prove that your typewriter is yours. And I know that your younger sister has a camera, well it would be a good idea to...

"Well, just leave me in peace!"

The lady with the pointed nose hurries along. Her feelings are hurt. Perhaps she is right; she wanted to help. Or so we say. My smallest worry is bigger than that.

My God, what will happen to Aunt Reményi?

Their washer woman is waiting for us at the door of the veranda. She is sitting on the steps and crying. The house is a mess, crates, suitcases, clothes tied in bundles, demijohns, clothes baskets filled with jars.

They know already.

The tiny old woman stands straight and defiant in the kitchen door. There is not a single tear in her eyes.

Dear son, we have to leave. We are allowed to take two hundred kilos of groceries, two hundred kilos of clothes and bedding, and other things. We are allowed to load everything on a wagon, furniture for one room and dishes. Help us pack.

The old closet doors open. My God, what order! Embroidered decorative shelf cloths, the underwear carefully ironed and piled high...yellow damask table cloths.

They were hardly ever used. "I was saving them for my daughter-in-law," says Aunt Reményi. Then she takes out six men's shirts and begins to cry. "If my sons come home...they won't even have a shirt. I had these made for them. And shoes and socks and two blue silk night¬gowns. They are also "for my daughter-in-law."

"And I would like to ask you for another thing, my dear. In this small green crate, there are a few things from my deceased son. He died in Davos. I couldn't be there. We responded to the telegram and that's when they gave us these things...the warm, knitted stockings, the vest, the little duvet, in which he was always wrapped up and in which he used to lie, outside on the balcony. Here is his comb, his notebook, in which he used to draw, a few of his favourite toys. I have been guarding these for years. Try to rescue them."

I am looking through all the stuff, surely no one will take these from me. As I rummage around among the pencil stubs and pieces of paper, I find a lapel pin of the Hungarian tricolour. I can see in my mind's eye the terrace of a sanitarium in Davos, a little 10-year-old boy, who pins that Hungarian tricolour on his coat lapel on March 15, the Hungarian national holiday.

In the evening, no one eats even a morsel. The children are finding it hard to go to bed; they can't get used to the fact that Grandma Reményi is not with them.

Grandma Reményi is packing. The fine-scented, clean home is turned upside down, as the contents of all the closets are emptied on the floor. How difficult it is to pick out the few pieces that are the most valued among all the things she collected over a lifetime.

She stuck a piece of paper on top of one of the crates: "This box contains the clothes of my sailor sons. Please, if possible, do not disturb them."

The late night light is still on when the dawn breaks and Aunt Reményi lies down for a minute. She lies fully clothed on one of the beds. It's the one in which her husband died, the one which stood beside her own bed for forty years, and the one she will never see again. Because she is taking just one couch into the ghetto.

How hard it is to leave everything here. And Aunt Reményi gets up again, and is sorting again: it may be possible to take this, this could be useful, one must not leave this behind. either.

And at 6 a.m., the gendarme appears in front of the house: no one may go outside, you must hurry up and pack, because at 10 o'clock the wagon will be here.

The two old women struggle desperately with the heavy crates. Several wailing peasant women stand in front of the house. The gendarme does not let anyone enter.

Finally, the assistant village clerk arrives, all fancied up, to check that everything is going well.

"But look here, please," I turn to him, "Aunt Reményi and her sister cannot carry these crates. They won't be ready on time. We are helping, but we are also weak."

"I wouldn't recommend that you help them, madam! Only the official authorities may be in contact with the Jews."
"In that case, you should help them. After all, you have bragged enough about how big your muscles are. Help Aunt Reményi carry those crates out to the veranda."
The assistant clerk is taken aback. Well, he won't do that. But perhaps something should be done...
"I'll send someone," he says and runs out.
The old clerk comes in. Along with the gendarme, he helps to load the stuff on the wagon.
It's eight o'clock...nine...ten...
The Reményis are still loading.

There are more and more wailing women in front of the house. One old woman shakes her fist at the sky.

"During the last war, when my husband died and I was left here with two children and nothing else, I got food from Aunt Reményi. I don't know if there will be as much decency among the new masters."

The loaded wagons pass in front of us in a long procession. There go the Farkas, the Frankel, the Weisz families. They are accompanied by the local peasants, who are walking beside them, with their hatless heads bowed. It looks like an endless funeral procession through the village.

Aunt Reményi is trembling from head to toes. She sits down in the kitchen for the last time. Her deathly pale sister starts to serve some food. Some soup, a few bites of meat and some hurriedly opened preserves.

Aunt Reményi is eating at home for the last time.

The gendarme pulls me aside and whispers to me: "Why are these poor people packing up like this? After all, when they get to Pentele, it will be taken away from them."
But he doesn't have the heart to say anything other than: "Let's hurry up, madam."

When everything is ready, the driver is seated at the front, the furniture and crates all loaded on the wagon, Aunt Reményi kissed the two children and, for the last time, looked around her messed up home. When she started toward the wagon, to step up on the axle, the bell began to toll.

The clerk is taken aback. So is the gendarme. "Well, not now...Let's wait a little..."

Aunt Reményi's eyes are dry as she stands erect, looks up somewhere and says: "I am also dead already...we can go!..." And the wailing peasant women accompany her, too, through the village.

The gendarmes search the Jews of Rácalmás once again at the Poor House Square at the edge of the cemetery. Then they take them to Pentele, where the authorities, through the local police, search them again, right at the village border. They are divided into houses, with five or six families to each. They are living in crowded, but human conditions. Their food supplies last and their friends from Rácalmás and Pentele drop in to visit the Jewish houses from time to time. Later, when the custody becomes tighter, it is possible to sneak parcels to them through the pharmacy, thanks to the good will of the pharmacist.

One day, a detachment of detectives arrives from Székesfehérvár.

From now on, no one may speak to the Jews of Rácalmás.

It's only from the district doctor of Pentele that we find out: one of the children died of peritonitis, because they didn't allow the doctor near him soon enough.

The Jews now are living in the mill, crammed in. It's here, in this mill, that the detectives from Fehérvár are working with them.

They chase old Mrs. Fränkel around a table for hours and beat her with a truncheon. They pull Farkas, the retired chief clerk up on a rack, with his hands tied behind his back. They beat the nails and fingertips of the women.
They are looking for jewellery. We hear nothing about Aunt Reményi.

The last time anyone sees her, she is on the Székesfehérvár highway, covered in dust, stooped over, carrying a small bundle.

I find it difficult to make any comment on this text. It does such a powerful job on its own. How lucky we are to have this. There were hundreds of thousands of these stories in Hungary alone and so many are just unknown.

However there are a few things which need to be said.

In post World War II Hungary the communist regime was not too willing to admit to the anti-Semitic atrocities perpetrated by the former Hungarian Government. As far as they were concerned the holocaust was a German phenomenon and had little or nothing to do with Hungary and Hungarians. Of course this was untrue and in the light of this attitude Margit Izsáky was courageous to write about Mariska Reményi. She may have got into a lot of trouble for this. We just do not know.

When Steve came back from his trip to Hungary in 1974 he said that he had found a few family friends. These people must have been in Rácalmás. It is true that Steve did live for a few years in Budapest finishing his school and preparing to be a radio officer. But his family friends would have been in Rácalmás. He did mention that they were old and that they were a doctor and a pharmacist. I suspect that they were the same people who were referred to by Margit Izsaki. It is clear that even in a little village like Rácalmás medical ethics meant something to the doctor and a pharmacist who no doubt took great risks to treat the Jews. These are the unsung heroes of the war. Steve said that these people and their families had been reduced to total penury which he found distressful. Could that have been the result of their being sympathetic to the Jews or was that just the plight of Rácalmás in general? By the time I got to Rácalmás there were no signs of poverty. It is interesting that Steve had gone to look them up. Perhaps Steve knew about this chapter in Margit Izsáky's book describing Mariska and mentioning the doctor and the pharmacist.

I also think that the so-called local peasants referred to by Margit Izsáky were probably the same people who spoke to Klára Szende and who said quickly and emphatically that "We did not kill any Jews". In fact the great tragedy is, I guess, that so few people killed anybody and so many people were caught up in the anti-Semitic climate which allowed the gangsters and the thugs to do the killing. Bernard Shaw said something to the effect that the greatest crime against humanity is indifference.

Going back to the dusty, sleepy little village of Rácalmás today it is hard to believe that the dreadful events described by Margit Izsáky happened. But there is no doubt at all that they really did and that they are remembered.

Hungary's Story –
The slippery road to hell

At least in one sense the Story of Steve is the story of one of those "lucky" Jews who got away. But like so many others of this sort he only got away in part. He had to carry a lot of emotional baggage with him – although it must be said that he was good at hiding it. He did not easily relate to the Hungarians whom he met from time to time and although we were used to this and didn't find it all that strange, we thought it was because he was such a private man. And there is no doubt that he was a thoroughly closed lipped, need to know, individual. Having come from a country where his family was discriminated against and where their neighbours shipped them off to the gas chambers can only have left deep scars.

When I look back on it there were a number of interesting remarks which were made about Hungary. On one occasion in Durban, Patsy had met some Hungarians through the book shop and had invited them around for drinks. Two couples turned up. After a few drinks they began to talk about how dreadful the Russian occupation of Hungary was. "It was bad in 1956", said one of them but "it was much worse in 1945", said the other. It was clear that there was no love lost between them and the Red Army. These people had come out of Hungary as a result of the 1956 revolution. One of the women who had not previously spoken said, "You know, no one can deny how awful the Russians were in our country but what happened to the Hungarians needs to be put in context. From the earliest times Hungarians have treated other people around them badly. If you go back to when the Magyars first came to the fertile valley which is today Hungary, it was already settled. The Magyars took no prisoners and wiped out everyone who was already there. Through the years the Magyars showed this attitude again and again. Look what happened during the Second World War".

These comments brought the conversation to a halt. The Hungarians in the room looked a bit uncomfortable and they started to talk about something else.

Of course as a young teenager, what this conversation was about went completely over my head.

It is interesting to note that Steve had kept himself well informed about international affairs leading up to the war. He was also able to talk authoritatively about the course of the war. But he had little to say about the aftermath. I once referred to apartheid as being fascist and he gave me a lecture on how the Italian fascists treated their opposition. On another occasion I asked what was so terrible about the eastern block Governments and he told me about people being dunked into baths of concentrated acid. But the discussion never went much further[17].

I was again reminded of this a couple of years ago when I was in Budapest and I had picked up a tourist news letter at the airport. This news letter had decided to give a short rendition of Hungarian history. I was fascinated to read about Hungary up to the end of the First World War and then again from 1947. But this account of Hungarian history just left out the period between 1918 and 1947. Hungarians want to stop the clock and pretend it just didn't happen. I could see the ghost of George Orwell smiling approvingly at the author.

This chapter provides some historical background on Hungary. It tells how attitudes towards Jews in Hungary changed and it describes how anti-Semitism grew in Hungary. It also describes some of the events related to how Hungary slid into the Second World War on the side of the Third Reich, how they realised their mistake, how they were taken over as a Nazi puppet state and some of the consequences of this. It is of course a very incomplete rendition of that period.

Few people would know where they would find Hungary on a map of the world. Those who do would probably describe it as being located somewhere in the centre or to the east of Europe. They might say that it is a little country known for its goulash – which is a strong beef or pork soup, often well spiced with paprika. They might know that Hungary has famous horses and horsemen. They might know that there is some wonderful violin music which comes from Hungary. It's unlikely that they would know that some of it was written by Brahms and the most famous piece is his Hungarian Dance No 5, but they might recognise the version, which was made famous by Allan Sherman as Hungarian Goulash No 5. Some people might remember the joke about the Hungarian in the Monty Python film Monty Python's Flying Circus where there was a rogue Hungarian-English phrase book sketch. The hapless Hungarian using this

---

[17] I have always assumed that Steve had no particular reason for being Russophobic. It just seemed to me to be human nature that the citizens of a small country which were under the shadow of the giant Russia would be fearful of them. I have not met a Hungarian with a kind word for a Russian.

rogue Hungarian-English phrase book thought that he was asking "Can you direct me to the station?" which was translated by the rogue phrase book as, "Please fondle my buttock." This resulted in the Hungarian getting his face slapped and caused considerable hilarity in the audience. But not much more would be known about Hungary or Hungarians and their history by anyone outside of the country.

Hungary is a small country approximately 93,000 square kilometres located directly east of Austria. Today it is bordered by some six different countries. The country has been described as lying in the drainage basin of the Danube. The capital city is situated on both sides of the Danube and is a twin city of the two settlements of Buda and of Pest. It is a colourful country with a vibrant population that is often regarded as high achievers. Hungary has recently joined the European Union and it is believed that the Hungarians will make a positive contribution to 21st century Europe. However Hungary has a dark history which is not well known to non-Hungarians. This dark period started at the end of the First World War and has persisted until recent years.

As the Second World War approached Hungary was a good place to leave. For a period of somewhat longer than fifty years from 1919 or 1920 until the 1990s the country went through a traumatic time during which many of its people were put through what might be considered as hell on earth and the details of this are not at all well known.

Hungary had been an integral part of the Austro-Hungarian Empire. Although not as big in land mass as the British, French, Ottoman or Russian Empires, it was probably no less complex than any of the other early 20th century empires. It had Germans, Magyars, Slovenians, Croats and Serbians, Czechs, Slovaks, Poles, Italians, Ruthenians, as well as some other nationalities. Within the Austro-Hungarian Empire there were millions of Jews, Muslims and Christians. Many of these people did not like each other at all. In fact there were many old grudges due to historical struggles among the people of the Austro-Hungarian Empire.

The Hungarians are the descendents of an ancient tribe called the Magyars who are described as a Finno-Ugric tribe, whose occupation of the Danube valley dates back to the late ninth century. This tribe spoke Magyar from which modern Hungarian is derived and which is a unique language that shares grammatical constructs with Finnish and Estonian. Hungarian and Finnish sound the same although they do not have many, if any, words in common. The speaking of this language as a mother tongue is what primarily defines a Hungarian and it is generally recognised as being a difficult language to learn.

Unfortunately this part of the Danube valley in Central Europe had been disputed from earliest times and had been subjected to countless tribal, national and international struggles, battles and wars. The Magyars were converted to Christianity at an early date. Later the nation was honoured by the canonization of one of its monarchs, King Stephen the Great – an unusual event. It seems that Stephen, as well as being truly pious, had undertaken a programme of church construction. He also suppressed pagan revolts and he had latinised the language. At one point in the Middle Ages a part of Hungary was occupied by the Turks and the rest of the country became part of the Hapsburg Empire. When the Turkish influence in continental Europe withered away all of Hungary fell into the hands of the Austrian-Hapsburg Empire. During the reformation period the Hungarians mostly converted to Protestantism but this caused problems with the Catholic Hapsburgs and, as part of the counter-reformation, the Hungarians converted back again to Rome's version of Christianity and have remained ardently so since that time.

Uncomfortable with being a subject-people the Hungarians, after years of agitation and struggle, managed to obtain a new status for themselves in this Empire which famously became known as the "Dual Monarchy" when Emperor Franz Joseph addressed the Hungarian Diet (parliament) in 1867 in the Hungarian language and declared the Austria-Hungary Empire a loose federation of the two nations. The Kingdom of Hungary enjoyed self-Government and proportional representation in joint affairs with the western and northern parts of the Austrian Empire under the Emperor, Franz Joseph (who was also King of Hungary) of the Habsburg dynasty. The full name of the federation was The Kingdoms and Lands Represented in the Imperial Council and the Lands of the Holy Hungarian Stephen's Crown. Within this Federation or Empire the Hungarians had their own dominions and their own subject peoples who are not known for speaking fondly of Hungarian rule. Within the Kingdom of Hungary there were many non-Magyar speaking people. The Magyar speakers hardly had a majority and the rulers were conscious of this and strongly felt a need to increase their numbers. To ensure their majority the Hungarians counted Magyar speaking Jews in their number. In fact they encouraged Jewish immigration into Hungary and any criticism of this was countered by the fact that Jews quickly learnt the language and counted themselves as Hungarians. This worked well. During the latter part of the 19th century Jews were being offered civil and political rights in Hungary which they were generally denied in other European countries. The laws were changed in Hungary to accommodate this new progressive attitude including a law passed at the end of the 19th century which declared Judaism to be a received religion which gave it the same status as other religions, except Catholicism which for many years had a special status on its own in Hungary. Considering how badly Jews were being treated in other parts of Europe at this time Hungary was a good example of how well people of different religions could co-exist.

It needs to be remembered that there were still large numbers of non-Magyars in Hungary and many of these resented the Jews aligning themselves with the Magyar speakers.

The years between 1867 and 1914 were a golden period for Hungary when the country industrialised and Budapest expanded and became one of the more important cities in central Europe. This unfortunately came to an end when Hungary was drawn into World War I as the Austro-Hungarian Empire invaded Serbia on August 12, 1914.

The Hungarians participated in this war apparently having no idea of the dreadful consequences it would have for them. It was not possible for the old European empires to continue in the 20th century and the empires of the losers of the Great War were the first to be swept away. In fact this war had greater global consequences in terms of the reconfiguration of political and economic power. The war precipitated the loss of the dominance of Europe which had been a feature of global politics for the previous five centuries. It mobilised the resources of the USA and it put it on track to become the world power that it is today.

At the end of the hostilities the Austro-Hungarian Empire imploded. It was just not possible to keep so many different people together in a modern society and anyway each of these groups wanted their own national Government. On November 11, 1918, the empire was officially dissolved and five days later the national council proclaimed the Hungarian Democratic Republic. Within a few months there was a communist coup and the country was run by the Council of People's Commissars of the Hungarian Soviet Republic. In the hiatus that followed the coup titles and ranks were abolished, banks were expropriated, business enterprises employing more than 20 people were nationalised, newspapers were banned and general confusion reigned. These reforms were accompanied by widespread violence. A number of the leaders in this brief attempt at a soviet type Government were Jews and in subsequent years anti-Semites used this fact to label all Jews as Soviet Communist sympathisers. Asso-

ciating this label with Jews was a way of insinuating that they were enemies of the Hungarian state.

Taking advantage of this chaos the Czechs invaded Hungary from the
north and the Romanians invaded it from the south. The Government in
Budapest collapsed on August 1, 1919. Three days later Budapest itself
was occupied by the hated Romanian Army, who retained control over
the city until November 14. In this short period the Romanians had thoroughly looted the country carrying off, in particular, much of its rolling-
stock.

From the victorious Allies' point of view this Romanian occupation was
unsatisfactory and under Allied supervision, an interim Government, rep-
resenting various political parties was formed on November 25, 1919.
This new Government was placed in the hands of the conservative leader
Admiral Miklós Horthy, a former Commander in Chief of the Imperial
and Royal Adriatic Fleet of the Austro-Hungarian Empire, who immediately instituted reprisals against communists and others. When general
elections were held in 1920 the idea of a republic was abandoned and the
country was proclaimed an independent monarchy, with Horthy the Regent until a King was found. A King was never found. It didn't suit Horthy to look too hard for a King as the position of Regent was really quite
comfortable. He would hold that position until the end of the Second
World War. The failure of the Hungarian Soviet Republic did a great
amount of damage to the political climate in the country and moved the
political discussion in the country materially to the right.

As a minor player in the First World War, Hungary was not dealt with at
Versailles with those countries considered to be the main culprits responsible for this conflict. In June 1920, the Hungarian Government reluc-
tantly accepted the Treaty of Trianon imposed on it by the Allies. As a
result of this Hungary lost territory to Czechoslovakia, Romania, and
Yugoslavia. The loss of these Hungarian-speaking lands, which
amounted to two-thirds of the country's pre-war territory, was bitterly
resented by the Hungarians. The size of the loss of territory can be well
understood by the numbers of people which remained in the reduced
country. Whereas Hungary had a population of nearly 21 million according to the 1910 census, after the treaty of Trianon the population had been
reduced to 8 million.

This resentment towards this treaty fuelled nationalist feelings and a
sense of aggression grew against the country's neighbours. A mantra
"Nem, Nem, Soha!" which translates into English as "No, No, Never!",

was used at public meetings and in schools to keep the population focused on not accepting the territorial provisions of the Treaty of Trianon. In the 1930s these nationalist sentiments fed directly into the hands of the fascist orientated political groups in the country. This was the period when Fascism and Nazism were transforming Italy and Germany. Horthy and others saw how apparently successful these extreme political stances were. The right wing had brought some economic prosperity and a type of stability to these countries. Anti-Semitism was an integral part of this nationalistic fervour.

Despite decades of Jews and gentiles living successfully side by side during the 1920's anti-Semitic laws began to appear in Hungary. The Numerus Clausus (Latin for Closed Number) Law limited the proportion of Jews in Hungarian universities. As it happened this law was not strictly enforced and was repealed eight years later. However by the 1930s there was a new wave of anti-Semitism and Hungarian anti-Semitics were further encouraged by how easy it was for Hitler to plunder the Jews in Germany. As a result a new wave of anti-Semitic Laws were introduced. These laws were intended to address the issue that the right wing believed there were too many Jews in industry, in banking and in commerce. The story was put out that Jewish success was somehow achieved at the expense of other Hungarian welfare. It was stated that while only five percent of the population were Jews, they held about 20 percent of the important positions in the country. Of course this belief has to be seen in terms of the backdrop of there being a severe economic recession in Hungary. Someone had to be blamed and the Jews were a relatively easy target. The misconception that if wealth was taken away from the Jews the rest of the country would somehow benefit was encouraged. Thus there were limits placed on how much economic activity a Jew could be involved with. Another set of Laws required Jews between the ages of 20 and 48 to work in forced labour units. Then the Hungarian Government showed its lack of concern for Jewish life when gendarmes capriciously murdered 1,000 Jews.

Of course the open wound of the Treaty of Trianon continued to fester. After the Munich Pact of 1938, in which the Third Reich's territorial ambitions were placated which resulted in the break up of Czechoslovakia, Hungary appealed to the Western countries to help it reclaim sections of Hungarian speaking Slovakia that had been previously awarded to Czechoslovakia at Versailles. However the Hungarians' claim for this territory was ignored. Hungary simply did not have the clout of Germany.

As Nazi Germany was the foremost power in Central Europe, Hungary now appealed to them. With the help of fascist Italy it was agreed by the First Vienna Award in 1938 that Hungary should have a section of Slovakia with a large Hungarian population. This was accompanied by a massive programme of re-armament in Hungary. At the Second Vienna Award in 1940 Hungary was given a large section of Hungarian speaking Romania. In return for this territory, Hungary agreed to support Nazi Germany and Fascist Italy in future conflicts. Hungary had decided to dine with the devil, but it didn't have a long enough spoon.

In fact in the late 1930s and early 1940s with the help of the Nazis and the Fascists, four so called 'corrections' were made to the Treaty of Trianon, the last one being when Hungary participated in the German invasion of Yugoslavia in April 1941.

Towards the end of the 1930s Hungarians and especially the radical right wing became obsessed with the "Jewish Problem". From 1939 there had been other waves of anti-Semitic legislation prohibiting Jews from various aspects of professional and commercial life including being teachers. The Hungarian official line was that "Jews were practising economic and cultural terror against the ordinary people". Quite what this might have meant is not clear. Privately Hungarians would say that Jews were just too successful with anything they touched. It is true that Hungarian Jews had been successful in almost all the walks of life they chose to pursue with large percentages of the top positions being filled by them. This did not apply so much to the Government and the Army where there were not that many Jews, but even in these institutions there were successful Jews. It is clear that Jews were not seen as so called team players, but were thought to be exclusive and elitists and it was said that they owed more allegiance to their fellow Jews and their ancient religion than to the country in which they lived. There had always been multiple aspects to anti-Semitism, one of which was taking property and therefore wealth from Jews. This was behind these new moves. Except for the richest Jews these measures where making life hard for the majority of the population.

Now the Hungarian Government made its biggest mistake. In support of its Nazi ally, Hungary declared war on the Soviet Union in June 1941 and on the United States of America and the United Kingdom in December of the same year. So for the second time in just over twenty five years Hungary had joined a war in which it had little direct interest, on the side of the Germans. These declarations of war were at least in part intended to be gesture-like rather than based on any real belief that Hungary could successfully make war against either the Soviet Union or the United

States of America. And it was a dangerous strategy. However it did appear that Germany might, like it had done in the First World War, inflict sufficient damage on the Soviet Union to cause a redefinition of boundaries and the Hungarian Government wanted to be in on this. Within weeks the Hungarians had sent the Second Hungarian Army, consisting of some 200,000 troops to the Soviet front.

And as was to have been expected, the war did not go well for the Hungarians who suffered heavy losses, with about 40,000 deaths and most of the other troops being captured or wounded on the Russian front. Putting this loss into context, the Germans had only weeks before lost the battle of El Alamein in the desert and they would lose even more men at Stalingrad within a few weeks. Hungarian judgement about the Germans' prospects in the war was astonishingly poor to say the least.

Having lost the Second Hungarian Army, by 1943 Hungary was effectively neutral in the war. In August that year the Government was trying in secret to negotiate a separate peace with the Allies. But despite the recognition that they had been badly mistaken to enter the war on the side of Germany, the Hungarian Government continued with anti-Semitic legislation and practices. It is difficult to imagine why they wanted to punish the Jews further and it is hard to know how the Hungarians thought that the Allies would let them out of their military predicament. The Hungarians had made a substantial, although ineffective commitment to the German war effort and they were now big time losers. The attempt to make a treaty with the Allies infuriated the Germans who, correctly felt, that the Hungarians could not be trusted when it came to German strategic interests.

Germans had never really trusted the Hungarians and had established and nurtured a network of pro-German Hungarian Nazi spies and collaborators who would directly help with the forthcoming invasion. There was some debate in Berlin as to whether to break up Hungary as a country by handing back the territories which had recently been reclaimed by Hungary through the Trianon corrections, but it was felt that this would probably cause an active rebellion in Budapest and make Hungary a direct enemy and therefore another liability to the Third Reich. It was decided to take the country over in a different and more subtle way without the need to face a major Hungarian rebellion.

On March 19, 1944 German troops occupied Hungary. They were met in Budapest by Laszlo Baky, a leading pro-German Hungarian Nazi. Baky, who had advanced warning of this and had been preparing to help the

Germans, had prepared a list of moderate Hungarians who might not support the German invasion. These individuals were immediately arrested. The new German Minister for Hungary began to replace Government ministers and other officials right down to the level of provincial Government and town mayors as well as civil servants. Almost all moderates were cleansed from the Hungarian political system. Extremists were put into every important post. This amounted to Hitler forcing Horthy to install a puppet Nazi regime of members of the Hungarian Nazi Party called the Arrow Cross Party. This was done without direct military intervention in order to give the Nazi's coup some degree of apparent respectability or legitimacy and Horthy was hardly in a position to resist or refuse to cooperate. It was a complete take over and Hungary had effectively become an extension of the Third Reich.

The country was now fully in the control of the Hungarian radical right wing which was effectively Nazis and they were taking their orders from Berlin.

This new Government immediately began to terrorize all dissidents and commenced the systematic implementation of the Final Solution. This hell was to last until the Soviet armies invaded Hungary and Budapest was surrounded by the Red Army on December 26. Pest was liberated on January 18 and Buda in February of the following year. Even then German troops and certain elements of the Hungarian army continued to fight the Soviets into 1945 as they retreated towards the Austrian border.

It has been estimated that at the time of the German invasion of Hungary there were 750,000 Jews in the country. There were also about 100,000 converts to Christianity, but in the eyes of the Nazis these people were also Jews. Hungary was the last country to be occupied by the Germans and it is sometimes said that up until that point the Hungarian Jews had been relatively unscathed. As may be seen from the previous pages of this chapter the emphasis needs to be placed on the word 'relatively'. Hungarian Jews had certainly suffered considerably. But from 1944 Hitler's Final Solution was applied to Hungarian Jews with a vengeance, and the main centre for this purpose was to be Auschwitz. To this end the railway track into the concentration camp was extended so that a great volume of Jews and other undesirables could be processed faster. And the Germans and the Hungarian Nazis showed considerable efficiency in dispatching Jews.

At this time there was a substantial gathering of Jews in Budapest. It was not the Warsaw ghetto, but it was a concentration of Jews in the big city.

Nearly a quarter of the population of Budapest had been Jewish. So the Hungarian Nazis decided to start their elimination work on the rural Jews and the Jews in the smaller centres. There were hundreds of thousands of these people operating little businesses, keeping shops or running small farms and the Nazi killing machine focused on them. They were easy prey.

The Government in Budapest declared that these Jews were to be sent abroad to work. Of course by this stage of the war everyone knew that being sent abroad to work meant deportation and that, in turn, deportation meant extermination. No one knows exactly how many Hungarian Jews were murdered but a guess of five or six hundred thousand would not be far off.

As an indication of how seriously Hitler wanted to exterminate the Hungarian Jews, by April 1944 Adolph Eichmann himself had arrived in Budapest. Now the gloves were off and any remaining vestige of common decency was dispatched. From that month Jews over the age of 6 had to wear yellow stars of David on their arms so that they could be identified. Jews from the countryside had been moving into the Budapest "Ghetto", which had swelled by this time. However, there were a number of buildings in the city, not necessarily contiguous, that had stars of David displayed on them. Generally speaking, they became part of the ghetto, once the ghetto was officially designated. There were a number of "safe" houses in Budapest, under the sponsorship of Sweden, Switzerland and the International Red Cross. People who were sheltered in these houses were thought to be protected by the sponsoring organization or country. The Nazis did not ghettoise the Jews of Budapest as it was believed that by spreading them around the Allies would be discouraged from bombing the capital city. Of course this did not discourage the bombing.

Outside of Budapest, there were many Jews who were moving to neighbouring larger towns in the various regions of Hungary. Ghettos were being established in these towns as Jews were being evicted from their properties. These ghettos were sometimes in abandoned warehouses and factories. The British were bombing Budapest and Eichmann was evicting Jews from their homes in the city to give houses to Hungarians who had been bombed. When Jews were evicted from their homes they were often given ten minutes to pick up a few pieces of clothes and food. Many of them left behind most of their most treasured belongings which were then stolen either by the Hungarian gendarmes or by German troops. It was said that Jewish property was to go to the state but much of it went to individual anti-Semites who were doing the evicting. This made it attractive in an economic sense to be involved in kicking Jews out of their homes. Of course the really rich Jews were dealt with by the senior Nazis who, in some cases sold safe passages to neutral countries for huge sums to those Jews who could afford it. The loot collected from the Jews of Hungary became a separate issue in its own right when it was transported out of the country on the Gold Train.

As the Hungarian gendarmes rounded up the rural Jews the Hungarian Roman Catholic clergy made appeals to the Pope in Rome. After all Hungary was a staunchly Roman Catholic country and the German killing machine at Auschwitz was being fed with Jews and others by ostensibly "religious" Roman Catholic Hungarians.

At that time the Shoes of the Fisherman were being filled by Maria Giuseppe Giovanni Eugenio Pacelli or Pope Pius XII who had assumed the Throne of St Peter on March 2, 1939. He was a patrician who had lived in Germany for a number of years and had a number of ties with that country. Pius XII's actions and inactions during the whole of the World War II have become a matter of major controversy. He was asked many times to speak out against the Nazis but on every occasion he refused to so do. An early request was from Edith Stein a few weeks after Adolf Hitler came to power. She was a Catholic convert from Judaism who became a Carmelite nun. She wrote to Pius XII seeking his condemnation of the Nazi ideology. Edith Stein herself did not survive the war and died in Auschwitz in 1942. She was canonised in 1998. In her letter to Pius XII she stated that the whole world was "waiting and hoping that the church of Christ would make its voice heard." But the voice of Christ's church was never heard. The argument proffered by Rome for not speaking out against the Nazis was that it would simply have made things worse for everyone in the occupied territories. Catholic Bishops of Holland had jointly issued a statement in 1942 denouncing the deportation of Dutch Jews. The bishops had instructed the clergy to read this out in public at Mass on Sunday, July 26th. Prior to this event, the Dutch Bishops had procured an exemption from deportation for Catholics of Jewish origin. Nazi reprisal came quickly. On August 2nd, Christians of Jewish origin were arrested and carried off by the Gestapo. The Nazi General-Commissar announced publicly that this was a specific reprisal for the pastoral letter. "We are compelled to regard the Catholic Jews as our worst enemies and consequently see to their deportation to the East with all possible speed." There was no easy way out of this dilemma. But in general it is not felt that the Catholic Church behaved as honourably as it should have and that it could have done more to help the victims of the Nazi machine.

When appeals were made to Pius XII to intervene on the part of the Hungarian Jews nothing was forthcoming. However the local clergy on the ground in Budapest made some efforts and offered help. Some safe houses were established and papers were issued by the Nuncios on behalf of the Holy See to offer some protection. There was also large scale or mass conversion to Catholicism – one church alone performing 3,000 baptisms in 1944. However by and large no amount of holy water could wash away a person's Jewishness in the eyes of a Nazi and many convertees were picked up and despatched to the gas chambers anyway.

Eichmann had envisaged a dramatic end to the 70,000 Jews in the Budapest Ghetto. He had decided that they should all be destroyed on one single day by a large-scale assault by the occupying German Army under the command of General August Schmidthuber. It seems unlikely that even with German efficiency and their proven ability to murder on an industrial scale, they could have disposed of 70,000 people in just one day. It is clear that less than 70,000 people were killed when the atom bomb was dropped on Hiroshima and even less deaths occurred as a result of the hydrogen bomb at Nagasaki. But no doubt Eichmann would have tried hard to achieve his target.

Eichmann's plan was never put into action. Raoul Wallenberg, a Swedish citizen with business connections in Hungary who had come to Budapest shortly before and who had been responsible for rescuing thousands of Jews, heard of the Eichmann plan. He approached General August Schmidthuber saying that if the German Army attempted to prosecute Eichmann's suggestion, Wallenberg would ensure that Schmidthuber would be hanged for war crimes. By this stage it was obvious to everyone including Schmidthuber that from the Third Reich's point of view the war was lost and he didn't want to have a dedicated, energetic and aggressive Swede leading a post-war hunt for him. Without Schmidthuber's support the Eichmann plan was a non-starter and the Budapest ghetto was not totally destroyed.

Wallenberg's achievements in saving Jews were quite remarkable and one wonders what a Papal Nuncio with the full backing of Pius XII might have achieved. Many regard the conduct of Pius XII as being a particularly low point in the recent history of the Catholic Church.

There is a dreadful and ironic twist to the Wallenberg story. When the Soviets occupied Budapest he disappeared. The Swedish Government pressed the Soviets for information but they claimed that they did not know what happened to him. However stories from people previously imprisoned in the Soviet Union suggested that he had been taken by the Soviets. Eventually the Soviet Government admitted this in 1957. They then claimed that he had died in Lubyanskaya prison on July 17, 1947. No evidence was ever forthcoming to corroborate the fact of his death. He is still regarded by many as being a missing person. It is not known why Wallenberg was kidnapped by the Soviets other than he was a heroic figure to whom much was owed for his work against the Nazis. Perhaps the Soviets didn't want such a figure to be around who might detract from the glory of the "liberators".

The retreating German Army implemented a policy of scorched earth leaving as little as possible for the invaders. Everything that could be dismantled was loaded on to convoys of freight wagons or trucks or barges and these were taken westward. They also took food stuffs, animal feed and anything else they imagined that could be useful. It is estimated that 100,000 head of cattle were also transported out of Hungary. The retreating soldiers not surprisingly took with them what portable wealth they could put their hands on. This amounted to a major stripping of the economic infrastructure of Hungary from which it was going to take years to recover. The theft of these economic assets and reduction in production capacity were to strengthen the Third Reich for its final struggle against the Allies. It is worth mentioning that at least some of the Germans believed right up to the last few days of the War that somehow they would win the day. The Germans were being told that the coalition of American, British and Soviets would not hold and that they would begin fighting among themselves. The Germans were told that any minute their scientists would discover the wonder weapon and that this would defeat their enemy. Even if they had produced the atom bomb it is unlikely that they could have delivered it on London, New York or Moscow.

As the Germans left a Soviet Army arrived. Horthy decided that the Hungarians should surrender unconditionally as the Rumanians had done shortly before. On August 23 King Michael of Rumania, a number of army officers, and armed Communist-led civilians locked their wartime leader Ion Antonescu into a safe and seized control of the Government and surrendered to the Allies. The Germans were not prepared to accept the proposed Hungarian surrender. Although the Hungarian Army had effectively ceased to exist, the Germans began to incorporate Hungarian units into both the Wehrmacht and the Waffen SS. Then the Germans decided to make a stand west of the Danube at Budapest. The residents of the city faced bombardment from outside and looting and murder from the remnants of the Arrow Cross or Nyilas troops left in the city. At the same time the Hungarian Nazis who had been for years picking up a range of valuables such as diamonds, jewellery, wedding rings, some gold coin and bullion and masses of silverware, fur coats and Persian rugs decided to move this plunder out of the capital. A train which is now referred to as the Gold Train comprising some 44 trucks of former Jewish owned property was loaded and moved west out of Budapest. The official motivation for this was the removal of Hungarian State property from an area which was likely to fall into the hands of the Red Army. This final attempt at grand theft was masterminded by Árpád Toldi who had been a career officer in the Hungarian gendarmerie and who had become one of the most active persecutors of the Jews. After a considerable amount of confusion the Gold Train fell into the hands of the Americans and exactly what happened to all its contents is still a matter of some speculation. Little of this loot was ever returned to its former owners.

Eventually Budapest fell. Large numbers of Soviet Troops poured into the city as liberators. They certainly couldn't have been any worse than the Nazis and the Soviet troops were there to kill Germans. A large number of them remained in the country after the fighting was over. Under the armistice Hungary had been assessed to have to pay reparations to the Soviets of some 300 million dollars. Of course there was no usable money. Thus the Soviets took this in 'kind' valuing in their own way what they decided to take. It has been said that Hungary was stripped of property worth much more than the sum demanded at the armistice.

The arrival of the Soviet Army brought considerable trauma to the Hungarians. Many had seen the Russians as a natural enemy and the Red Army which was described as the 'liberators' hardly treated them with kid gloves. In fact it is said that the first wave of fighting Red Army solders treated the civilian population as well as could be expected. But these soldiers were subsequently followed by the Soviet Army of occupation troops and the local civilians did not get on with them as well. There was the usual bounty in goods and women taken by the victors. However peace was restored and elections took place. The Peace Treaty, which was eventually signed on 10 February 1947, reinstated the Trianon frontiers with a further small but important piece of territory going to Czechoslovakia.

But the elections were not particularly satisfactory to many. In the following years there was considerable political unrest and uncertainty until in 1949 the communists assumed control of the country. Hungary was declared a People's Republic bringing it into line with other countries that were under the "rule" of the Soviet Union. The army, the judiciary and the civil service were purged. The trade unions were emasculated and the

Catholic Church's influence enormously reduced. Any notion of freedom of speech was a distant dream.

This was not a happy period for Hungary as the Soviet Union under Joseph Stalin exerted more and more control. The Soviets had their own version of Auschwitz in the Gulags. Many regard the reign of terror perpetrated by Stalin as being second to none – not even second to Hitler. So in a sense it was out of Hitler's frying pan and into Stalin's fire.

With Stalin's death there was hope for more liberalisation and when this was shattered the 1956 revolution followed. Budapest once again saw fighting in the streets where revolutionaries, mostly using small arms and petrol bombs, fought against Soviet tanks and heavy armour. And tens of thousands of people were displaced as they tried to flee the country.

It was to take nearly 40 long years before a more liberal and democratic Government was elected in Hungary, and it was to become part of the European Union.

A final note concerning the Jews and concentration camps. Since the end of World War II across Europe nearly 40,000 individuals suspected of war crimes have been investigated and tried, and more than 19,000 have been found guilty.

What happened to Mariska?

I was a bit puzzled by the fact that everyone including the officials in 'Rácalmás' 'town hall'' believed that Mariska was murdered in Auschwitz. I was able to believe that Mariska was shipped off to the concentration camp but did she ever make it to that destination? Margit Izsáky's account suggests that she may not have got there. My sister had attempted to find out if Mariska was on the roll of Jews murdered in Auschwitz and Mariska apparently is not listed. I didn't have the know-how to make any further investigations and in any event I was uncertain if I actually wanted to do that. But it did seem to me that to understand what had happened to Mariska it was important to make a journey to Auschwitz.

I had no idea of where Auschwitz was and how do you get there? It's not exactly on the main tourists' trails of Europe. So the first step was to ask a travel agent and sure enough the answer came quickly and easily and was "Auschwitz is in Poland and you get there by flying to Krakow". An easy answer – but of course where exactly is Krakow and which airlines go there? The city is in the south of Poland towards the west near the border with Slovakia. There are many flights to Krakow. From London there is one direct flight every day by LOT, the Polish Airline and a couple of direct flights per week with British Airways. These days it is relatively inexpensive and out of season there are plenty of seats. The flight time is about two hours travelling east and a little more coming home when you have the prevailing winds to fly against. The travel agent was not able to supply details of how to get from Krakow to Auschwitz but he was confident that there would be plenty of different ways of getting there. Of course none of the flights' times really suited what I wanted to do, which was to go to Auschwitz for a couple of hours and come straight home. I didn't want any further contact with Poland which I have always seen as a rather strange country, too far east of Europe for my liking. In the end it was necessary to go to Krakow for two nights. I really didn't want this stop over at all but in retrospect Krakow turned out to be a wonderful city and the Poles were largely welcoming. I eventually ended up by spending the two nights in the now small Jewish quarter and getting some impression of that area.

Krakow is an old city. Some scholars believe that it was a human settlement as far back as 50,000 BCE. In more recent times it was an important cultural centre of Poland. Although the Nazis intended to destroy the city as they had destroyed Warsaw, the arrival of the Red Army forced them to withdraw sooner than they had expected and the city was saved. Krakow has the largest central market square in Europe, which has the necessary collection of restaurants with tables overflowing into the square like those in the Grande Place in Brussels. On one corner there is a large church – cathedral sized – and when I stuck my head in the door it was packed with people. Catholicism is alive and well and living in Poland. In the centre of the square there is a remarkable building which houses a significant number of small vendors from which you can buy every sort of tourist trinket you can imagine, including statues both of the Virgin Mary and of Rabbis in various costumes and poses. The Poles are serious about their income from tourists!

The Jewish quarter is small and it is mainly noticeable by Jewish restaurants. I found a great place to eat with the best borscht I have ever had. There are of course several synagogues and some signs in the street in Hebrew. When I asked if I could see one of the synagogues I was told apologetically that there was a service going on and that I could come back tomorrow when I would be welcomed. However I was flying away the following day. There were a number of antique shops whose windows were jam packed with what looked to me like bric-a-brac. There were not many people around in the streets in that area so it felt rather empty. I tried to engage the people in the hotel about the war years but they were unprepared to talk and brushed me off with the comment "terribly bad times". There had been many Jews, 20,000 I was told, in Krakow but now it was a small number, although they didn't know just how many.

There were indeed plenty of ways of travelling from Krakow to Auschwitz. Auschwitz is about a ninety minute train ride from Krakow or somewhere between a 2 and 3 hour bus ride. Auschwitz is actually the German name for the Polish town of Oswiecim but everyone seems to know it as Auschwitz. There are a number of tour companies who will pick you up from your hotel and take you there for the day. There are also taxi touts at the airport and at the central station looking to take foreigners there for some large sum of money. Taking people to Auschwitz is an important part of the industry of Krakow.

The advice from the Krakow information or tourist bureau was that if I didn't want an organised tour then I should go by bus and I decided to take this advice. I was also told there was a bus on the hour and that it would cost me 16 zlotys return. So having spent the night in the Jewish quarter in a family hotel I made sure that I arrived good and early at the bus station. The bus station is immediately next to the train station. It is a bustling place, much like a marshalling yard, with buses coming and going all the time. There are many people milling about and others in queues waiting for buses. Here were the little old ladies dressed in 1930 frocks or over coats with tight scarves around their ears and two over-sized shopping bags in their hands. These were my archetypes of the typical middle Europe peasant. There are a number of officials who seem to be busy directing the buses. I went up to one of these officials and I said "Auschwitz, where do I get the bus?" I had already at this stage worked out that quite a few people understood a few words of English and I was pleased to hear him say "Ticket" and point towards a large building only 20 or 30 metres away. It was a big official building with people coming and going and it had some international signs such as the big "I" for an information office. So off I went enthusiastically. Some way down a long concourse I found a counter with a glass front behind which there was a helpful looking woman who I approached with the words "Auschwitz please". She nodded and reached for a ticket which she began to stamp. I followed up her action with the words "Return. Return today." And she seemed to understand and issued me with the ticket. However when I gave her a 50 zlotys note I noticed that I hadn't been charged the 16 zlotys which I had been previously told by the tourist people was the cost of the bus trip. However I didn't think much of this – maybe the price had gone up or she had taken a small commission and I rushed back to where the buses were loading. I looked for the official who had sent me for the ticket and I could not find him. However there was a different official who was directing buses and I rushed up to him with my ticket in hand with the word "Auschwitz". Looking at my out-stretched ticket he said "Yes. But you have in your hand a train ticket to Auschwitz and the train station is 200 metres over there and you had better move as the train goes in less than 10 minutes". There was no pigeon English here. Travelling in a foreign land without a word of the local language is indeed a challenge and there are often surprises.

But it was not a big deal to run to the railway station and I arrived there with several minutes to spare. The Auschwitz train was standing at platform No 2 and there were 20 to 30 people hanging about next to the train waiting to be told to board. One elderly couple caught my eye and to re-assure myself that I was on the correct platform I said "Auschwitz". They both replied together in a broad Scottish accent "We hope so". These were Mick and Margo originally from Aberdeen but now retired to the South of England and who were enjoying their retirement in several ways including travelling to unusual places. And so a few minutes later I boarded the train and sat in an old, worse for wear, almost dingy carriage with Mick and Margo on our way to Auschwitz.

The train from Krakow to Auschwitz is not an express. It is very similar to many of the trains in Ireland - it travels slowly and it stops many times. It was by no means full, with people getting on and off at the various stops. The countryside through which it travels is agricultural but there are occasional huge piles of coal next to the railway tracks. This reminded me that it was cheap Polish coal imports which were said to have been one of the triggers for the mine closures which had started the Great Coal Miners' Strike in the UK which devastated the mining communities in the 1980s.

Mick and Margo were easy talking people. They had travelled the world since they had retired, with their most recent long trip having been to Boston (Massachusetts) which they had liked. They had seen an advertisement for a one week break to Krakow and they had taken the opportunity to see a part of the world they had not visited before. Although very attractive, Krakow is not a big city so they were now exploring other parts of the country. They had taken a day trip by train to Warsaw on the previous day and they commented on how the agricultural activity which we could see as the train passed by was more modern and opulent than what they had seen on the way to Warsaw.

It seems that Margo had only recently heard about Auschwitz and that was one of the reasons they were on this train trip. As a young man Mick had been in the British Army and he had known about Auschwitz since that time. Margo asked a number of times if I thought that many people knew about the concentration camps. I felt that concentration camps were well known, certainly to my generation and that one didn't have to be in the British Army to be told about them. I took Margo's lack of knowledge about concentration camps to signal that she wasn't likely to be Jewish or to have known any Jews. But even so I am still puzzled as to how anyone gets to adulthood, never mind the early seventies without having been informed as to what happened in the Nazi camps.

It was a strange feeling being on a train to Auschwitz. The last member of my family to have made this journey was probably Mariska and she would have travelled in a cattle truck with another 100 people squashed in. I was apprehensive as to how I would react to what I found there and just wanted to sit with my own thoughts. But I was now engaged in conversation and Margo wanted to talk more about concentration camps.

Margo began to talk about how terrible the concentration camps must have been and Mick was of the view that it was sort of what one might expect of Germans. Germans according to Mick were aggressive, pugnacious and belligerent. Concentration camps were to have been expected of them. I really didn't want to argue. I did want to point out that many historians believe that concentration camps had been invented by the British during the South Africa Boer War at the turn of the nineteenth and twentieth centuries. The British treatment of Boer women and children in the final year of that war and during the immediate aftermath was utterly abysmal. But making any remark which could have been interpreted as trying to reduce the horror of the Jewish Holocaust would not have been appropriate.

But I couldn't let the remark about Germans being aggressive, pugnacious and belligerent go entirely unchallenged. It was after all this sort of blanket ignorance, prejudice and bigotry which allowed the Nazis to say that all Jews were rich, mean, avaricious, eaters of Christian children, etc.

"You know Mick" I said, "I wish it was just as simple as that. But it really isn't. There were Hungarian Nazis who murdered many Jews. There were French Nazis who handed Jews over to the Gestapo for deportation. I wonder if you knew that there was a concentration camp just outside of Paris called Drancy. The Frenchman Klaus Barbi had been awarded the Iron Cross for his services to the Third Reich. And then there was our very own William Joyce or Lord Haw-Haw as he was better known. Then there was Oswald Mosley and his British Union of Fascists. I could go on and on. On the other hand there were hundreds of thousands of Germans who spoke out against the Nazis and not all of them were communists either, many of them died in concentration camps themselves. It's just not fair to group all Germans together". Mick was not really convinced by my words, but neither of us wanted to strain a newly made acquaintance with an argument, especially an argument like this. So we both watched the passing country side.

Eventually we arrived at Auschwitz railway station. It is a strikingly unattractive place. This modern station building is an eastern European rectangular box which epitomises the lack of style of the architects of the communist era. The banal exterior is only broken by the equally banal Coca-Cola vending machine. The small group of us who are visiting Auschwitz proceed into the building where Mick and Margo decide that it would be a good thing to have a cup of coffee. There's a large railway station café in the corner with the usual sort of sweets and sandwiches for sale. Margo buys the coffee and comes back with three cups and saucers in her hand. As we sit there sipping our coffee out of fine china cups, Margo points out the fact that on their recent trip to Boston they could not find coffee offered in a café which was served in anything other than a paper or polystyrene container. Here in the back waters of Poland we have been served coffee in quality china cups with saucers and the cost has been a zloty or so each. We sit there and contemplate the irony and other philosophical implications of this.

The Auschwitz concentration camp which since July 2, 1947 has been a state museum is a few kilometres from the railway station and there is a sizable sign at the station door stating that a taxi will take you to the museum for 10 zlotys. So we jump into a cab and ten minutes later we are unloaded in the museum car park which has several tour buses, people carriers and taxis all parked in a row. There is no doubt that this is a well visited place. It is not difficult to find the entrance and the ticket desk. Here you pay for a tour and then you wait for the next one to begin. The next English tour was to start in about 15 minutes with a film to be shown in the auditorium which sat about 100 people. Near the ticket desk were posters showing the concentration camp and faces of some of the victims. You had to walk past these to get to the auditorium and then go through an open area where there were more wall hangers and posters describing how Jehovah Witnesses were murdered in Auschwitz. Margo is surprised that Jehovah Witnesses were victims of the holocaust. "What did they do?" she said. I replied, "Well the point is that Hitler had a lot of different peoples who he considered undesirable. It is sometimes said that 15 million people were murdered in the concentration camps of which 6 million were Jews. So there were 9 million others. The Jehovah Witnesses were part of a great mosaic of victims of the Third Reich." On the wall in this area of the camp there is a poster which shows the number of people deported to Auschwitz and from which groups they came. The numbers are 1,100,000 Jews, 140,000 Poles, 23,000 Gypsies, 15,000 Soviet POWs, and 25,000 prisoners of other nationalities, etc. There is no mention of the number of homosexuals murdered there.

The film we were shown is about twenty minutes long and it was made by Soviet cameramen as the Red Army liberated the Auschwitz camp. There is very little new in this film for me. There are piles of dead naked bodies. There are some skeleton-like emaciated people walking around the camp after liberation. The only truly new piece of information which I picked up was to do with the warehouses which were found at Auschwitz. The Soviets found several large warehouses which contained the clothes of the victims of the gas chambers. The Nazis were great collectors – clothes, tooth brushes and spectacles by the million. The clothes were gathered up by the Nazis, folded and carefully stored in warehouses. There were hundreds of thousands or maybe a million sets of clothes. The

Soviet commentator on the film asks "Who would have wanted to wear dead Jews' clothes?" This is a puzzle.

After the film we are assembled and we are introduced to our guide. She is a middle aged Polish woman who speaks heavily accented English. She introduces herself as a guide, interpreter and as a historian. She is certainly very knowledgeable but she is also emotional and I felt on a number of occasions that her emotions sometimes got in the way of her explanations.

She begins by telling us that there were actually three concentration camps at Auschwitz. The camps were Auschwitz 1 which was the oldest and was constructed on the orders of Himmler in 1940 to detain the Polish intelligencia. This was well before the Final Solution to the Jewish problem was conceptualised by the Nazis. The second camp was Auschwitz-Birkenau which was built later in 1941 to process Jews. This camp was also known as Auschwitz 2 and then there was a third camp, Auschwitz 3 - Monowitz, built in 1942 and placed adjacent to the IG Farben chemical plant. Auschwitz 3 was a slave labour camp created to ensure the profitability of IG Farben. IG Farben, which is short for Interessengemeinschaft Farben was one of the most powerful German enterprises in the first half of the 20th century. The German word Interessengemeinschaft means "Association of Common Interests" and was a powerful cartel of BASF, Bayer, Hoechst, and various other German chemical and pharmaceutical companies. The IG Farben organisation was the single largest donor to the election campaign of Hitler, donating 400,000 marks to Nazi party coffers. IG Farben made the gas used to poison the prisoners in Auschwitz 1 and 2. For the directors of IG Farben, concentration camps were about profit. They made the gas using the slave labour of Auschwitz 3 and then they sold it to the gas chambers next door for Auschwitz 2 to murder those who were not strong enough to be slaves.

Auschwitz 1 and 2 were built to eliminate undesirables. The original method of elimination was starvation and working to death. But this was later changed in the case of Auschwitz 2 to rapid mass murder when the Final Solution was implemented. Auschwitz 3 was not directly about elimination but rather about slave labour. A large part of the workforce required to support the war effort was provided by various subject-peoples who worked in factories under slave like conditions. People in Auschwitz 3 were generally better fed than those in Auschwitz 1 and 2 and they lived longer.

Our first stop is outside the famous gates with the words "Arbeit Macht Frei" which is translated for us as *work makes you free*. These are the gates of Auschwitz 1 which is a compound of a few dozen prison buildings. The barbed wire and the guard towers are immediately apparent. Our Polish guide takes us into a number of these prison buildings. It is hard seeing these reminders of the atrocities carried out here. But little is new as it has all been filmed and shown in cinemas and on television many times. However one of these buildings houses walls of photographs of Polish victims. As mentioned above Auschwitz 1 was built to eliminate the Polish intelligencia. Hitler saw Poles and other Slavs as being some sort of sub-human group who were only fit for slave labour. Thus for Nazis, Polish doctors, lawyers, architects and professors were oxymorons and needed to be exterminated. One of the interesting aspects of these photographs is that each photo has the person's name, and the date on which they were incarcerated and the date of their death. The average survival period in Auschwitz 1 seems to have been less than a few months. Some people died a few days after arrival while others survived years and even walked out when they were liberated.

What I found very interesting was the fact that these Polish prisoners were photographed and their dates recorded. When the objective was to eliminate a few tens of thousands of the Polish intelligencia by starvation and hard work it was still possible to record their details. When the objective was to murder hundreds of thousands of Jews and other undesirables, then there was no time for the niceties of any recording of personal details. These people usually went directly to their deaths in the gas chambers or at the very end were simply shot.

One of the prison huts now houses a large map of Europe showing all the different places people were transported from to the concentration camp. It is interesting that they came from all over Europe. This map really helps explain why the town of Auschwitz was chosen. The town is surprisingly central when looked at from a total European perspective and it is very well connected by the network of railways which criss-cross Europe. Once people were put in a railway cattle truck then the Nazis knew that they could get that truck to Auschwitz. The Nazis didn't care if they cooped people up for two days or two weeks. The trains would eventually end up in Auschwitz. In the same building there were photographs of children who were used for "medical" experiments. But these were no investigations into how to improve human health. Some people say that these "medical" experiments were really a form of torture given another name. No respected members of the German scientific community were involved. Nazis like Josef Mengele an SS officer working for inter alia the interests of IG Farben led this work.

Auschwitz 1 has its torture block and we were taken through that by our guide. In this block we were shown the cell where Maximilian Kolbe lived his last days until be was murdered. He was a Polish Franciscan priest who as a prisoner in Auschwitz volunteered to take the place of a man condemned to death by the Nazis. In August 1941 a prisoner appeared to have escaped from the camp and as a reprisal the Nazis selected 10 other prisoners to be killed by starvation. One of the 10 men selected to die by the camp wardens was a Franciszek Gajowniczek who broke down and cried: "My wife! My children! I will never see them again!" At this the priest Kolbe, who had been already imprisoned, stepped forward and requested that he should take Gajowniczek's place. Surprisingly his request was granted. Kolbe survived confinement and torture for two weeks, much longer than most others and was actually still conscious in his starvation cell when he was murdered by lethal injection. It is interesting to note that Franciszek Gajowniczek survived his time at Auschwitz, returned to his family and lived to be an old man. According to our Polish guide the irony of this incident concerning the death of Kolbe and the other nine prisoners is that there had not been a successful escape or even an attempted escape from Auschwitz[18]. The missing prisoner was later found dead in the lavatories.

Our visit to the torture block was at a very fast pace. We rushed down dark and damp passages of the building. This was a very depressing place and it was just as well to move quickly. Some of our group began to flag and one of our group, a young French woman, began to cry.

Then we were taken to the gas chamber and the ovens block. After the five minutes in here there was more than one woman crying. There was not much to learn from seeing the gas chamber and the ovens. Our guide stressed the poisonous nature of Zyklon-B and the large quantity which

---

[18] Although the Polish guide stated that no one escaped from Auschwitz this is not true. Maybe some meaning she was trying to communicate was lost due to language differences. Or maybe no Poles escaped. Emotions were quite strained during the tour of the camp. In fact some sources say that as many as 600 people escaped and that nearly half of them were not recaptured. Those who were captured were generally returned to the camp, then tortured and executed. Also it appears that in some cases the guards gratuitous murdered a number of people from the unit from which an escape had happened. Consequently escape was not a frequently occurring event. In particular it was extremely difficult for a Jew, who would have been from Hungary or some other foreign lands to survive in German occupied Poland. They would have had no infrastructure to support them in any attempt to get back home. So perhaps the greatest chance of survival was to stay put in the camp.

was used in the camp. We were told how busy the other section was to keep up with the disposal of the bodies and how it couldn't cope and how bodies had to be disposed of in nearby mass graves. What I hadn't known was that the bones of the victims did not burn in the ovens and that they were then ground down and used as fertiliser on farms in the neighbourhood. Was this a sort of once or twice removed cannibalism?

As we were leaving this block we heard a loud noise which appeared to be a bugle call. In fact it was some sort of animal horn called a Shofar that was being blown. Among the groups on the official tours which were being conducted by the museum staff, there was a group of people dressed in prayer shawls and yarmulkes who had come into the gas chamber and were holding some sort of remembrance service. We moved quickly on.

When we finished our tour of Auschwitz 1 we were taken by bus the few kilometres to Auschwitz-Birkenau. Our Polish guide told us that during the Nazi administration of the camps there was a 15 kilometre exclusion zone around the camps so that ordinary people could not get near them. Auschwitz-Birkenau was much bigger than Auschwitz 1 and it certainly needed to be. This was the camp for the Final Solution. We have a building pointed out to us where the colour of the bricks is permanently stained by Zyklon-B, the gas used in the gas chambers. We are shown where the extension to the railway track was laid to bring in the Hungarian Jews. The Hungarian Jews were not really brought to Auschwitz-Birkenau for labour in the same way as they had been brought to Auschwitz 1. A small number of Jews were used as labour but mostly this camp was for death. In any event by the time the Hungarian Jews arrived in number everyone sort of believed that the war was lost and that the murder of these people was something the Nazis was doing for the benefit of post-war Europe. Of course this does not take into account the fact that a material number of Nazis thought that they would develop the "Wonder Weapon" which would save them. And indeed if they had developed the atomic bomb they would certainly have used it.

Auschwitz-Birkenau was built for the processing of very large numbers of people. Unlike Auschwitz 1, the railway actually goes into the camp at Auschwitz-Birkenau. The victims were unloaded from the cattle carts where they were faced with SS guards with clubs and whips and fierce dogs. There they were processed by the activity which the Nazis called selection. This took place on the railway platform. Selecting was a simple business. Anyone who could provide a hard day's labour was selected to work. Children, old people, or anyone who was sick or in other ways incapable of a day's hard labour were selected for gassing. Those who were to live were then tattooed with their camp number.

But whether you were selected to live or die you were immediately separated from your property, in most cases a suitcase. As soon as the victims were moved away from their suitcases the Nazi looters arrived and took any valuables – including old clothing - they could find. Many of the Jews who arrived at Auschwitz-Birkenau had some money or some jewellery in their luggage and it is clear that stealing this was an important part of the Nazis' objectives. Then the non-valuables were scooped up and stored in the warehouses mentioned above.

Many thousands were arriving every day. Only about 10% of the Hungarian Jews were subject to selection procedures. The majority were taken directly to the gas chambers. In fact the gas chambers could not always cope with the numbers and so people were shot in the open and their bodies thrown into mass graves. It seems that the Nazis' High Command felt that they had to redress the fact that the Hungarian Jews had been left alone during the earlier years of the war and they called for the immediate murder of as many of them as possible.

The guide describes the conditions in this camp, but by this time I had largely lost interest. One of the few remarks that I can remember is that she says Hungarian Jews were lucky because Budapest is close and therefore they only had to endure two or three days in a cattle wagon. Some other Jews had a seven or even ten day journey from their home city before getting to Auschwitz-Birkenau. I was sure that there was a language difference between me and the guide and that she did not intend this to sound so callous.

The tour has now been running for four hours without a break and we are all exhausted, physically and even more so, emotionally. There is just so much that anyone can take in. There has been no intermission or a chance for a sit down or a simple drink. It was a forced march. It was just too intensive for everyone. We were grateful that it was over and we were dropped off near the railway station. No one had much to say as we waited for our train.

So what did I learn from my trip to Auschwitz?

First, it is very unlikely that Mariska was ever an inmate of the camps. As a middle aged woman coming to Auschwitz-Birkenau in the second half of 1944 she would almost certainly have been transported directly to the gas chambers. It is hard to know whether this makes me feel better or worse. The whole thing is so grotesque that it is hard to believe what actually happened. Since time immemorial human beings have been murdered in the most atrocious ways. And not only by individual murderers, but also by armies, the police and by state bureaucrats. But the massive scale of these murders is hard to comprehend.

Being at Auschwitz makes me once again ask why did this happen and why did it happen in the way that it did. Of course there is really no answer to this question. In a sense the Nazis did this because they could. Would it have happened in other places at other times if raw power had fallen into the hands of a few people? Were the Nazis "mad" or were they just "bad"? There are many other questions which are equally unanswerable and which are equally haunting such as: How many Nazis were there? Does someone have to have been a member of the Party to be considered a Nazi? Was Party membership enough or should we reserve the name Nazi for someone with real blood on their hands? What made someone become a Nazi? What made someone work in a concentration camp? Having been recruited or seconded to a concentration camp could you as a person opt to leave? I suppose not.

These are some of the other reflections which arose from this trip.

There was more than one motive behind the Nazi attitude towards the Jews. But even taking all their objections to Jews into account the intensity of the hatred of the Jews is hard to understand. It seems that one of their primary missions was to murder Jews at almost any cost. It has been pointed out that the resources used at Auschwitz and the other 5 extermination camps, if used for military purposes would have strengthened the German war machine considerably and could maybe have changed the course of the war. The intensity of the hatred is a real puzzle. But it does show clearly how hatred is so self-destructive.

Can Nazism be understood rationally? Nazism grew up during a period of unimaginable deprivation in middle Europe during the 1920s and 1930s. Economic and social conditions were not good during much of this period anywhere in the world. Western Europe was in a state of post World War 1 recession. Although the USA was relatively sound in the period immediately post World War 1, by 1929 the Great Depression had set in. Whatever problems existed in Western Europe and the USA, Germany and Austria, the rest of middle Europe was in a really dreadful state.

Life in middle Europe was for a large number of people dominated by hunger; it was cold; it was damp; it was joyless; it was grim beyond our ability to understand it. Disease was rampant and there was little medical service available. Furthermore there was little hope for improvements to the ordinary people's lot. Alongside this deprivation there was evidence of certain groups of people doing well and living rich lives. The hapless politicians were not poverty stricken. Civil servants and other functionaries had regular incomes. Conditions may have been difficult for professionals, bankers and merchants, but they were coping well enough with the depression. Shopkeepers were surviving. In essence society was deeply divided and the lower echelons had genuine grievances and they needed someone to blame for their plight.

Among the groups who were doing well even during this period were Jews. Although it is a classical anti-Semite myth that all Jews were rich, many Jews were middle class – only a small number were poor. For a very long time Jews have had several compulsions which led to prosperity. They have generally worked very hard. They have prized education more than others. They have been entrepreneurial in their outlook. They have been highly self reliant. From time immemorial Jews have been excluded from whole swathes of civil and economic life. There are different views as to the reasons for this, but whatever they are, Jews have created societies for themselves which have been seen by some as remote and uncaring about their neighbours. Jews have been accused of only looking after themselves.

Along comes power hungry, money grabbing unscrupulous politicians. These people recognise no limits to the use or rather the abuse of power. Might and only might was right to them. They needed a scapegoat for the conditions in middle Europe and a scapegoat that couldn't defend itself. They could take money and property away from Jews and they could use them as slaves. When you take this situation and combine it with Nazi concepts of racial purity then you have something to sell to the depressed and hungry masses. Also once you have stolen what you can and have people as slaves the idea of the Final Solution is not far away. Slaves wear out, especially if you don't feed them. Worn out slaves are useless and can be disposed of like worn out property.

Mixed up in this quagmire of unacceptable thinking is the fascinating myth that if you steal things from the rich (or even people who are not that rich but have a bit more than yourself), somehow the situation of the poor will be improved. But theft does not bring wealth. If anything theft is a destroyer of wealth. Getting out of poverty is not a function of how much jewellery, furniture, clothes you can get your hands on. Taking property from the economically successful has often made the underprivileged or poor even poorer.

The need to steal from the Jews was brought home to me by the film made by the Red Army when they discovered the hundreds of thousands or millions of sets of clothes belonging to the murdered Jews and the mountain of spectacles, shaving and tooth brushes the Nazis so carefully kept. Our Polish guide repeated what had been said in that Russian film – "Who in Germany would have wanted to wear the old clothes or use the shaving or tooth brushes of murdered Jews?".

There seems to be no end to human depravity, stupidity and greed.

Although I am energetically agnostic my final reflection on the train back to Krakow having left Auschwitz was just how wise are the admonitions – Thou shall not kill and Thou shall not covet thy neighbours' goods. It's a pity that people have not followed these ideas over the generations.

Chapter Twelve

The Epitaphs!

This has been an attempt to tell a personal story, as much as it is known. No doubt masses of detail have been left out and thus it is by no means a complete story and I am very aware that the tale begs a number of questions to which I do not know the answers. Furthermore it is not only the story of Steve but also some of the story of those who were around him. But it is not really the story of Patsy (there is much more to tell about her not included here). Nor is this the story of Jean or Brendan, although it has described some very small parts of their lives. Also as I have written this story it has to be, by its very nature, some of my story, but again only a small part of it.

I have been trying to find a few words to describe this story. It is clearly a biography but it is in at least one sense much more than that. I clearly remember as a child in Ireland a number of people talking about death and they would say, "Well if there is anything going on after death I will do my very best to come back and tell you about it". Of course this was always said in jest although there is probably a greater interest in the occult in Ireland than in many other parts of the world. The Irish are certainly very superstitious. The reason that I mention this is that as I said before I believe that Steve effectively reached out from beyond the grave and touched his three children. He touched Brendan by setting him up with the name of the village in which he was born and in so doing allowing him the opportunity to visit and discover his background. Brendan's experience in turn touched me and resulted in my visiting Rácalmás a couple of times, finding family friends in Canada and eventually writing this book.

But I think that Jean's life was changed more than the rest of our's which I will describe later.

In a sense Steve's memory haunted us and probably still does in a quite real way. I use the word haunted with care as I do not believe in ghosts in the normal sense of the word. It seems to me that a ghost is not an objective external entity but rather an internalised idea, perhaps some sort of a memory which someone lives with successfully or unsatisfactorily. If this is the case then the question becomes, to what extent can we live with our memories or ideas about the past? It was for this reason that I have begun to think of *The Story of Steve* as more than a biography. It is both a biography and a ghost story and the ghost in question is my memories and ideas of Steve and our past. Can this ghost be put to rest? Do I want it to?

Maybe this type of ghost is like a genie - not the sort of thing that can easily be put back in its bottle – if ghosts ever go back into bottles!

This book is quite a different one to what I thought it would be at the outset. I thought that I would just write down some memories about the family when we lived in Ireland and the early days in Africa. But that would have been so incomplete. The story simply spread into a much bigger arena. It has taken me into areas of which I previously knew very little about such as Hungarian history. I knew absolutely nothing about what had happened there between the end of the First World War and the end of the Second World War. I had only the vaguest idea about concentration camps and I certainly knew nothing about what actually happened at Auschwitz.

I quickly wrote the first draft of this story over a month or two while I was travelling abroad on business and then it has taken me 7 years to return to the second draft which I have found considerably more challenging. Originally I had not envisaged that writing this story would make me want to return to Hungary or to go to see Auschwitz for myself which was no simple thing to do.

I have become aware that it would be useful to make some sort of sense of this story as a whole rather than just seeing it as a series of tales. This is hard to do. Nonetheless I will try to do it now.

I have tried various ways of describing the story but none of them seem adequate. At one level it is just the story of one of the millions of central and eastern European refugees who were displaced before or during or after the Second World War. Steve was just one of the Jews who, unlike his mother, got away. Mariska was a woman of some foresight – at least when it came to her children. I don't know if Mariska foresaw her fate. Many Jews didn't. But I see in the photographs of Mariska's face a stubbornness which says to me, "To hell with these people, they are not going to make me run away. I can take whatever they can dole out".

Steve like many refugees tried, pretty successfully, to completely leave his history behind - at least during his own life. He became an Irishman through and through. I have heard people say to him in Dublin, "You are from County Clare, aren't you?" Like the old Irish saying he actually, in some respects, became more Irish than the Irish themselves. But this denial of the past usually can't be achieved without paying a price. It is difficult to know just how uncomfortable it was for Steve to leave everything and everybody he had previously known behind. It was not as though he had had an unhappy childhood or that he had no circle of friends back home. He did not appear to have any real emotional problems so we don't know whether he paid any price or if he actually felt quite comfortable living his secret, which he successfully took to his grave.

Interestingly enough Steve did not take what is perhaps the final step of assimilating into Ireland, which many others had done over the ages. His own grandfather and even his brother had taken this step. These members of his family changed their surnames. As mentioned Steve's paternal grandfather had changed his name to Remenyi from Hoffer and his maternal grandfather had changed his name from Cohen to Kalmár. And on becoming an American citizen Imre had become John Remy – a name much easier to cope with than Remenyi.

Steve could have changed his name to O'Reilly or Ryan which some would say are not all that far from Remenyi. The name Remenyi has always produced spelling problems and life would have been easier with an Irish name. This would have been another step in firmly closing or rather locking the door to his past behind him. If Steve had changed his name then it would have been difficult to find out about the family's past. So if he really wanted to bury his past why didn't he do a complete job? He was after all a very thorough man. Maybe he didn't want the past totally buried. There is also the issue of why tell his son, Brendan that he was born in Rácalmás? Without that clue we would never have learnt about his family. It is very unlikely that Magda would have told us as Steve had made her swear (whatever that might mean) that she would not tell us about his family.

This is also the story of how consistent hard work and a lucky break can drag one and one's family, out of post-war poverty to the middle class. It wasn't easy and he found the going quite tough at times. Steve always gave great importance to his work often at the expense of his own leisure time. In fact thinking about the way he lived, work often appeared to be more important than his family. The lucky break, the good fortune in Ireland with regards the Irish Sweepstakes, was in a sense paid back by the misfortune in travelling some 6,000 miles to South Africa to find that the promised job wasn't there. On reflection he wasn't an especially lucky man and although he had for a short period of time a minor entrepreneurial streak with the charcoal business in Ireland during the war he subsequently did not take risks with his family's income.

In the end Steve achieved a comfortable standard of living and in some sense he was able to help his children obtain the qualification they seemed to want. His values were sufficiently traditional that he didn't really see the need for Jean to obtain a university education and he was far too set on Brendan qualifying as an accountant which delayed Brendan finding a more appropriate career niche for himself. It is possible that taking his family to South Africa may be seen as a mistake when looked at from the long term point of view. None of the children settled there. Of course Steve did not go to South Africa with a long term perspective or aim. Thus it was rather ironical that both he and Patsy died in Port Elizabeth in the Cape Province.

It is also a story of how someone who has come from a family which was destroyed by the Nazis was nonetheless prepared to live and bring his own family up in countries which treated many of its citizens very badly. Some people say that apartheid was nearly as bad as Nazism. I do know that Steve and many other people, for that matter, objected strongly to comparing apartheid to Nazism. But I have never heard a black person object to that comparison. It is always whites who got and still get annoyed. Steve was not unusual in this respect. I have tried hard to understand this tolerance of Apartheid and I think that I may now have an explanation. Steve was a man of his times. When in Southern Africa he was a white middle class male European who was born in the early years of the 20th century. At that time Europe thought of itself as the cradle of civilisation and the centre of knowledge and culture. After all, the great empires of the world, if you ignore Egypt and Babylon and a few other spectacular centres of culture and civilisation, were European. In Steve's youth there was the British Empire and the French Empire. The Russian Empire had morphed into the Union of the Soviet Socialist Republics – the Russian Empire under any other name. The memory of the German and Austrian Empires were fresh in the European consciousness. He would not have seen it as incongruous that black people should be the "hewers of wood and the bearers of water". That is how the world was for thousands of years and in some senses it still is. It was simply a matter that Steve was unquestioning. I have also given some thought to what made the world change from its deep seated racism – this does not suggest that we have been able to eradicate racism. Clearly it is unlikely that there has been one cause. Perhaps an important cause was the way black or Afro Americans' became soldiers in the Second World War. They were particularly visible in England as was racist attitudes against them. They fought for their country so they expected to be treated like other citizens. They came home to the USA knowing that the time for them to speak up had come and this steadily spread into the American consciousness. Certainly my awareness of the injustice of racism was influenced by not only what I saw in South Africa but what I knew people like Martin Luther King Jr were saying and doing in the USA.

Furthermore many Jews lived very comfortably under apartheid hardly ever empathising with the blacks and perhaps never wondering about what it felt like to be at the receiving end of the oppression of the regime (of course there were leading members of the political opposition who were Jewish, such as Helen Suzman, but their vision of freedom in South Africa was not acceptable to the black majority). To my mind what Apartheid and Nazism had in common was that they both were oppressive political systems that had total disregard for specific people as human beings. Nazism was more extreme. Further the German character with its tendency to or need for industrial efficiency totally out performed Apartheid.

No matter which perspective one takes apartheid was untenable. A few million whites couldn't keep tens of millions of black and brown people down for long. Also the world powers had clearly set their faces against overt racism. Not that there wasn't plenty of implicit racism in other parts of the world then and even today. That the apartheid regime couldn't last was patently obvious even in 1958 but Steve was only coming to South Africa for a "few" years. Apartheid ended miraculously peacefully which is a great credit to the ANC with some credit also due to the white leaders of the day. But the legacy which apartheid created is a country in which many of its citizens of all races are directly affected by the fear of violent crime. To be exposed to a mugging or a car hijacking or a burglary or some other crime is always a real possibility for anyone. South Africa is today a country with problems for all its citizens.

On another level it is just another story of a pretty dysfunctional family. This dysfunctional family stuck together, at least in some senses, for quite a long time before it relatively gracefully drifted apart. There was relatively little major drama. There was no divorce. Steve and Patsy bonded well. It's hard to really know why as they were so different. It probably has something to do with the fact that they started their married life under such difficult circumstances that they felt that they shared a lot. Steve was not a quitter and he was always hopeful that things would get better. But most of the time Steve simply closed his eyes to the family problems. 'Keep the peace at any cost" seemed to be his motto. 'Don't argue with your mother' was another one of his refrains. I felt that there was a high degree of moral cowardice in this approach of his. Thus the children just simply drifted away. No doubt there are millions of even more dysfunctional families around who didn't manage to stick together for such a long time and in which the children were even more disgruntled than those of Steve and Patsy. Steve would certainly not have seen his family as dysfunctional. He had a sense that families should stick together, and despite the fact that he left home for a voyage which he and Mariska must have known might have taken him away forever at the tender age of 19, he often pointed out that is was not a bad thing for children to live with their parent until they married even if that was in their 30s or 40s. According to him this was common in Ireland.

It is also a story how one can live within a family and never really know the individuals who comprise it. More or less, everybody just got on with their own lives and didn't get round to knowing or understanding each other very much. It is not too clear as to who should take a lead in making a family more interested in each other. Perhaps this lack of closeness is not really unusual. But on the other hand it wouldn't have taken much for Steve to have created some sort of family self awareness of each other within and between the members of the family. There is not much likelihood that Patsy had any real insight into how other people felt or worked. She was just too self preoccupied. She was not a unifying type of person. Her nature was fundamentally divisive. She was the archetype of what the Irish call a Mé Féiner.

Another way of looking at this story is to question why the children didn't ask more about their father and his background. I am surprised that we didn't. I am surprised that he didn't want to tell us. To look at Steve or to hear him talk you would never had known that he had a deeply hidden secret. How he sustained this secret is, to me, one of the more interesting elements of Steve's story. At least I am very grateful to Steve that his secret was that he was a Jew and not a Nazi. It would have been a major problem for me if Steve or his father for that matter had been an official in the Arrow Cross or an officer in the Hungarian Gendarmes. After I met Imre in New York I had for just a moment the awful feeling that there may have been Nazis in my family. As an old man Imre's bitterness was all encompassing and he could have been a Nazi. At that time I immediately dispelled that idea. This would have been just too much. I am very grateful that we do not have such a situation in the family. At the end of the day secrets within a family are essentially unhelpful if not down right destructive.

And Steve was quite passionate about keeping his secret. The explanation of the row in France between Patsy and Jacques Kalmár described in an earlier chapter, appears to have been a great red herring. I know that this is speculation but I would bet that Jacques told Pasty some of the information about the family background and also said that Armand and Steve were Jews. Steve would have objected very strongly to this. He would have seen such a revelation as a major infringement of his right to privacy. This caused Steve to break contact with Jacques and I believe that he put out the story that the big row between Patsy and Jacques was over some trivial matter like the choice of a restaurant. I had actually asked for details of the row and I had got nowhere. And of course, we all believed Steve's story. It was after all the sort of thing that Patsy would or could have done and was thus perfectly believable.

No doubt being a cautious man he had some justification for not telling us in the early years when we were children. It may be that the Irish would not have been accepting of him as a Jew. Marrying Patsy as a Jew would have added another layer of complication to their already difficult situation. He certainly could not have married Patsy so quickly if he had been of another faith. Were the Irish in 1942 anti-Semitic or perhaps to what extent were the Irish semi-Semitic at that time? It is said that the last pogrom[19] in the British Isles was in Limerick[20] but that had been in 1904 when, Father John Creagh, of the Catholic Arch-Confraternity of Limerick delivered a sermon in which he referred to Jewish merchants as "leeches" and accused them of sucking the blood of the Irish. The Jewish quarter in Collooney Street was only saved by the Royal Irish Constabulary who had to intervene. Although there were about 4,000 Jews in Ireland during the Second World War the Irish Civil Service were not enthusiastic in allowing more Jews into the country. There seems to have been a restrictive policy towards helping Jews fleeing the Nazis, as there was in most countries during that period. When writing about Ireland and Jews and Nazis there is one incident which should be mentioned. On hearing of Hitler's death, Eamonn de Valera went to the German Embassy and presented his condolences to the German people. Attempts

---

[19] Some sources define a pogram as a riot whiles other describe the word as meaning a massacre. The word pogrom is used here to mean riot.

[20] There have been some anti-Semitic riots in the United Kingdom in the 20th century. One of the better known events was the riot at Brynmawr in South Wales in August 1911. It was a time of intense social unrest in the United Kingdom in general and the Valleys of Wales in particular. One Saturday night a bunch of people who were later referred to as "young hooligans" broke the windows of all the Jewish shopkeepers in the village, while singing Welsh hymns. The story goes that this may have got further out of hand if it were not for the good offices of Sergeant Thomas Price who helped build barricades to prevent the "young hooligans" from inflicting further damages on Jewish property and maybe even people. In June 1917 there were riots in Leeds after the Chief Constable claimed that nearly three quarters of the Russian Jews in the city had refused to enlist in the British armed forces to fight in the Great War. In autumn 1947 further riots occurred in Manchester and Liverpool. In general the Jewish community leaders played down the significance of these events.

have been made to explain away this unimaginable act of folly but none of them make much sense. The most convincing explanation was that Eamonn de Valera was so obsessed with Ireland's neutrality that he had to appear to be moved by the death of the man who destroyed tens of millions of people and destroyed the lives of hundreds of millions. Both Ireland's Jewish population and Israel seems to have forgiven de Valera and a forest has been planted in Israel in his name[21].

It does seem that it was wise of Steve not to have declared his former religious/cultural connections in Hungary. But when the Remenyi children became adults it would have been appropriate to allow us to know about our roots.

There is a flip side to Steve's secrecy. Is it possible to keep a secret for 40 years from a family who have an active interest in finding out about the past? Did we, the family not have any interest in his past? As we didn't why did we not? I don't know the answers to these questions. The record shows we had virtually no interest in finding out about Steve's family past. I am puzzled by this; I wonder where our curiosity was. Are all children like this? Do children not care about their roots? Or do they just not perceive themselves as having roots? Maybe, to some extent at least, our antipathy towards our immediate family was a sort of barrier to our actually wanting to find out more about the further-away-family and the past. Learning more about your wider family is not guaranteed to be pleasant. For me this was well proven by meeting Imre in New York.

Perhaps this is also a story of someone who actually wanted his family to know about his roots but was just unable to bring himself to tell them during his lifetime. Just perhaps, Steve's telling Brendan that he was born in Rácalmás was not really a slip of the tongue. Maybe Steve decided to

---

[21] I have only just become aware of a documentary film made by Tile Films called *Ireland's Nazis*. It would appear that Ireland in the late 1940s and the 1950s admitted a number of Nazis who seemed to have been directly involved in genocide of Jews and others. It also argues that the Catholic Church were directly complicit in supporting the escape of these people from European authorities. One of these was Otto Skorzeny of the Waffen-SS. Skorzeny was one of Hitler's personal favourites for his bravery at the Eastern Front and for his role in the escape of Mussolini from imprisonment at Gran Sasso. The film was broadcast by RTE in early 2007. The film makers point out that although requested the Irish Government has refused to make the immigration files on these individuals public. In so doing they are making it impossible for us to know just how sympathetic the Irish Government of that time was to Nazi criminals. The refusal to make these files public suggests that there is material in them which is embarrassing to the Irish Republic. This film clearly suggests that Ireland as a Catholic country was antipathetic to Jews. It would appear that a material number of the Irish population felt that accounts of the Holocaust may have been exaggerated and that these stories were in some way pro-British. The film points a finger especially at two senior civil servants whom it describes as strongly anti-Semitic.

give Brendan a clue. He knew that Brendan would not rush off to Hungary to visit his old home village, but maybe it gave Steve some sort of pleasure to know that he had planted a seed that might grow into something surprising to us. It's very hard to know what was really going on in his mind. I guess whether or not this was the case, it was more or less inevitable that once we knew about Rácalmás then we would get to know something about the Remenyi family's history. We will never really know but Steve may have been playful enough to have created the possibility of our finding out about his past, but much later.

Now that Steve has been dead for more than 20 years I believe that I now have a more balanced view of him. Patsy used to say that I and her other children thought that Steve was St George and that she was the Dragon. This was the way she expressed her resentment for the imbalance of esteem and affection which was clearly visible in the later years and as they were living in the St George's Club this allusion to St George and the Dragon was actually quite amusing and perhaps pertinent, and furthermore this was a pretty accurate description when he died. Through the lens of passing years views can change. Looking at Steve today, with the benefit of some years of reflection his positive contribution to the family is not so wonderfully clear. There has been a very substantial deterioration in my view of Steve and his role in the family. If I were to write the epitaph of Steve Remenyi today I would say,

"It is surprising how little a father has to do, to have his kids love and admire him".

Maybe all parents are just lucky in that way.

As said before in effect, Steve was a good enough father. And good enough, no matter how you define it, is all that can be hoped for. He had his own personal problems which he masterfully hid from us. What has also happened to my thoughts on Steve is that I now wonder if he was actually a good enough husband. He kept this relationship with his wife and with his children fairly separate and didn't try to integrate them. Steve never complained about Patsy and except for one conversation he never said one word that was critical of her. Patsy never complained about him either although she did complain enough about the circumstances (her having to work and having to leave Durban and again a few years later leave Salisbury) which to some extent he created.

What it really amounted to is that as children, Steve gave us a little bit of his time, in that he took us swimming or something similar. He always found a few pence to buy his kids an ice cream and he didn't rush around with a cane to beat us as Patsy was once prone to do. And maybe that's really all that most kids need from their parents.

What Steve had to offer to his adult children actually remained the same; it was the grown up equivalent of an ice-cream and a swim. He would have the time to have a drink and a chat with us and he would find a few quid if we needed it. Sometimes this money was on loan but other times he would give it with no strings attached. He often said not to tell Patsy that he had given us money as she would be jealous. Steve's cult of secrecy was never far away.

And then there was Patsy.

Patsy has been dead about 10 years. An epitaph for her is more complicated. Maybe it should read like this.

Although severely damaged by child poverty and paternal beating she managed somehow to survive although at some considerable cost to others.

This would hardly be a compliment to Maurice. There is certainly no point in demonising Patsy or for that matter Maurice. She was simply a victim of her childhood and also of her times. Some people rise to the challenge of poverty and over strict fathers and teachers, Patsy didn't. It would seem that Patsy spent her whole life worrying about no one other than Patsy, well, maybe occasionally about Steve. Whenever she thought about her children she seemed to feel that they were primarily impediments of some sort and I guess the truth was that we actually were impediments to her. It seems that she also thought as we went through school we were getting the education she deserved and never got.

Of course we all have to live our lives with the hands we are dealt and sometimes they are quite awful hands.

But exactly what else she would have done with her life is hard to know. There is no doubt that she was a victim of the Sheehan family circumstances in the 1920s and the 1930s. But her history was not the fault of her children, although she behaved as though it was. It is all too easy to take your resentment at the deal that life has given you out on your children.

It is probably true to say that Patsy would have been better off if she had not been married. Having no children would certainly have suited her better. She was most resentful of me because I was the one who forced her into a marriage and a domestic life. She probably should have been a spinster writer. If she had lived 45 years later her dyslexia would have been noticed and she would have been taught strategies to cope with it. She would also have had a word processor with a spell checker and she could have written to her heart's content, instead of struggling through her short stories and articles.

It is now not clear to me that Steve was actually such a good husband to her. There was no doubt a very strong bond between them. He certainly provided for all her worldly needs as best he could. But he was not really sympathetic to her being lonely and isolated in Salisbury or in the initial years in Port Elizabeth. In fact even when we lived in Durban his jobs always entailed long unsociable hours and he just left her up to her own devices – which is of course what he had done in Ireland for the 10 years he worked at sea for Irish Shipping. In his defence this was a time when men were men who went to work and the women stayed at home waiting.

I once asked Steve why he had put so many hours into his work and whether he had done this so that he did not have the time to spend with Patsy. Of course he did not give me a straight answer. But he did say that the problems which he had had with Patsy were over. I didn't understand this and once again I am surprised with myself for not pressing him for a clearer answer which I might have actually understood. In fact for many years I had wondered why Steve and Patsy had stuck together as it seemed to me that they didn't have much reason for so doing. Perhaps they were scared of starting a new life on their own. Maybe they actually didn't need any more out of a relationship than what they gave each other.

Jean once asked me why our family was in such a mess. My reply at that time was that when Steve married Patsy she was still 19 years of age. She was far too young or immature for the responsibilities of being a wife and a mother. It seemed to me that somehow Steve's love and attention had somehow inhibited her personal growth and maturity. But I am not sure anymore whether there is any sense in that view of what happened. On the whole probably not.

Steve and Patsy may have been a handsome couple in their youth. But they were very complicated and in many ways a great challenge to their children.

As for the three siblings, it is hard to know what effect having parents as complicated as Steve and Patsy really have on children. Maybe quite a lot and then maybe not much. It's not difficult to imagine a more tranquil childhood but whether it would have made much difference to what we are today no one can tell.

There is no doubt that all three siblings are complicated mixtures of Steve and Patsy and products of having lived in more than a dozen houses and in my case having gone to six different schools. Jean has of course the added challenge of physically looking just like Patsy and she perhaps more closely resembles her in other ways too. Jean, who had never really expressed much interest in religious matters, converted to Judaism as a result of the revelations about Steve's past. I have found this action a great puzzle and can only believe that prior to her conversion she must have been enormously unhappy. I wonder if Patsy would not have been more contented if she had done the same and became a Jew as well. It has always seemed to me that there is a lot of theatre surrounding Judaism and that would have appealed to Patsy's nature.

There is no doubt that having Steve and Patsy as parents has given all three an interesting, colourful and challenging legacy to live with if not live down.

And wouldn't life be boring without challenges. I am acutely aware that there are many lessons for me from reflecting on the story of Steve and Patsy and I do hope that I will be able to learn something from them. But who knows if I will be able to so do. Learning is always a difficult process and its effects, if any are never guaranteed. Knowledge does not always bring with it the required wisdom to deal with a changed reality.

Chapter Thirteen

On reflection

I told a half dozen friends about Brendan's experience in the Catholic grave yard in Racalmas and the subsequent discovery of our Grandfather's headstone in Hebrew in the Jewish cemetery. I also gave an early draft of this book to several friends. I received a number of supportive comments. Only one friend and I should say a good friend of long standing said something to the effect of, "Good God! You are a Semite!" These may not have been his exact words but he decided that the discovery of my connection to Jewry was a good issue with which to pull my leg, forever. I certainly do not feel Semitic and of course I am not a Jew except in the eyes of Hitler or one of his cronies.

On a more serious note only one friend asked me how I felt about this genealogical discovery. This question which stood out among the other comments as it put me directly on the spot. Without having time to think I replied that I was saddened by the fact that my father was not able to share his Hungarian family history with the rest of us. I had felt for a long time that there was something in the family background that was waiting to be revealed and I was indeed most grateful that none of my ancestors were Nazis. It was quite bad enough been related to that old bigot in New York, which was Imre.

But as time has passed I have had more thoughts about Steve, his background and how he spent his life. There is also more to be said about Mariska.

In some ways I wonder at Mariska's ability to send her youngest son away at the relatively tender age of 19 to face on his own the uncertain world of 1938. Of course my view is fashioned by my own life experiences. I have not directly felt the impact of a war or an impending war, nor have I been the object of intense hatred[22]. The courage and the faith which was needed to send her last son away was considerable. Obviously she knew that World War Two was coming and she lived in what was essentially an anti-Semitic country. But virtually no one including the

---

[22] I am aware that from the mid-1930 the Kindertransport moved perhaps as many as tens of thousands of Jewish children out of Germany, Austria, Poland and Czechoslovakia. Some were fostered and some were old enough to take up work. Most of the children never saw their parents again. Some went to the United Kingdom while others were sent to the USA, Canada and Australia. About 1,000 of these children who were resident in the Isle of Man were interned as aliens. Some of the boys when they became old enough were allowed to join the British Army and thus fight against the Nazis. There is a memorial to this initiative at Liverpool Street Station in London.

most worldly-wise Jews were able to envisage the forthcoming holocaust. The application of 20th century technology to mass murder had already been established in the Flanders Fields and in the Valley of the Somme and other parts of Europe[23]. However these were battlefield situations and as such were acceptable to the majority of Europeans. The idea of using mass transportation, large extermination camps and the other ways of killing non-belligerents on a multi-national and multi-million scale were simply outside the imagination of most people until it actually happened[24,25,26]. So, Mariska didn't send Steve away to avoid Auschwitz, but to help him find a better life away from an anti-Semitic country and an impending war. Imre had already gone away and so the idea of immigration was already established.

Steve's acceptance of this instruction to immigrate is also worthy of reflection. Nineteen is very young to go abroad on ones own. Imre was then already 35 years old and didn't have much interest in Steve. Getting away from Racalmas was a great idea as it could only have been stifling to any young person who wanted to experience the "world". Steve had already lived in Budapest for a few of years and Budapest was and still is a particularly fine city with much of what the world has to offer.

Nonetheless Steve went away to find a new life. Having reached the United States of America Steve did not find that country to his likening. He didn't have a long list of complaints about America, rather he said the quality of life there was not good. He pointed to the materialism of American culture which led to some people having to do two jobs to

---

[23] It is estimated that there were 40 million casualties during World War One of which 20 million were deaths. This was the first real evidence of how many people could be murdered through the use of modern technology. World War Two is said to have cost 50 million lives and reflects the further technological development and industrialisation of warfare and murder.

[24] It has only recently become common knowledge that in the early years of the 20th century the German settlers in Deutsch Südwest Afrika (German South West Africa) now Namibia, in the name of ethnic cleansing murdered Herero and Nama people. Although estimates differ it is thought that at least tens of thousands perished with 80% of the Hereros being murdered in 1904 alone. It was in Deutsch Südwest Afrika that the term *Lebensraum* was first used. It is said that this experience in colonial Africa prepared the Germans for the thinking needed for the much larger holocaust to come.

[25] I do not want to give the impression that the Germans were the only colonial power which abused the people whose land they had taken. I do not know of any colonial power which did not. Horrific stories are told about what happened on every continent. The German attack on the peoples of Namibia seems to have been motivated by a desire to annihilate the indigenous population of a whole tribe and this resonates with that happened 30 years later in their own country.

[26] Considering genocide during the 1930s and 1940s it is only fair to mention that the Japanese murdered an unknown number of Chinese. The latest estimates of the Massacre at Nanking suggest as many as 500,000, and this is only one incident in an 8 year war. Also, the Japanese had their own forced experiment unit where they were producing biological weapons. The centre, referred to as Unit 731, was located at Harbin in China, and is where an unknown number of people were tortured and murdered. This period also saw Stalin exterminate tens of millions of his own people.

make ends meet. I don't know how common this type of working life was or is in America but this practice offended Steve sense of a balanced life. Steve also expressed dismay at the high crime rate in that country. This was the America of the late 1930s and early 1940s. He said that there were a number of pressures on Americans which contributed to this high crime rate. There was the materialism mentioned above. There was the size of the country and some of the bigger cities. Steve did not like big cities. There was the presence of many cultures which had not integrated as well as it was often claimed and there was not enough respect expressed for all these groups. I am not at all sure just how genuine he was on this issue. I suspect that deep down he also didn't want to go to America because Imre was there. Looking back he didn't want anything to do with his brother and only went to meet him after Armand's death due to Patsy's enthusiasm that there might be an inheritance involved.

Steve's antipathy for America was balanced by the regard in which he held the British. A number of times he expressed the view that the British Empire was a remarkable achievement especially by such a geographically small country. He admired British courage, pluck and inventiveness. He did not share the ideals and ambitions of the Republican movement in Ireland. He did not believe the Irish nationalist claims made frequently during my schooling in the 1950s that Ireland had won its freedom from England. His comment was, "The English just came to realise that keeping Ireland was more bother than it was worth. So they decided to let it go". He told me more than once that he had met many people in Ireland who privately regretted Ireland's independence and withdrawal from the "Empire". I am sometimes surprised that he didn't move the family to England.

I remain puzzled by his moving his family to South Africa and by his "settler mentality" although as an anglophile being a settler would almost naturally follow. There is no doubt that South Africa is a beautiful country with a magnificent climate. South African's are on the whole a warm and, when they can afford it, a generous people. But South Africa was and still is a troubled land. It is not possible for me to regret having gone to South Africa as I have so many great friends there and wonderful memories of having lived in that country. But I do recognise that there are ways in which my life would have been better if we had not moved to that unstable society. There is also the fact that white immigrants were used by the Nationalist Government as a source of skill and thus at least in part removed the necessity to train their own, black, Indian and mixed race people.

There is also the issue with regards to Steve believing that he could make his "fortune" in South Africa in a few years and then return home to Ireland. In general he was not a naïve man but this thought was unrealistic. Few immigrants achieve that level of riches. Admittedly immigrants work harder when they go abroad. Steve would say that, "At home an Irishman enjoyed nothing more than a leisurely life and a few jars at the end of the day. Abroad they worked long and hard". But nonetheless there are not many immigrants who hit the jackpot. Most immigrants, and definitely not all, have a better life in their new country but they work hard all their lives for it. It could never have been possible for Steve to make a fortune, not that he didn't have a lot of talent and the energy to work very hard, that is never enough. He just wasn't ambitious enough. He was also concerned about the welfare of people working for him and this does not help if you are going to make yourself very rich. After his experience with charcoal in the 1940s he never showed an entrepreneurship flair. I once asked him, "Why didn't you start your own restaurant? You have been successful in turning around restaurants for other people for relatively little reward. Why did you not do that for yourself?" His reply was, "With a wife and three children to support, how could I take the risk?"

There is another interesting effect of having lived in South Africa related to the number of Jews who had immigrated there over the past 100 years. Until the 1948 victory of the Nationalist Party South Africa was reasonably well disposed towards Jews[27]. As a result there was a relatively significant number of Jews among the white population[28]. I have heard it said that Jews composed more than 10% of the population. For no reason to which I can point I acquired a number of Jewish friends over my South African years. At one time I would have had at least as many Jewish friends as non-Jewish friends. A couple of these friendships have survived 30 years. I cannot explain this affinity. As a result of these associations I learnt that there are in most ways little difference between Jews and any other part of the population. Human characteristics seem to be normally distributed though any group and thus most anti-Semitic comments are nothing more than expressions of ignorance. In simple terms most anti-Semetics do not know any Jews. However I feel that I need to comment on what a self styled liberal acquaintance said to me recently

---

[27] Although not openly expressed the Nationalist Party were known to believe that they could not rely on the loyalty of the Jewish population. By the way a similar attitude was frequently expressed about English speaking South Africans who were said to be able to go back to their original roots in United Kingdom.

[28] I have recently been told that South Africa and Ireland had a large percentage of their Jewish population from Lithuania. No explanation as to why this should be the case was offered.

which was, "All Jews are nice. All Jews are good people". This statement is as unworthy of serious comment as are the opposite anti-Semitic remarks.

Although Steve abandoned Judaism he did not adopt Catholicism. Until he was well into his 50s he did not attend church frequently. In the early days in Durban the family attended mass on Sundays. This was largely driven by me as I left Ireland a devout Catholic. When I look back I am truly impressed by just how complete a job the Christian Brothers aided and abetted by Lilly (my grandmother) had indoctrinated me with what are clearly nonsense ideas about God and humankind's relationship to Him[29]. Catholic guilt has to be experienced to be appreciated and the Irish church in the 1950s knew how to plaster it on. Steve had no interest in any of the formal functions of the church. He did not recognise the Catholic requirement to abstain from meat on Friday which was said by the church hierarchy to be punishable by condemnation to the fires of hell for all eternity[30]. Later in life, from the end of his 50s he could frequently go to mass on Sunday. When I asked him why he did this he said, "The hour's service gives me a peaceful interlude in the week, when I can be alone with my own thoughts". He had previously told me that he didn't need a Priest, Rabbi, Guru, Imam or Fakir to help guide him to the after-life. I pressed him as to why he went to the Catholic Church for mass on Sundays and he replied, "It is near by and your mother has friends there". I suspect that there are many people who like him go to church for rather superficial reasons, although few would admit it. The fact that he received the last rights of the Catholic Church was no indication of his religious beliefs. Steve would not have liked to have been put on the spot with a question directly enquiring about his religious beliefs. His behaviour did not show any connection to an active belief in a god. I believe that he would have described himself as an agnostic, as I do.

Reflecting on the chain of events that led Brendan to that Catholic grave-yard in the Hungarian countryside in a cold, windy late autumn afternoon is fascinating. Several people to whom I have told this story have said that Steve gave Brendan the name of his village as he wanted the rest of his family to find out about this Jewish childhood. I cannot make my mind up on that issue, believing this is like believing in conspiracy theory. I am inclined to believe that the world is driven by incompetencies and mistakes rather then by plots. I don't think that if I had been given the village name I would have gone exploring the Hungarian countryside.

---

[29] I hope that readers will appreciate that I use a capital G and H ironically.

[30] It is hard to believe that the Catholic Church was able to make adult men and women believe this.

Maybe Steve saw a greater need to visit family roots in Brendan than in me.

There are many more questions which I would like to be able to ask Steve but alas his death took so much information to the grave. If I were now asked "How I felt about the discovery of his real background", I would answer differently. I still feel sad that he was unable to tell us about Hungary but this is not my only feeling about the situation. When I think about it I am frustrated by not knowing more about the details of his family. Fortunately I don't it think about it very often. On the other hand I have thought about it enough to have put hundreds of hours into writing this book. There is no doubt that in a sense the writing has been somewhat therapeutic and definitely quite educational. But the situation is still unsatisfactory. It becomes even more unsatisfactory if the suggestion that Steve deliberately gave the name Racalmas to Brendan with the intention of our finding out about his background in the future.

Indeed writing this book and reflecting on the events have helped me understand my family and myself better. But it has not supplied me with many answers. Of course there are none and this is the only conclusion at which it is reasonable to arrive.

I leave it to a friend of Steve's who has tried to sum him up in a poem at the end of the final chapter.

After the story was over?

I hadn't known the name of the ship on which Steve travelled to Dublin until a few weeks ago. The ship had only been mentioned in the family as the Finnish ship which was trapped in Dublin and eventually impounded and then taken over by Irish Shipping. I needed to find out her name.

I surfed the web and easily found a picture of the ship and its name, the Vicia, and the picture is now in the front of this book. I was initially surprised at how small she was and how old she looked. Clearly this was no modern ocean going vessel. The ship was purchased by Irish Shipping on April 20, 1942 but she did not go into service for three years as she needed extensive repairs. It took all that time for the ship repair company at Rushbrooke to get the necessary steel and engine parts to make her sea worthy again. However during my research I was assured by men who had sailed onboard her that she was a fine ship for her time.

In exploring the web on this subject I found some wonderful websites and as a result of this I met (telephonically and by e-mail) some great people. The first man I met had a special interest in the history of shipping in Ireland and who was in contact with a number of Irish seafarers. He had not met Steve although he told me that Steve's name was well known in the community of older seafarers in Dublin. I was surprised by this as I would previously have said that Steve's 12 year service would not be known outside his close friends. Also as Steve's stay with Irish Shipping ended nearly 50 years ago I was expecting him to be well forgotten. But this is clearly not the case. This first man pointed me to a copy of the Irish Shipping in-house magazine which carried an article in which Steve was mentioned and described as one of the officers suing the owners of the Vicia. This man then passed me on to another and within a few days I had spoken to about a dozen people most of which were ex-Irish Shipping and all of whom knew Steve or knew of Steve. The youngest of these men were septuagenarians and the others were octogenarians. I was told several times, "If only you had phoned two or three years ago so-and-so would still have been alive and would have loved to talk to you".

Every one of these men spoke of their sea going experience with great fondness even though a number of them had been treated very badly by their ship owning employers. Seafarers seem to have a special bond with the sea, with their ships and with their ship mates.

I was delighted as to how open these men were with me about what they knew of Irish Shipping in general and of Steve personally. Several of these people told me how well thought of Steve was. It seems that Steve had a great reputation in the company for his professionalism and also as a good shipmate. A number of these men told me that Steve was known and remembered for his consideration and generosity. This made me remember that he was always very generous to the people who worked with him in his various jobs in South Africa and Rhodesia. Hearing several times how popular he was and how well thought of he was made me feel a little embarrassed. I hope that none of these men thought that I was fishing for compliments about my father.

I was also reminded that Steve used to check the shipping column of the news papers when we lived in Durban to see which ships were expected that day. On several occasions he had gone down to Irish ships and met crew members with whom he had previously sailed. He continued to do this when he moved to Port Elizabeth. He had obviously treasured the friendships he had made many years before in Dublin. He also knew how nice it was for seafarers to know someone in a distant port.

One man had information for me about Steve's charcoal days. Another told me that Steve had mentioned that moving to South Africa would be good for his back complaint. I had never heard this before and I thought it put another interesting spin on the story. I was pleased to hear how well Steve had been accepted by his colleagues in Irish Shipping as I know that some foreigners have not been all that well received.

I learnt interesting things about these Irish ships on the North Atlantic. It could take 6 or it could take 12 days to cross the Atlantic. It depended on the wind. It could be a comfortable crossing especially if the ship was full but if the ship was empty, an ocean swell would lift the propeller out of the water and that would produce an unsatisfactory effect. This made even hardened sailors uncomfortable. But this was all part of the way these men were prepared to live and they got very little consideration for their efforts. Of course in those days everyone's pay and conditions were poor.

I began to ask about the Irish Hospitals Sweepstakes ticket and counterfoil operation. I was not at all successful in this endeavour. About half of the people I spoke to said they had no knowledge of this aspect of the company. I received a very interesting e-mail from a man who opened his message to me by saying he had no knowledge of this operation and then he wrote a page telling me about it. I expect that he meant that he had no personal knowledge of the operation. The other half of the people I spoke to were very unforthcoming. The Irish Hospitals Sweepstakes is a taboo subject among these seafarers. I could feel that nearly all of these people believed that this was not an issue about which they felt at liberty to speak. There was definitely an element of fear that some how there could be a reprisal for spilling the beans. Not wanting to be impolite I did not press the matter. A couple of them said that they understood that the mafia was involved and that it was unwise to bring this subject up. I found that hard to believe. But even if the mafia had been involved, the Irish Hospitals Sweepstakes affair is long over and it is hard to image them taking a contract out on anyone for talking about how tickets were smuggled into North America nearly 50 years ago.

One man did tell me with some pleasure that in the old days, and I presume that he was referring to pre-World War Two the tickets used to go to the USA on the original Queen Mary. I was also told the story of the Irish Elm and how the men arrested in the USA were fired and re-employed on their return to Ireland. I was told that the tickets were always sent early as the distribution channels in the USA and Canada were slow and if a ship was caught there would be time to send another consignment. Thus a ship would be carrying tickets for a Sweep eighteen months or two years ahead of the date of the race. There were often between two and three million tickets shipped at a time. These were carefully stored away out of sight. In general Irish Shipping did not take the tickets into the USA as the ships were met by high speed launches off shore, presumably just outside territorial waters and unloaded at that point. Obviously there were exceptions to this as happened when the Irish Elm was caught. Once again, in general, no money changed hands in the Ballsbridge Head Quarters of the Sweeps. Cash was taken down to the ships where it was handed over to the chief stewards. The chief stewards worked with a small team of hand picked men who were given a few week's pay for a few hour's work. And there was a generous allowance for drinks for the boys. According to Steve there was at least one occasion he was paid in Balls Bridge and he received a larger amount than he was expecting. The sums of money do not sound much in today's terms but in the currency of the times it was substantial. My informant told me that Steve would have been earning about £700 a year from his official company salary but that he could have been nearly doubling that on one ticket trip alone. The chief stewards who were chosen for this work usually got two or three trips a year. Some may have had four trips.

The original man I spoke to sent me a URL (a reference to web pages) to the Irish Film Board which had details of their documentary film on the

Irish Hospitals Sweepstakes. The Irish Film Board was very kind to lend me a copy of the film called *If You Aren't In You Can't Win*. This was first broadcast in 2003. It is a remarkable film which exposed the way that the Irish Hospitals Sweepstakes operated. I had not realised just how much money was involved with the Sweeps. Neither had I known that the Sweeps started in 1930 and that in the early years the United Kingdom had been the main overseas market for the tickets. Over its life time there was tens-and-tens of millions of pounds involved and the film suggests that the promoters where effectively given a blank cheque by the Irish Government to spend whatever was required to make this project a success. Also the film points out that there were thousands of people involved with these tickets from every strata of society in Ireland. Steve and the other seafarers in Irish Shipping were very small fry indeed in this huge pool of ticket handlers. I did learn that some of the people at Steve's level in this operation had made enough money to fund themselves in business when they left the sea. This reminded me of the fact that Steve often spoke about how some people were avaricious. Steve was never avaricious. He had a clear sense that his colleagues needed to have a fair share of whatever was available. So he never attempted to keep more than he believed was his reasonable share. He always felt, I guess a bit like Voltaire's Candide that things would turn out all right in the end.

Another one of my newly found contacts informed me that Pearse McLoughin had written a poem as a tribute to Steve when he had heard that Steve died. I knew Pearse from the time I went with him and his family and friends around Ireland's Eye on the fishing trawler. I had remembered him from that event fondly – despite the fact I was sea sick. I had a clear picture of him in my mind as not a very big man but quite rugged with a chiselled face of one whom had had a hard life. I would have said that he would be cast well as Popeye in a Hollywood film. While still fishing Pearse had turned his hand to poetry. Pearse had some success with this despite the fact that he was a great Irish Nationalist eccentric who did not have confidence in what he regarded as the English ISBN numbering system. As a result Pearse published his own work. I was sent a copy of *Shafts of Light Through Moving Clouds* in which the poem Sorrow Flows Across The Seas, appears. This poem is a tribute to Steve. I have reprinted the poem on the following page.

It is fitting that Pearse's words should end this book. I cannot comment on this so I leave it up to readers to make what they will of it.

For Steve Remenyi -
Sorrow Flows Across The Seas
By   Pearse McLoughin

Across the seas in mourning now my heart is flowing o'er;
Tragic news has reached my ears of friend on foreign shore.
I mind his kind and gentle ways, his humane soul and heart;
His generous impulse forged a link which time could never part.
I stand on cliff-top near my home and gaze across the sea;
A passing ship invokes a prayer as Steve comes back to me.
The ocean rises 'neath my feet; we are back at sea once more,
On board the Irish Hazel we are bound for Baltimore.
Again I hear him calling as I end my "watch" below -
My body caked with coal-dust and the sweat from furnace glow.
"A cuppa-tea; a drink of coke; we've had a dirty night;
Now, thank God, the storm has eased, and shore-based birds alight."
Friendship born in ship-confines forge everlasting ties –
Burdened down with sorrow now I face the seas and skies.
My tears are for you Steve my friend, 'tis grief our shipmates sip,
And pray that God will calm the seas, on this, your last long trip.

The Irish Oak, part of Irish Shipping's War time fleet. Irish seamen braved the elements and the possibility of belligerent action to work on these old ships.

The Irish Poplar, part of Irish Shipping's War time fleet. The word Eire and the Irish flag were used to signify neutrality.

The Irish Willow, part of Irish Shipping's War time fleet.

Steve on the Bridge.

Steve at the age when he arrived in Ireland.

Members of the crew of the *Vicia* taken shortly after their arrival in Dublin in 1941. Steve is the second from the right. Four members of the crew sued the ship owners for breach of contract and repatriation expenses to the North America.

Maurice Sheehan in his later days of working for an international oil company. He retired in 1965 and received a pension of £10 per week.

Lily Sheehan in her late 70s.

Ted Sheehan's wedding breakfast party. Steve is standing immediately to the right of Ted. Patsy is to the left of Steve. Lily is directly behind Ted. Paddy is the man at the extreme left of the front row.

Steve and Pat at the Ring of Kerry in the mid 1950s

Jean Remenyi dressed for her first Holy Communion in the mid-1950s

Patsy and the three children on arrival to South Africa

Patsy, Jean and Brendan in a Zulu Warrior Rickshaw in Durban at the end of the 1950s.

Patsy's first job in Durban in 1958 as a bookshop sales person.

Steve, Patsy and Armand Kalmár (Mariska's brother) in Paris in 1968. This was taken during the student and workers riots that year.

A picture Postcard for sale in Racalmas

Steve's middle school. The man in front is Lajos Remenyi. He was Steve's uncle and he taught at this school for some years before being sent to Auschwitz. Steve is in the back row. He is the fourth boy from the left. This was a catholic school and it was here that Steve learned something about Catholicism.

The Remenyi House in Racalmas. The top photo shows the shop and the road in front of the house. The second photo is the rest of the house which extends away from the road.

Steve with friends while swimming on the Danube. Steve is the boy standing on the right. Imre is the man standing behind Steve and Klára Szende is seated on the ground in front.

Steve in Budapest in the late 1930s with his friend and neighbour Klára Szende

The only known surviving photograph of Mariska Reményi taken in the late 1930s

This is Jean Cooke (ne Remenyi) at the Gravestone of Oden Remenyi found in the Jewish graveyard in Racalmas.

This is Ibi who survived two concentration camps,
Auschwitz and Alendorf.

This is the Seaman's' Identity book of Imre Remenyi
issued in 1922.

Magda Remenyi who has been living in Australia
since 1939.

Steve and Patsy in the St Georges Club not long before he retired.

FOR USE BY WHITE PERSONS
THESE PUBLIC PREMISES AND THE AMENITIES THEREOF HAVE BEEN RESERVED FOR THE EXCLUSIVE USE OF WHITE PERSONS.
By Order Provincial Secretary
VIR GEBRUIK DEUR BLANKES

DANGER!
NATIVES, INDIANS & COLOUREDS.
IF YOU ENTER THESE PREMISES AT NIGHT, YOU WILL BE LISTED AS MISSING.
ARMED GUARDS SHOOT ON SIGHT. SAVAGE DOGS DEVOUR THE CORPSE.
YOU HAVE BEEN WARNED!

whites
blankes
non-whites
nie-blankes

U.S. POLICE FIND 20 CASES OF SWEEP TICKETS

Police in Wilmington, North Carolina, said that a conspiracy involving £672,000 worth of Irish Sweepstake tickets has been uncovered. A Wilmington cab driver, a labourer and a waitress had been arrested for alleged participation in a plan to unload 20 cases of sweepstake tickets from an Irish ship, the Irish Hazel, stated the police. The cases were found hidden in a hut.

Police added that the three would be charged with possession of lottery material.

Just before the arrests, the Irish Hazel, owned by Irish Shipping, Ltd., sailed from Wilmington for a British port.—Reuter.

SHIPPING OFFICIAL DENIES REPORT

Irish Shipping official described as "fantastic" the reports concerning the visit of their ship, Irish Hazel, to Wilmington, North Carolina, and the reported finding there by the local police of cases of sweep tickets.

Reports in the Wilmington papers had stated that the police alleged a plan to unload 20 cases of sweep tickets from the Irish Hazel—a load which would be worth about £672,000, if the tickets were sold. The Irish Hazel is now back in Dublin.

These two articles, which first appeared in the Independent newspaper in 1956 are published with the permission of Independent Newspapers, Dublin.